# RADICAL SECRECY

## Electronic Mediations

Series Editors: N. Katherine Hayles, Peter Krapp, Rita Raley,
and Samuel Weber
Founding Editor: Mark Poster

*(continued on p. 246)*

# RADICAL SECRECY

## The Ends of Transparency in Datafied America

**CLARE BIRCHALL**

**Electronic Mediations**

University of Minnesota Press | Minneapolis | London

Portions of chapter 2 are adapted from "'There's Been Too Much Secrecy in This City': The False Choice between Secrecy and Transparency in U.S. Politics," *Cultural Politics* 7, no. 1 (2011): 133–56; copyright 2011 *Cultural Politics* and the present publisher, Duke University Press; reprinted by permission, www .dukeupress.edu. Portions of chapter 3 are adapted from "Data.gov-in-a-Box: Delimiting Transparency," *European Journal of Social Theory* 18, no. 2 (2015): 185–202; copyright 2015 *European Journal of Social Theory* and Sage; reprinted by permission. Portions of chapter 4 are adapted from *Shareveillance: The Dangers of Openly Sharing and Covertly Collecting Data* (Minneapolis: University of Minnesota Press, 2017), published under a Creative Commons Attribution 4.0 International License. Portions of chapter 4 are adapted from "Shareveillance: Subjectivity between Open and Closed Data," *Big Data and Society* 3, no. 2 (2016); copyright 2016 Sage Publications; reprinted by permission. Portions of chapter 5 are adapted from "Aesthetics of the Secret," *New Formations* 83, January 2015: 25–46; copyright 2015 *New Formations* and Lawrence & Wishart; reprinted by permission. Portions of chapter 6 are adapted from "Transparency, Interrupted: Secrets of the Left," *Theory, Culture, and Society* 28, no. 7–8 (2011): 60–84; copyright 2011 *Theory, Culture, and Society* and Sage Publications; reprinted by permission.

Published by the University of Minnesota Press
111 Third Avenue South, Suite 290
Minneapolis, MN 55401-2520
http://www.upress.umn.edu

ISBN 978-1-5179-1042-6 (hc)
ISBN 978-1-5179-1043-3 (pb)
A Cataloging-in-Publication record for this book is available from the Library of Congress.

Printed in the United States of America on acid-free paper

The University of Minnesota is an equal-opportunity educator and employer.

For Christine Clarke and Roger Birchall

# CONTENTS

# PREFACE

This book troubles the vectors of secrecy and transparency to make room for more equitable distributions of power. I completed it just before the impact of Covid-19 started to reveal itself in the UK, where I live. It is now October 2020 as I write this preface, and the intervening period has made me think about the concerns of this book in new ways. In the early days of the pandemic, watching the virus topple health care systems and economies like dominoes, I wondered if aspects of the neoliberal political settlement challenged in this book would be displaced. There was a small chance that high levels of state intervention seen in otherwise capitalist democracies would survive the crisis and normalize socialist solutions and wealth redistribution. That now seems like wishful thinking. While the pandemic is far from over, it has become clear that most states are likely to revert to precrisis behaviors. The United States, the primary focus of this book, may even rebound further—embracing aggressive forms of disaster capitalism and more intensified marketization and privatization—or shift toward state monopoly capitalism. The calls to civic duty, altruism, and collective action could not reverse years of individualism and atomization or interrupt the logic of competition. Forms of antiglobalization, nationalism, and xenophobia are undermining the ideals and efforts of international cooperation. Right now, the prospects of a postpandemic progressive covenant in the United States appear to be less than promising, although much will depend on the (mis)management of this crisis over the coming months and on the forthcoming election.

Radical Secrecy interrogates the state's claims *to* transparency and *on* secrecy, particularly as these are mediated through digital data. This means I am concerned with how the state makes data visible and how it justifies covert data surveillance via invocations of security. So far, the current crisis has focused more attention on health and the economy than security. Nevertheless, it casts new light on the book's concerns with how transparency and secrecy policies and practices serve as carriers of ideology, prescribing the relationship between citizens and the state, but rarely in ways that favor the former. Indeed, the split between data surveillance and open data collapses in the current crisis as certain nation-states repurpose their surveillance capacities for tracking and limiting the spread of infection, in turn making that data available to citizens to enlist them in the fight against the virus.

Biometric monitoring is part of a wider technological solutionism at work in this crisis. Many are looking to big tech, social media, A.I., drones, and blockchain to assist in the epidemiological, economic, informational, and social challenges posed by Covid-19. In addition to the well-documented surveillance technologies in China, many countries—including the United States, the United Kingdom, Israel, Poland, Austria, and Italy—have either implemented or entertained the possibility of biometric monitoring courtesy of smartphone data. The ease with which data surveillance is being repurposed is having the unintended consequence of revealing just how broad the existing surveillance capacities of private tech platforms and state-sponsored intelligence agencies are. Whistle-blower Edward Snowden's revelations in 2013 precipitated scrutiny of these capacities, but the desperation and fear produced by a pandemic lower barriers to their acceptance. To what end will biometric data be put once the health crisis subsides?

The fear of future outbreaks may well secure acquiescence to extended, perhaps indefinite, forms of data surveillance, meaning what few legal constraints remain would be removed. Perhaps these relaxed regulations will be complemented by measures designed to ensure ethical data tracking: truly anonymized data, or nonretention of data beyond a time-limited, explicitly identified purpose, based on meaningful forms of consent. Whether such forms of "transparent" data surveillance or sharing would go far enough to avoid the antipolitical tendencies described in this book is unclear.

In *Radical Secrecy*, I explore tactical opacity and obfuscation as methods of interrupting demands to share and engage with data. Such strategies are undoubtedly harder to justify in the context of health data sets compared with a security function that casts its gaze, and applies algorithmic discrimination, in uneven ways. Privacy is a weak defense in the face of mass suffering. But how can we be certain that these two uses of our data will be kept separate when the demands of health and security have become increasingly intertwined as viral bodies are configured as security risks? Indeed, a U.S. Department of Homeland Security report from February 2020 warned that white supremacists were discussing how to use Covid-19 as a domestic bioweapon (Walker and Winter 2020), and plenty of people have been arrested for coughing or spitting at those enforcing mask wearing.

As well as fashioning opacity as a tactic that can resist calls on the data subject, I also invoke opacity as Martinican philosopher Édouard Glissant understands it: an irreducible singularity of the minoritarian self, which remains illegible despite attempts to understand and articulate it. One cannot help but note a grim lack of respect for singularity in broad categorizations like the "herd" of "herd immunity," or reductive, catchall terms like "underlying conditions," or the casual racism, used to deflect accountability, of "the Chinese virus." This opacity is also violated every time Black Lives Matter protests, which have intensified during the pandemic following the police killings of George Floyd and Breonna Taylor, are subject to multiple forms of surveillance, including social media monitoring.

Alongside data surveillance, this book looks at the role of open government data. The Covid-19 pandemic shows us that while the openness of data is important, the way that the data has been gathered is even more so. Useful though it is, the Johns Hopkins Covid-19 map (https://coronavirus.jhu.edu/us-map), for example, which keeps a running count of cases, recoveries, and deaths, does not include details of how widespread testing is in each location, nor how deaths are recorded. It offers a valuable snapshot, but it makes comparisons across countries seem simple when they are not. Similarly, the model developed by a team at Imperial College London shows the likely outcome of different measures taken, but it "explicitly limit[s] the scope of analysis to narrowly tailored questions framed within the dominant social order. By design, [it fails] to capture the broader market forces driving outbreaks and the political decisions underlying interventions" (Wallace et al. 2020). This is why *Radical Secrecy* calls for thoroughly contextualized transparency and open data in whatever format; for transparency and open data that above all deliver social benefit; and for transparency mechanisms that help to highlight inequalities, rather than make inequitable systems work more efficiently. Containing a pandemic and fostering fairer political and economic systems in its wake require all of these.

In essence, this book represents a move away from the familiar opposition between the promise of transparency and the threat posed by secrecy. The innovative forms of both transparency and secrecy that I explore have the potential to interrupt the political settlement that state-prescribed forms of transparency and secrecy prop up. At the end of *Radical Secrecy,* I show why the opposition between these two sides of the secret—revelation and concealment—collapses under scrutiny; more importantly, I show how to move away from old regimes of visibility to open up a new form of politics. If the newly disrupted coordinates of partisan ideologies and economic orthodoxies settle back into old patterns after the crisis—reliant on neoliberal political-economic modes and concentrations of data power—and if the burden of surveillance continues to fall on minoritized people and those committed to social justice, we will need such an approach more than ever.

# INTRODUCTION
## Transparent Times, Secret Agency, and Data Subjects

A few years ago, I ran a workshop in London on mediations of transparency.[1] Among the participants I had invited to speak was a woman named Simona Levi, one of the founders of Xnet, a Spanish activist organization. Xnet had come to my attention as a group campaigning for, and putting in place the digital tools to achieve, meaningful transparency and direct democracy as part of an anticorruption and antiausterity agenda in the wake of the 2007 financial crisis. Two years after meeting Levi and hearing her talk engagingly about Xnet's campaigns, I received a newsletter with details of the group's work concerning the outlawed Catalan independence referendum, an event that required Xnet and others to consider the role that secrecy as well as transparency might play in the exercise of direct democracy.[2]

The newsletter described the events leading up to and during the referendum. What emerges from Xnet's report, and confirmed by other news sources, is that in a bid to prevent the referendum from taking place, the Madrid government, with the backing of Spanish courts, implemented internet censorship, blocking original websites with the .cat suffix, mirror sites, and any voting apps that had been developed to assist with the referendum.[3] On the day of the referendum, Catalan polling stations found their connection to the internet interrupted and had to rely on smartphones to access vital census information. When interviewed by *Wired* about possible developments, Levi said, "If the Spanish government does restrict Catalan autonomy—especially if it bans Catalan political parties—we will probably have a clandestine government. The internet would be an important part of that" (qtd. in Armstrong 2017). With the benefit of hindsight, we know that this clandestine digital independent government did not in fact emerge; but what I find interesting about Levi's prediction is the way she imagines secrecy in the service of radical democracy in the same conjuncture in which she lambasts the Spanish government for internet censorship and also campaigns for greater transparency. Her tactical approach, rather than moral attachment or aversion to either secrecy or transparency, is notable because of its rarity. Often transparency and openness are uncritically lauded as morally superior to secrecy, which, as I will show in chapter 1, has accrued negative values.

I wrote this book in an attempt to answer three connected questions. How might transparency, in contrast to the high hopes placed in it by a range of political pundits, organizational and management theorists, and campaigners, actually delimit the scope of the political and serve agendas that are far from transparent? Can we imagine, or think with, a secret or secrecy that could act in the service of, rather than against, a progressive politics? And finally, how can we represent the relationship between secrecy and transparency in a way that avoids the dead ends of current debates? Together, these questions prompt a reassessment of secrecy and transparency as ideas, practices, and resources.

The narratives attached to both secrecy and transparency have intensified in the era of digital data. Datafication has solidified the monopoly the state (in collaboration with big tech) has on secrecy qua surveillance and has multiplied the power and value such concentrations bestow. Transparency in this sense means transparency of citizens to the state. Even attempts to make transparency more symmetrical, through open government data, tend to offer responsibility without power in a way that curtails rather than increases agency. Alongside the pressures that datafication places on narratives that assume transparency is an unequivocal good, we are also living through a moment in which visibility and revelation have lost much of their force. Transparency is spent. The "ends of transparency" I use in this book's title refer to both the means to which transparency has been put, and how and why the story we have told ourselves about transparency has already expired. We encounter zombie transparency every day, but we still act as though it were alive and well.

As a tactic of defiance—a way of interrupting the current uses and abuses of transparency—I propose radical secrecy. I use the term "radical" in the spirit of Natalie Fenton: to indicate movements or phenomena that seek "democratic gains over global capitalism" (2016, 9). Because I lean on Jacques Rancière's "distribution of the sensible" (2004b) in this book, I would like to add an emphasis on the necessarily redistributive capacities of the radical. Such redistributions should move beyond commitments to equal shares and treatment from here on in, to offer reparative solutions that adhere to principles of social justice. I am also asking "radical" to point toward something other than the everyday contextual secret. In the last two chapters of this book, therefore, I examine the role that other configurations of the secret and opacity might play in this idea of radical secrecy as well as a reconfiguration of the relationship between secrecy and transparency.

In temporarily reversing the values and promises of secrecy and transparency, I go against the conventions of routine discourse. This critical and recuperative experiment is a necessary stage in a move toward the state of what I call postsecrecy, to which I turn in the concluding chapter. I imagine postsecrecy as a politics free from the cycle of concealment and revelation and from the opposition between secrecy and transparency. It is not a space beyond secrecy and transparency, but rather one that mobilizes radical incarnations of both secrecy and transparency in a way that makes their separation nonsensical. Over the course of this book, I will explain how radical secrecy enacts a "right to opacity" (Glissant 1997, 189) in communitarian forms, while radical transparency is one that plays a part in structural transformation. Postsecrecy serves as a utopian horizon throughout my discussions of the contemporary hegemonic invocations, as well as the radical manifestations, of secrecy and transparency. It is postsecrecy that would be the necessary condition for imagining, finally, an alternative vision of "the good," equality, and responsibility, as well as a demos not framed by neoliberal instantiations of transparency or undermined by secret state surveillance. Postsecrecy, I will argue, offers the possibility of reimagining collective resistance in the era of digital data.

Rather than fixed opposites (though at times they will certainly appear and operate as such), I have found it useful to think of secrecy and transparency more as conjoined twins: each singular and unique, but essentially connected, sharing vital functions, and only severable by extreme measures and at some considerable risk. They move together, though not necessarily facing the same way or with the same intention. I try to pay attention to where they connect as well as the spaces between them; how at times they operate together in balance and at other times are in conflict; how historical context determines which twin, at any moment, is the favored one; and how we might think with secrecy and transparency beyond the meanings attributed to them by that context.

Secrecy and transparency are malleable, floating signifiers that take form in certain ways at particular times, harnessed by various actors and rooted within different discourses. In these discursive, technological, and aesthetic manifestations, they shape political institutions, realities, and subjectivities. Moreover, as floating signifiers, secrecy and transparency are subject to an ongoing contestation over meaning and can be articulated to radically different political projects (Laclau and Mouffe 1985). Secrecy and transparency therefore have no essential meaning outside of the discursive formations that invoke them. This is not so unusual. But what makes secrecy and transparency more complex as signifiers is that they each refer to form rather than any specific content, any individual piece of information that might be called secret or transparent. They are not themselves information; rather, they label and determine the value of the information they carry. Nevertheless, they cannot be located in isolation from that information to which they refer. While we can point to the infrastructure of state secrecy and transparency measures and mechanisms (there is a certain materiality to secrecy and transparency), it is not possible to look directly at either transparency or a secret if they are to retain their identity. This is because a secret dissolves on discovery and transparency denotes a medium that is supposed to be seen through rather than directly at. The form of the secret and the mode of transparency outlive any particular revelation or transmission of content. We could say that they are nothing in and of themselves.

Elaborating on Claude Lévi-Strauss's ideas, Ernesto Laclau uses the term "empty signifier" to indicate how certain floating signifiers become central within a discursive field. In recent years, we might think this particularly applicable to transparency. Signifiers are empty (or almost empty) because they can come to mean literally anything. The example Laclau provides is the idea of "order" in the work of Thomas Hobbes, which is never defined but called for as a solution to disorganization (2007, 44). It signifies the lack that must then be filled by various hegemonizing functions. He offers other examples of empty signifiers, including "unity," "liberation," and "revolution." This helps to explain transparency's force. While the meaning of transparency is still more circumscribed than these examples, its current overuse and lack of specificity suggest a future of emptiness in which transparency comes to "incarnate the (impossible) symbolic unity of a community or society" (Howarth 2004, 262). In other words, transparency, like freedom and democracy in the United States (and elsewhere), comes to organize and lend coherence to the discursive field. It enables the community to think of itself as a politically coherent entity ("We are a transparent liberal democracy!") but ultimately has no content.

I will chart the ascendency of transparency as an ideal and practice in chapters 1 and 3. Here, I simply want to acknowledge its discursive pervasiveness. Today we are told that transparency can solve all our problems. Patrick Birkinshaw (2006), a professor of law, has gone so far as to claim that transparency constitutes a human right. It is invoked with "soteriological optimism" (Tsoukas 1997, 840) and entrusted with the task of fostering accountability and strengthening participatory democracy. It is expected to weed out and prevent corruption—or, to invoke early twentieth-century U.S. Supreme Court justice Louis Brandeis's (1913) famous phrase, to disinfect public life. More specifically, in recent decades, it has been called on to foster economic growth (European Commission 2004);[4] prevent the undue influence of lobbyists on U.S. representatives (OpenSecrets. org); pave the way for financial recovery after the 2007 crisis (Keeley and Love 2010); thwart the abuse of British MPs' expenses (Brooke 2010); democratize aid (Barder 2010) and assist global development (Ingram 2018); prevent food waste (Dave Lewis, CEO of Tesco, qtd. in Mace 2016); curtail drug price rises (OECD 2017); fight fake news (HLEG 2018); and help tackle global warming (see, for example, Transparency International's Climate Governance Integrity Programme). These offer just a few examples. Indeed, it is hard to argue against more transparency when it is presented as a universal, common(sensical) good. To question transparency in liberal democracies today is to be opposed to progress (conservative in the general sense), corrupt (if there is nothing to hide, why fear transparency?), or antidemocratic (the link between transparency and liberal democracy has become unassailable).

In contrast to the capacious hope placed in transparency, secrecy is invoked apologetically, as an unfortunate necessity for exceptional circumstances, or as a strategy of last resort. Of course, the ubiquity of secrecy in the state and corporate sectors, whether in the form of security agencies, covert operations, classified information, black box technologies, opaque algorithmic discrimination, trade secrets, and so forth, means that secrecy is a staple rather than exceptional. In many contexts, secrecy is called on, and appealed to, with caution because of the opprobrium it has accumulated and excites in moral, personal, and political settings. Privacy has become the only acceptable version of secrecy for individuals; the state has to justify secrecy via the discourse of security. In such a climate, it becomes difficult to think politics outside of calls for more of the same old transparency and imagine an ethical, radical secrecy. I have set myself just these tasks.

With regards to vocabulary, I use a constellation of terms in this book. Though they are connected to one another (and in and of themselves somewhat plastic), they are not interchangeable. There is an already substantial and increasing body of work on transparency that tries to define it. Debate arises from the fact that it "incessantly wavers between a factual requirement, and a normative claim, an optical impression and a metaphorical promise" (Alloa and Thomä 2018a, 4). Emmanuel Alloa (2018) identifies ten aspirations now associated with transparency, including accessibility, procedural fairness, accountability, truth making, and authenticity. In this book, "transparency" refers most often to the different processes and mechanisms for information and policy provision put in place (ostensibly at least) to render society, institutions, and politics free of malfeasance and corruption. In practice, it functions as a form of what Mikkel Flyverbom terms "visibility management" for the way that it "foreground[s] strategic and dynamic attempts to govern through vision and observation" (2019, 22). Indeed, transparency, as Byung-Chul Han warns, exceeds any administrative role: "Whoever connects transparency only with corruption and the freedom of information has failed to recognize its scope," he writes. "Transparency is a systematic compulsion gripping all social processes" (2015, 2). In order to take on the idea of transparency as more of a pervasive project or ideology, I also discuss transparency as it is understood in philosophy: the idea that an individual can know or encounter herself, an other, language, information, or the world in ways that are free of distortion. This epistemological ideal, and the desire for immediacy that it reflects, bolsters the turn to transparency in all kinds of contexts. Transparency is "a powerful metaphor that drives and shapes the desire for a more perfect democratic order" (Fenster 2017a, 6) and the dream of optimized, frictionless communication.[5]

I use "openness" to indicate an ethos or spirit that draws on a broad spectrum of ideas—including administrative and philosophical transparency, to be sure, but also the idea of a Popperian open society and science that supports the wide dissemination of knowledge, as well as open critique and critical inquiry; stalwarts of liberal democracy such as Freedom of Information and open meetings; and more recent digital affordances that enable open repositories and exchanges of knowledge. At its core, openness "implies accessibility or lack of restrictiveness with regard to communication" (Long 2001, 5). Publicity plays a key role in this atmosphere of openness and clearly has much in common with contemporary forms of transparency fashioned as oversight. As publicity gained traction during the latter half of the eighteenth century in tandem with representative governments, it is best understood as that which provides assurance to citizens that they are being adequately represented, and that political business is subject to public scrutiny (Baume 2018).

"Secrecy" is the state and perpetuation of keeping certain information from becoming public. Such secret keeping can involve a community of knowers however large or small and the idea of intentionality, a requirement that both Sissela Bok (1982) and Pamela O. Long (2001) invoke. But concealment can also be systematized, instituted, technologized, and routinized through various mechanisms so that secrecy becomes less dependent on individual secret keepers—what Matthew Potolsky calls "the secret without a subject" (2019, 138). "Secret" is the name we give to information that is kept from us, or that we keep from others—information that is in principle knowable.

However, in later chapters, I will also discuss the idea of the unconditional secret as that which exceeds and resists knowledge in absolute terms. As chapter 5, on an aesthetics of the secret, makes clear, secrets take on various forms, including commonplace, open, and unconditional. I try to pay attention to the differences when describing particular secrets.

I work with a definition of "privacy" that indicates a state of existence free from intrusion that has been fashioned in the United States as a personal possession, but I recognize that it is not a stable, transhistorical concept (Igo 2018). As will become clear, I take issue with the concept of and appeal to "privacy" at various points in this book for its inability to adequately challenge or capture what is at stake in contemporary forms of data surveillance. I use "opacity" to denote a state of illegibility, taking inspiration from Édouard Glissant's use of the term in a postcolonial context. "Obfuscation," too, suggests an interference with reading practices by flooding a system with distracting or distorting information. In this way, the goal of much obfuscation is opacity, but not all opacity involves obfuscation. For all their specificity, each node in this network of terms can be seen to manage visibility and information (Flyverbom et al. 2016).

My interest in "secrecy" and "transparency," it should be clear, is not simply at the conceptual level. The conceptual force of both terms certainly grounds my reading of certain situations and case studies within this book, particularly when I challenge the idea that secrecy and transparency are opposites in any uncomplicated manner. However, I am primarily interested in secrecy and transparency as they inform and shape the parameters of the political first and foremost, but also different experiences and environments. They may be floating (or even empty) signifiers at various points, but they are also mediating modes that produce (unevenly distributed) affects and effects. This means that alongside the role that secrecy and transparency play in discursive terms, I also pay attention to the material practices that enact either secrecy or transparency; the institutions and technologies developed to imagine and implement them; the subjectivities and dynamics they presuppose, and how these subjectivities might marry with, or challenge, other narratives and experiences of selfhood available today; and the structures of feeling that secrecy or transparency (as well as secrecy *and* transparency) engender.

I approach secrecy and transparency in this multilayered way be-cause I see them as crucial to the political and technological distribu-tion of power in the global north today. The balance between secrecy and transparency at the level of the state has long been positioned as a political question in the sense that every government must decide on the amount, tenor, and granularity of information it covertly col-lects and publicly releases. I am not primarily interested in this peren-nial debate. While the tension between security and, first, the right to know, and second, privacy, is evident in chapter 2 when I consider the three U.S. presidential administrations of the twenty-first century so far, and the information imaginaries that mediate the social con-tract, I explicitly seek to interrupt it in chapter 5. My focus is some-what different. It is not only that the balance between secrecy and transparency is a political question, or that the terms "secrecy" and "transparency" become mobilized within the discursive field of poli-tics. It is also that secrecy and transparency are, in and of themselves, politics. I mean this in the sense that they are distributive modes that determine what is sensible to us (Rancière 2004b)—what is available, knowable, and actionable. They are gateways and barriers, forms of mediation, which determine in uneven ways (depending on various axes of social difference) what share we have in information and data. This in turn shapes our ability and agency to determine the scope of the political itself—which questions, actions, and debates are deemed properly political. More than this, secrecy and transparency, not al-ways in ways we might expect, curtail or enable our ability to work collectively on issues we may care about; they shape our agency and how we think of ourselves as political beings. They are prime vectors of contemporary subjectivity, operating at macro and micro levels at once, across individual and collective identities.

Paying attention to secrecy and transparency today entails rec-ognizing that they fail to stay pure at both the conceptual and ma-terial level. At various moments in this book, I therefore expose the internal limits of secrecy and transparency. Returning to the image of conjoined twins, each might decide to perform as the other; or they might be mistaken for one another. Some secrets, for example, can be classified as open, what Michael Taussig names "public se-crets," or that which "is generally known, but cannot be articulated" (1999, 5). Equally, some transparency measures offer up so much information and data that it may as well be secret, never finding an audience.

Understanding contemporary secrecy and transparency also means reading them through and alongside digital technologies. These technologies optimize transparency or secure secrecy (for states, private sector companies, or individuals), but they are simultaneously shaped by secrecy and transparency at both the discursive and infrastructural level. Discursively, there has always been an ideological tussle between hopes for an open and free internet against its manifestation as an arena for enclosure, capture, and control (Chun 2006; Franklin 2015).[6] In terms of design, the internet is finely balanced between the possibilities for encryption and anonymity on the one hand and decryption and tracking on the other. As well as functioning as key coordinates within digital design, secrecy and transparency are central to debates and decisions concerning datafication. As will become clear, I am particularly interested in the ways that open and closed data sharing (data shared with citizens in the name of transparency and data that the state covertly collects about its citizens) produces an antipolitical settlement that, to use a neologism that I explain in chapter 4, I call shareveillance.

At the very outset of this project, I wanted not only to describe a political-technological settlement but also to intervene in it, in whatever limited way an academic book can be thought to intervene. That is, I hope that in thinking secrecy and transparency against the grain, in reimagining their political potential at a time when transparency has been exhausted by empty invocations and secrecy is overly aligned with repression, securitization, and abuses of power, I can recognize, collate, and further instigate the possibility of (albeit modest) redistributions of the sensible in the twenty-first-century global north.

The first chapter sets out how secrecy and transparency have accrued particular meanings and values in transatlantic political and cultural thought. The intention here is to explore the negative and positive meanings ascribed to the two key vectors of this book in order to question such logic. I offer a selective account of secrecy and transparency, of the values they have accumulated, and of the relation between them created in particular Western discourses. How have they been envisaged and articulated together? How has the balance been managed at particular moments in time? And how has discourse about secrecy and transparency shaped the political culture and public sphere of the United States? Asking such questions opens up the possibility of thinking secrecy and transparency otherwise. In later chapters, this will mean revisiting the respect given to secrecy and wariness of some forms of openness evident in pre-Enlightenment Europe, for example (without any nostalgia for the attendant despotism, ignorance, and the occult).

Chapter 2 picks up where chapter 1 leaves off: on the threshold of the twenty-first century. By focusing on the American political context, this chapter considers the different approaches to secrecy and transparency evident in the administrations of U.S. presidents George W. Bush, Barak Obama, and Donald J. Trump. I do this via the information imaginaries of each administration: the specific communicative forms enlisted to manage government information, the corresponding roles for citizens therein implied, and the ideological frame animating these configurations. I draw on arguments by Joseph Masco (2014) to show how the Bush information imaginary was animated by a fear of joined-up information in the public sphere, which prompted a struggle over the visibility of information and documents. Increased security concerns and high levels of suspicion left little room for citizens to be perceived as other than potential threats or vigilant spies. The Obama information imaginary declared a commitment to transparency, positioning open government data as the way to realize this. While pointing out all the ways in which Obama continued to utilize, rather than eradicate, the covert or obfuscating security measures employed by his predecessor, I concentrate more on the entrepreneurial position that open data creates for citizens. The Trump information imaginary, as it manifested during Trump's time in office, offered a different relationship to secrecy and transparency again. It was dismissive of day-to-day document- or data-based administrative transparency, yet it enlisted social media to offer the illusion of a president who is unequivocally unmediated—that is to say, transparent—to his public. At the same time, Trump's relationship with the traditional representatives of government secrecy—the intelligence agencies—was fragile and fraught, and his political campaign and administration seemed to rely on the opaque operations and logic of conspiracy and collusion. Flows of communication were used to misdirect, leaving citizens less informed, not better informed. Taken together, these case studies challenge any simplistic representation of a clear choice between secrecy and transparency at the level of policy and politics. Such representations fail to capture the complexity of the relationship between secrecy and transparency in action. Moreover, they show how the deployment of this relationship offers the public certain positions that shape the scope of the political. I conclude chapter 2 by asking if we can reconfigure the admittedly dangerous derailing of transparency by the Trump information imaginary as an opportunity to think about more radical forms of secrecy and transparency.

To further question the opposition between secrecy and transparency, the third chapter posits the less than transparent qualities—the secrecy even—of transparency as both a concept and a practice. I review some of the main critiques against transparency and connect them with the analysis of open government data introduced in the previous chapter. I do so in order to address the transparency imperialism that animates the circulation of open government data portals around the globe. I argue that ideas about publics and politics travel with this model of open data. Unless we want to export a political contract delimited by neoliberal formations of open government data, we need to imagine and experiment with more radical forms of transparency. To this end, I examine WikiLeaks, arguing that its legacy is more important with regard to form rather than content.

Chapter 4 proposes a name for the antipolitical settlement produced by covert data surveillance on the one hand and open government data transparency initiatives on the other. Shareveillance delimits the political experience and agency of subjects called on to share their data in order to be watched, and to watch and act on data shared by the state. The chapter links "sharing" with "veillance" in order to think about a form of contemporary subjectivity shaped by both open and covert digital data practices. After showing how these forms of sharing undermine agency, the chapter ends by calling for more progressive ways of dividing the distribution of data.

The close of chapter 4 marks a turning point. Chapters 5 and 6, which suspend the attempt to transform transparency, argue for an appropriation of secrecy—that is, to imagine the radical secrecy to which my book title refers. To begin this process of rehabilitation, chapter 5 takes the Snowden revelations about government data surveillance and considers how a meditation on secrecy—offered by different artworks in this instance—interrupts the debates that dominated the airwaves. I argue that we are better able to form a radical political response to the Snowden event and subsequent revelations about government data surveillance if we situate the secret within a distributive, aesthetic regime and imagine what collectivities and subjectivities the secret, rather than transparency, makes available. An aesthetics of the secret, with aesthetics read through Rancière (2004b), who understands it as a political "distribution of the sensible," presents us with a way to think about the productive possibilities of secrecy. What is freed up when we no longer have to concern ourselves with a hermeneutics of the secret (asking the secret to reveal what, why, and how) in favor of experiencing an aesthetics of the secret?

Chapter 6 examines various forms that a secrecy of the left has taken in the past and could take in the future. This involves looking at resistant experiments with secret societies, masking, anonymity, and opacity as well as digital experiments with secrecy that scramble the coordinates of shareveillance, and all of the different demands placed on us by datafication. I turn to Jacques Derrida and Glissant, who have worked with the secret and opacity, respectively, to offer new ontological and political possibilities. Through these examples of praxis and theory, I argue that the left needs to experiment with communities of secrecy rather than communities of transparency under the current conditions. Transparency under neoliberalism and securitization is no longer a viable clarion call around which the left can organize.[7] Given that secrets are aligned with singularity rather than community in Derrida's thought, the challenge here is to configure secrecy as a form of commons: a freely available resource that can be shared without depletion.

Because of the density of the discursive terrains that have determined the value and meaning of secrecy and transparency, much of this book is taken up with the quest to challenge them. My reversal of the opposition, however, is only an initial move before "a general *displacement* of the system" (Derrida 1988, 21). Such a displacement must wait until the Conclusion of this book, where I argue for postsecrecy. A rehabilitation of the secret is necessary as an interim strategy to interrupt the dominant configuration of transparency, secrecy, data subjectivity, and agency. However, this must give way to a new approach to the place of openness and opacity in the political. Postsecrecy would institute a right to opacity and require an openness to openness.[8] We should think of the openness of postsecrecy not as an end point, a principle to be celebrated in and of itself, as transparency has become, but as an openness *to* something: a new politics of visibility.

# CHAPTER 1

# THE CHANGING FORTUNES OF SECRECY AND OPENNESS

At the time of American independence, the fortunes of and values attributed to secrecy and openness were changing under the influence of Enlightenment ideas and metaphors. The Constitution is either praised for instituting provisions for open government and therefore oversight, or it is lambasted for embedding enough ambiguity and pockets of opacity to allow for abuses of power. But these evaluations ("praised" for openness, "lambasted" for secrecy) are decidedly modern, a legacy of the very Enlightenment thinking that shaped the American revolution and the new republic.

This chapter begins by drawing on research that shows how secrets and secrecy in pre-Enlightenment Europe were more often considered useful rather than signs of corruption. As Enlightenment philosophies proposed new modes of political accountability, concepts of the transparent subject, and the open application of reason, they positioned secrecy (as well as forms of irrationality and esotericism) as the outmoded other. Enlightenment philosophers privileged transparency (of the state, self, other, and world) as an ideal, and in the process, they ascribed negative value to secrets and secrecy. This shift in signification does not mean that secrets and secrecy were thereafter eradicated from public and private life, of course. Rather, it necessitated strategies to accommodate and justify denigrated secrets and secrecy.

In the latter half of this chapter, I explore the various ways in which openness was institutionalized and became a cultural norm in America even while the state effectively established a monopoly

on secrecy. This focus on how the broad shift in legitimacy from secrecy to openness played out in the American context will ground
the contemporary examples I draw on in later chapters. While there
are other national contexts that would provide fruitful insights about
the relationship between secrecy and transparency, I look to the
American example because it has exported its legislative and cultural approaches to openness around the globe in what I call, with
caution, transparency imperialism in chapter 3.[1] I close this chapter
by suggesting that the plethora of legislation and heightened moral
discourse about transparency in twentieth- and twenty-first-century
America can be seen in part as compensation for both the ambivalence toward openness in the original articles of the Constitution
and reliance on an ever-intensifying and expanding covert security
sector.

The purpose of this chapter is not to offer a comprehensive history of secrecy and openness as practices or as concepts, but rather to
show where the values attributed to secrets and transparency in contemporary America are rooted. I have selected examples that demonstrate how values have been articulated to, and disarticulated from,
secrecy and openness. I highlight the historically contingent nature
of the values attributed to secrecy and openness and the binary into
which these terms are constrained in order to pave the way for the
work of later chapters, in which I challenge how those values are mobilized in the twenty-first century. I explore the ideological work to
which they are put and attempt to better understand the relationship
between the terms in play.

## The Value of Secrets and Secrecy

So familiar are we with hearing negative evaluations of secrecy and
near universal praise of transparency that it would be easy to mistake
culturally produced values for essential qualities. An account of pragmatic, even celebratory, early modern approaches to *arcana imperii*
in the political realm and appreciation of secrecy in more quotidian
economies of knowledge offers an opportunity to understand the rise
of transparency's fortunes and fall of secrecy's reputation as tied to
the emergence of a new episteme.

*Arcana imperii*—secrets of the state, or, in Foucault's terms, "the secrets of the power" (2007, 356)—became a central component in the early modern practice of *raison d'état,* "a rule or an art . . . which makes known to us the means for obtaining the integrity, tranquility, or peace of the republic," in the words of Giovanni Antonio Palazzo in his 1604 book on the subject (qtd. in Foucault 2007, 257). While secular leaders benefited from a transfer of "the aura of sacredness from the *arcana ecclesiae* of the church, ritual, and religious officials" (Bok 1982, 172), political theorists "drew on the significance of the secret in Christian theology to further legitimate the confidentiality of state affairs" (Jütte 2015, 19). Political manuals also drew on instances from antiquity to illustrate the necessity of *arcana imperii* to secure the national interest. For example, German jurist and political theorist Arnold Clapmarius (1605) promised readers that they could learn the secrets of statecraft from the actions of the Roman emperors as reported by Tacitus.[2] Positioned by Clapmarius as distinct from elements of corruption, *arcana imperii* were, Eva Horn explains, "clandestine means for achieving laudable goals" (2011, 91). Under the influence of Clapmarius and other political theorists of the day (Horn cites Botero, Bodin, and Ammirato), *arcana imperii* became "less a body of dark secrets than a prudent code of conduct for princes" (111). In practice, this meant developing systems that could not only covertly discover the enemy's secrets and enable the state to intervene in unanticipated ways but also protect the state's own secrets. The latter included knowledge about what resources—manpower and wealth—the state had at its disposal. Foucault notes that "for a long time, statistics in particular were considered as secrets of power not to be divulged" (2007, 356).[3] Of importance is the way in which secrecy was aligned with, rather than pitted against, ethics, honor, and moral responsibility in this period (Jütte 2015, 21).

The practice of *arcana imperii* was therefore justified as a pragmatic instrument to maintain power and a necessary form of information control at a time when more and more knowledge about the state was available. *Arcana imperii* benefited from an association with theological secrets; were naturalized through references to their place in antiquity; and were praised for being the moral choice for rulers wanting to protect not only their own power but also their subjects' safety. Embedded in statecraft as secrets and secrecy were in the early modern period, their role in the realm of politics must have seemed secure, not least because they helped conserve the very regimes that placed so much value in them.

Secrets were also prized and praised in the early modern period beyond the power brokering of the court. Craft secrecy and proprietary attitudes and practices regarding inventions and designs, including patents, were developed in late medieval Europe; after the rise of the printing press, they coexisted with books and pamphlets dedicated to recording and disseminating technical knowledge (Long 2001). Indeed, early modern print culture was awash with titles that included the word "secret" (Jütte 2015, 18), which would often denote "technique" or "method." In this genre, "secret" signals the value of the knowledge being imparted. It is closely guarded, cautiously revealed, and needs to be handled with respect. In most cases, trade secrets would need to be accompanied by practical experience and apprenticeship to be of real use. The moniker also created interest for the esoteric sciences. In an account of magical texts, alchemical treatises, and Hermetic writings, Long (2001) finds that injunctions to keep knowledge of magical practices and recipes secret prevalent in the Roman imperial period continued to permeate texts of the seventeenth century.

The tension in examples of trade or esoteric secrets, of course, is that in being transcribed and disseminated, however limited the readership might have been, each point of knowledge is inflected by the possibility of being read by someone other than the intended, initiated reader.[4] Yet as Daniel Jütte points out, "Writing down and publishing secrets was by no means tantamount to disclosing them. Putting secrets into writing, especially during [the sixteenth century], is a relatively problematical criterion for claims about the 'open' character of knowledge" (2015, 13). He goes on to quote Leo Strauss (1988), who points out that writing between the lines existed in the philosophical and esoteric traditions. The wide translation and circulation of texts like *Magia naturalis* (1558) by Della Porta, the celebrated Italian magus and "professor of secrets," only increased the remuneration he received from patrons (Jütte 2015, 14). Writing about secrets, therefore, was a careful, creative art. It required vague, suggestive language in order to preserve the allure and power of those secrets.

Authors of secrecy literature approached these constraints creatively. In order to hide in plain sight, books on alchemy utilized methods such as illustrations in need of decoding (Obrist 1982), used cover names for technical terms, used elliptical descriptions of processes, and engaged in a disorienting overuse of synonyms (Long 2001). In addition, magicians, such as the Neoplatonist Cornelius Agrippa, used strategies of concealment: "Certain things are written with order, certain things without order, certain things are transmitted through fragments, certain things indeed are hidden, having been left for the investigation of the intelligent" ([1510] 1992, 65; qtd. in and translated by Long 2001, 160).[5]

Jütte's (2015) point that the rise of a literature of *secreta* did not equate to the decline in the fortunes of secrecy appears in a compelling account of how secrets in the early modern period were seen as positive and productive. He writes about an "economy of secrets" in Europe that created contact zones between Jews and Christians. Dealing with a wide array of secrets from the natural sciences, alchemy, magic, the military, and politics, Jütte shows how they counted as modes of useful knowledge exchange and value creation.[6] He writes: "No other period in European history, neither before nor since, has shown so profound a fascination with secrecy and secret sciences. Arcane knowledge was widely considered positive knowledge, and this notion of 'good secrecy' extended across all fields of life, including everyday life, scientific and economic domains and the political culture of the day" (viii). This vision of "good secrecy" is the one I want to hold on to as we approach the discursive production of more negative connotations that occurs at the end of the period Jütte is writing about. There were other practices and ways of handling knowledge available to people in the early modern period and earlier (Long's 2001 book charts the history of open knowledge), but the use of secrets and secrecy was valid and respected.

### In Praise of Openness

In vivid language, Foucault describes the prerevolutionary era in France as one mired in an opacity that allowed ignorance and malfeasance to fester and rulers to operate unchecked: "A fear haunted the latter half of the eighteenth century: the fear of darkened spaces, of the pall of gloom which prevents the full visibility of things, men and truths. It sought to break up the patches of darkness that blocked the light, eliminate the shadowy areas of society, demolish the unlit chambers where arbitrary political acts, monarchical caprice, religious superstitions, tyrannical and priestly plots, epidemics and the illusions of ignorance were fomented" (1980, 153). Foucault evokes this period through its central metaphors. In the work of European Enlightenment writers, light was no longer used "to symbolize divine salvation, but rather to express philosophical self-affirmation, it also transformed church and clergy from transmitters of true light into bearers of darkness" (Reichardt 1998, 110). During the so-called Age of Reason, the clergy were not the only ones to be designated as potential "bearers of darkness." Despotic monarchies and "obscure and invisible" governments, as Francis Bacon (1826, 213) terms it, were also aligned with the shadows. Politics was ripe for being rendered visible by nascent democratic forms and a burgeoning public sphere. Darkness and light were the textual and visual metaphors to capture the desired transition from legitimacy drawn from arbitrary sources and maintained by secrets and mystery to one drawn from reason or the will of the people and secured by accountability.

European Enlightenment thinkers offered openness in various guises as a guarantor of authenticity, truth, and freedom; they raised numerous objections to political and personal secrecy, shaping how both terms have been perceived since. By briefly considering some formulations in Rousseau, Kant, and Bentham, I seek not to further reify their canonical position (nor sideline non-Western modernities or other enlightenments) but rather to show how the canonical story of Western modernity rests on the apportioning of positive meanings and roles to openness, publicity, and transparency on the one hand and negative meanings and roles to secrets on the other.

Rousseau's fervor for personal transparency speaks to the way in which the Enlightenment orbited the theological language of Western Christianity that posited transparency as a state to be achieved before God (Geroulanos 2017). His belief in the transformative potential of transparency reached in directions spiritual and psychological as he attempted, in the *Confessions,* to "set before [his] fellows the likeness of a man in all the truth of nature" (Rousseau [1764] 1953, 1), to render his heart "transparent as crystal" (415), and to produce a self-coincident autobiography and "unveil" his "inmost" self (1). This idealization of the transparency of self, of lifting the veil of false appearances to achieve authenticity, extended to all realms of life. Rousseau saw such a bid for transparency at times as "a matter of personal reform," at times as "individual education," and at other times as "a matter of forming a political community" (Starobinski 1988, 13).

Capturing the far-reaching and holistic nature of Rousseau's approach, Foucault presents Rousseau's project as "the dream of a transparent society, visible and legible in each of its parts, the dream of there no longer existing any zones of darkness, zones established by the privileges of royal power or the prerogatives of some corporation, zones of disorder" (1980, 152). In his political theory, Rousseau ([1762] 2002) imagines a social contract based on the sublimation of the public's individual will to the general will. The general will, when brought into line with reason and free from impediments, would always aim for the common good. As Foucault notes, Rousseau thought that "each individual, whatever position he occupied, might be able to see the whole of society, that men's hearts should communicate, their vision be unobstructed by obstacles, and that opinion of all reign over each" (1980, 152).

As an expression of his distaste for intermediaries, Rousseau writes, "Sovereignty cannot be represented. . . . It consists essentially in the general will, and the will cannot be represented" ([1762] 2002, 221). If Rousseau's authentic self could tolerate no dissembling, then his social contract could not abide outsourcing or deputizing. Any form of mediation that would introduce friction into the fantasy of transparency ought to be banished. While confessional culture and government transparency often seem to occupy distinctive theaters in contemporary culture, they shared a home in Rousseau's utopian thought, and the positive meanings attributed in one realm became applicable to the other.

In "Answer to the Question: What Is Enlightenment?," Kant describes the obligation individuals have to "make *public use* of his reason in all matters" ([1784] 2001, 136). This means obeying one's civic duties or religious obligations, but it also means exercising one's freedom of thought, and most importantly one's freedom to critique those civic duties and religious doctrines in writing, to subject them to reason. "Religion through its holiness and legislation through its majesty commonly seek to exempt themselves from [criticism]," Kant argues; respect will only be granted to religion and legislation by reason when they have "been able to withstand its free and public examination" ([1781] 1998, Axi).

Whereas Kant's categorical imperative determines unconditional and universal moral laws, it is his hypothetical and transcendental publicity test that determines the viability of political maxims. In "Toward Perpetual Peace," he writes, "All actions relating to the rights of others are wrong if their maxim is incompatible with publicity" ([1795] 1996, 8:381). His formulation positions publicity as the condition that marks whether an action is ethical and just. He was not suggesting that all decisions and actions *should* be public, but rather that they be judged against the condition that they *could* withstand the scrutiny of an ideal, rational public. Just as the categorical imperative determines morality in place of religious doctrine, so too does the publicity test offer an alternative to *arcana imperii,* decided and kept by arbitrarily appointed leaders.

Bentham, approaching publicity from a utilitarian perspective, has been central to the cultivation of publicity and transparency as positive in all kinds of governmental and administrative contexts. He places great faith in publicity's ability to protect against poor administration and to secure justice (Baume 2011). In his "Draught for the Organization of Judicial Establishments," for example, he describes publicity as "the very soul of justice" (Bentham [1790] 1843, 316). It was his solution to potential abuses of power by public officials; publicity would serve a regulatory function. In "Of Publicity" ([1791] 1999), he advocates publicity with respect to political assemblies, seeing it as the most important method by which to secure public confidence and assent to legislation, and to keep malfeasant, tyrannous, and indolent men from occupying positions of influence. He recommends publication of individual votes by representatives on each motion as well as the content; public assemblies; and the publication and communication of the "issue" and "tenor of every motion" as well as the reports that inform the decision-making process (38). He advocates a free press, which would inform his imagined public opinion tribunal, and to keep judges in check, he recommends a quasi jury (Postema 2014). Bentham assumes that secrecy in public life indicates wrongdoing: "Suspicion always attaches to mystery. It thinks it sees a crime where it beholds an affectation of secrecy; and it is rarely deceived. For why should we hide ourselves if we do not dread being seen? . . . Calumny . . . collects its venom in the caverns of obscurity, but it is destroyed by the light of day" ([1791] 1999, 30). Unlike Rousseau's vision for transparency, Bentham stops short of calling for the law of publicity to be absolute, recognizing the limitations imposed by security concerns, but he concludes the paragraph in which he expresses that sentiment with the following dictum: "Secresy [sic] is an instrument of conspiracy; it ought not, therefore, to be the system of a regular government" (39).

Behind many of Bentham's plans and designs was the hope that publicity would ensure that an official's interest would align with his "duty to be humane" (Harrison 1983, 130). This is why the guards of the proposed panopticon prison design were to be under the "same irresistible controul" and subject to the same regimes of visibility as the prisoners (Bentham [1791] 1843, 45)—a factor that often gets left out of Foucauldian accounts. And while publicity is not synonymous with transparency, we could accurately say that Bentham's attempts to systematize and engineer visibility, writing it into the very fabric of his proposals and designs, resembles the way in which contemporary transparency procedures are thought best to operate. Moreover, Bentham's technocratic utilitarian vision for publicity's role is at the heart of justifications for contemporary transparency practices.

## Dirty Secrets

Of course I am not suggesting that the Enlightenment investment in openness eradicated secrecy and secrets. As Georg Simmel (1906) argues in his seminal sociological study, secrecy and secrets are essential to the functioning of and shape the very parameters of the social. Simmel imagines that "human associations require a definite ratio of secrecy which merely changes its objects" (467–68). Given this irreducible or structuring role of secrecy and secrets, it is more accurate to say that the Enlightenment cultivated a lexicon to represent them as suspect. I would not be the first to point out that the Enlightenment is haunted by the very obstacles it sought to banish. This long line of critique begins with Hegel ([1807] 1977), who saw the Enlightenment commitment to absolute freedom morph into the bloody chaos of the Reign of Terror. The Enlightenment, we might want to say, has its own dirty secrets. These include the epistemological and physical violence inherent in imperialist and colonial projects bent on eradicating indigenous knowledge (Comaroff and Comaroff 2003); the erasure of difference and singularity under universal liberalism; the way instrumental reason gave rise to technocratic totalitarianism (Adorno and Horkheimer [1944] 2002); and its coincidence with the turn to fossil fuels, meaning that "the mansion of modern freedoms" is built by that which will destroy it (Chakrabarty 2009, 208). The irreducible role of secrets and secrecy in the processes, claims, and logic of enlightenment is another dirty secret. I think of this secret as dirty not in the sense of being negative (as those secrets of the Enlightenment mentioned above are), but because the secret of secrecy's irrepressibility is seen to contaminate the purity of the transparency that serves, provisionally at least, as its opposite. It is also somewhat spoiled because it is not a real secret; it has been revealed before.

For example, Jean Starobinski (1988) finds that it is Rousseau's very claim to self-transparency that produces the impossibility of living a transparent life. In order to maintain (belief in) the purity of his transparent soul, Rousseau had to project opacity onto others—a situation that caused Rousseau much distress. Stefanos Geroulanos, who begins his history of transparency in French thought by looking at this case, writes, "Having declared himself transparent, [Rousseau] found the masks, separations, and veils he had banished from his soul all now rising up everywhere around him. . . . Step by step, this countergesture immobilized the transparent soul, making inevitable the increasingly solipsistic, paranoid, haunted self that Rousseau famously became" (2017, 2). Opacity returns as the repressed condition of transparency's claims, now manifested as external obstacles that interrupt the project of self-transparency. Steering clear of psychoanalytic frameworks, Geoffrey Bennington (2011) finds in Kant's work an awareness that the public can be duped by means of "a pseudo-transcendental publicity" or "a transcendental pseudo-publicity," which disguises the abyss at the heart of power, or the violence at the origin of the law and the state. In his reading of Kant's "Toward Perpetual Peace," Bennington suggests that it is a text troubled by the secret of transparency: "Uncovering secrets always might unveil the fact that the truth thus revealed is part of a greater system of secrecy, and merely a supplementary fold in the structure of veiling itself." He points out, "Enlightenment always might in fact be the dupe of apparent transparency, and transparency might still be a kind of veil" (27). With respect to the utilitarian thinking that informs Bentham's approach to publicity, we might draw on a fellow utilitarian, Henry Sidgwick, who remarked, "It may be conceivably right to do, if it can be done with comparative secrecy, what it would be wrong to do in the face of the world." But, crucially, under the principles of utilitarianism, this "should itself be kept comparatively secret" ([1874] 1907, 490). This metamaxim suggests that a secret should be made of the fact that exceptions to the rule of publicity—that is, the secret action taken to maximize the general good—are permissible under utilitarian thinking. For Sidgwick, secrecy about this "covert utilitarianism" (Gosseries and Parr 2018) is necessary because he harbored somewhat elitist fears about what such complex calculations will give rise to in the hands of what he named "the vulgar" (Sidgwick [1874] 1907, 489). The irony in these three readings resides in the reflexive imperative of enlightening. An enlightenment that cannot withstand its own call to dare to know or to cast light—scrutiny that might reveal the secrets and secrecy that make enlightening possible—risks becoming "a tool, serving the powers that be to preserve the order that is" (Malloy 2005, 58).

It is also worth noting, as Jürgen Habermas ([1964] 1991) and others have, that emergent Enlightenment ideals needed the cover of secrecy to be discussed before being put into practice in the eighteenth century (Koselleck 1988; Nowotny 2011). The public sphere, according to Habermas, existed behind closed doors to begin with "because it was a threat to any and all relations of domination" ([1964] 1991, 35). Wolfgang Hardtwig, too, points out that "the secret society facilitated—and this seems paradoxical only at first glance—an expansion and intensification in communications, as well as a proliferation and acceleration in the exchange of ideas" (1989, 74, qtd. in and translated by Jütte 2015, 250). The dilemma faced by such groups was that as their ideals were realized through the bourgeois public sphere, the ritual of secrecy, by then such an integral part of their identity, was no longer needed, and indeed threatened to undermine those ideals.

These examples remind us of the difficulty of parsing the terms at play in this book and point toward the secret as irreducible not simply in spite of transparency's ideals, but because of them. Moreover, they indicate something important about the cultural work that praise of openness and denunciation of secrecy performs. Starobinksi's interpretation of Rousseau, Bennington's reading of Kant, and Sidgwick's invocation of the utilitarian's dilemma tell us that publicity and transparency are not absolutes; they let secrecy in through the back door. They are not the absolute other of the secret, not least because the secret is not a stable object but, as Louis Marin writes, "an appearance or an apparition, a light, incorporeal envelope that floats over things, thoughts, discourses. . . . [It is] an incorporeality, a simulacrum, a nothing" (1998, 196). In light of this, revelation through publicity and transparency is merely one stage in a potentially endless play of secrecy effects. The case of secret societies reinforces the idea that secrecy is a condition of possibility of openness. We could read the moral and ethical force lent to openness by the philosophies of the time and in subsequent discourses inspired by them as a bid to obscure the fact that secrecy accompanies openness at every step. Light and dark, openness and secrecy—these oppositions had to carry weighty political and epistemological shifts.

Jütte, however, advises caution to historians who invoke a general "struggle of the Enlightenment against the secret" (Voigts 1995, 29, qtd. in and translated by Jütte 2015, 252). To make his point, Jütte claims that the secret sciences and arts (alchemy and magic) coexisted for a good amount of time with newer, open forms of science. Yet the fact that the secret arts coexisted with more open sciences highlights how the turn against the secret and secrecy occurred at the discursive level first and foremost. In practice, the secret arts proved as hard to eradicate as Rousseau's obstacles.

While Enlightenment thinking and practice did not (and could not) rid the self, politics, and society of secrecy and secrets, it certainly ensured that secrets accrued negative meanings as part of a far-reaching project of demystification. Secrets became the markers of courtly rule and outdated, esoteric knowledge—and for Rousseau and his followers, of dissembling and dishonesty. In theory at least, secrets became the apparent enemy of reason, truth, and progress. The American Enlightenment draws on this register, but its political institutions, like those in other regions, tolerate secrecy to a far greater extent than the positive rhetoric about transparency and publicity would suggest.

### "From Time to Time": American Ambivalence

Given the rising fortunes of openness during the Enlightenment, it is not surprising that the Founding Fathers instituted a principle of publicity in civic life when conditions allowed. Article I, Section 9, of the Constitution, for example, states, "A regular statement and account of receipts and expenditures of all public money shall be published from time to time." Section 5 of the same article reads, "Each House shall keep a journal of its proceedings, and from time to time publish the same, excepting such parts as may in their judgment require secrecy." The allowance for secrecy introduced here, however, displays an ambivalence toward openness—because oversight can cause issues for security and destabilize power—that is never resolved. As further markers of this ambivalence, Mark Fenster reads the qualifier "from time to time" as an indicator of "limited disclosure practices" (2010, 638), considers the separation of powers a block to "the creation of a uniform, comprehensive approach to public access" (637), and remarks on the uneven enactment of openness across different states. While its publicity provisions tentatively acknowledged the place and power of public oversight and open government, the Constitution also leaves a place for secrecy.

Like Fenster, Michael Schudson questions the efficacy of Article I, given that "the Senate proceeded in full secrecy for its first six years" (2015, 6). What Schudson does not provide, however, is an account of how the Senate was made to relinquish its proclivity for secrecy, which is just as telling. According to F. A. O. Schwarz, "Closing the Senate's doors prompted the first national debate about secrecy" (2015, 20). Bolstered by Madison and Jefferson, Philip Freneau, who edited the anti-Federalist *National Gazette,* conducted a systematic campaign against the Senate's closed-door policy. Using heated rhetoric, he condemned this form of secrecy, telling readers that it "is a worm which will prey and fatten upon the vitals of your liberty" and "is a masque to treachery"; only "honesty shrinks not from the public eye" (qtd. in Grotta 1971, 667–71). Schwarz notes, "At the core of Freneau's stance was an impassioned plea for an informed citizenry"

(2015, 21). Though the *Gazette* folded in 1793, Freneau's campaign against Senate secrecy staged a debate about open government in the free press—a key component of America's democratic design. The Senate opened its doors in 1794, at first only temporarily while the eligibility of a foreign-born senator was debated, and then permanently later that year after Senator Alexander Martin introduced a resolution. Federalist senators from New England changed their stance at the last minute and supported the measure, considering "the old, elitist style in politics" to be "obsolescent" (Schwarz 2015, 21), meaning that the Senate voted 19–8 to become an open institution. Schwarz concludes, "Power in the new America was increasingly based on publicity and openness, not the closed culture of aristocratic England" (21).

Blumenthal's (2010) history of transparency for the Sunlight Foundation emphasizes that "these early efforts to open government to the people relied on the simple revolutionary notion that ordinary people had an equal say in public life and deserved the information to craft informed opinions. The policies enacted may seem rudimentary by our standards today, but postal travel and open congressional sessions provided the meat of the information that fed public opinion and public debate." Much discussion centers on the question of whether the Constitution does or does not support transparency, including whether the separation of powers institutionalizes oversight (Marquardt 2011) or is more an effective mechanism for controlling the flow of information (Sagar 2013). Blumenthal and others sidestep this issue by concentrating on the conditions that had to be in place to make any oversight of government meaningful. Historian Matthew Connelly (2014) likewise locates the radicality of the founders' commitment to transparency in their attempts to create a citizenry that could read, understand, and discuss whatever material the government and the free press made public. The uneven application of this aspiration along racial, and for a time gendered, lines renders any talk of "universal" literacy, and therefore public oversight, deeply flawed. What we can say, rather, is that late eighteenth-century America boasted high literacy rates among free whites for the time. Connelly (2014) cites a well-documented estimate that 90 percent of white men could read and write by 1795 (Lockridge 1974), and he points out that the state subsidized and protected the postal service and the press, as well as encouraged schooling (Adams 1854), thereby help-ing to create the conditions of communication necessary for a (white male) public sphere capable of casting its gaze onto the government. Openness was as much a practical response to the informational and communicative needs of representative democracy as it was the en-actment of an Enlightenment ideal.

Claims of early openness or any new radical commitment to trans-parency are obviously flawed when contextualized within histories of racial and gendered occlusion and oppression. But they are also tempered by the fact that the early republic was reliant on secrecy for protection and security. In fact, the newness of the state, and es-pecially its hesitant promise of openness, made it vulnerable and in need of strategically deployed secrecy. Even the act of drawing up the Constitution was conducted beyond the glare of the public, with a majority of delegates agreeing to a mandate "that no copy be taken of any entry on the journal during the sitting of the House, without leave of the House. That nothing spoken in the House be printed, or oth-erwise published or communicated without leave" (Madison [1787] 2003, 58). What happened at the convention was therefore one ver-sion of an open secret. Citizens knew that the convention was taking place, but what was discussed remained confidential until decisions had been reached.

Secrecy was also present in the republic in the form of covert intel-ligence gathering, which was a central part of George Washington's strategy during the War of Independence and after.[7] As commander in chief of the continental army, for example, he established a spy net-work in New York known as the Culper Ring, and he spent 11 percent of his military budget on clandestine activity in 1776 (Knott 1996). Famously, Washington wrote in a letter, "The necessity of procuring good Intelligence, is apparent and need not be further urged. . . . For upon secrecy, success depends in most Enterprises of the kind, and for want of it, they are generally defeated" ([1777] 1983, 7). Though it would take more than another century to institutionalize intelli-gence operations (the FBI came into being in 1908 and the CIA in 1947), once free of British rule, the vulnerable young state put faith in the clandestine activities that had proved so useful during the fight for independence. Drawing on primary sources, Stephen F. Knott charts how, during the first hundred years of America's existence, clandestine activity included "intervention in the domestic affairs of foreign nationals through bribery and support for insurgent movements, kidnapping, employing journalists and clergymen for intelligence and propaganda purposes, and using secret service funds for domestic purposes" (1996, 5).

Whether it be the Federalist Papers repeatedly invoking the need for the executive to act with "secrecy and dispatch" (as in Jay in Federalist No. 64 or Hamilton in Federalist No. 70), covert intelligence gathering, or presidents claiming executive privilege to avoid disclosing information to Congress, America has always positioned some situations and information as exempt from a requirement for publicity or transparency. On the cusp of changing attitudes toward secrecy and openness, then, America applied a pragmatic approach to both at its inception. As secrecy accrued negative meanings, appeals to security and the public interest reigned as justifications for using it within government. But as openness accrued positive meanings, idealism and zeal entered America's rhetoric about its own openness. That is to say, while openness might have been a prerequisite for a meaningful representative democracy, it also became a key component of the mythology America told about itself—a myth that ignored all of the occlusions and exclusions on which it relied. The extension of America's Puritan exceptionalism to encompass American representative democracy positioned the latter as an act of enlightenment that could serve as a shining example for the rest of the world. Extollers might have concentrated more on the abstract concepts of "liberty" and "freedom," but attempts at open government and a free press played a significant role in realizing and illustrating those abstractions, at least for certain groups.

While the Constitution includes enough references to publication to bolster an interpretation that openness was an important part of the American project, Schudson and Fenster are right to point out that it lacks adequate legal provisions for transparency proper, and that the separation of powers leaves as much room for secrecy as oversight. This is why a range of measures geared toward rendering government more open in the twentieth century had to be vigorously campaigned for.[8] It is within the rationale given for openness and the rhetoric of those campaigns that we can find evidence of the moral register that increasingly comes to accompany issues of visibility. The moral certitude of these campaigns, which increases as the twentieth century progresses and reaches its zenith in the twenty-first century's transparency movement, seeks to overwrite the ambivalence regarding openness and publicity that has always dogged the American state. In fact, as we shall see, both the rhetoric of transparency advocacy and the investment in, reliance on, and reach of the covert sector intensify at an equal pace.

In 1913, Woodrow Wilson and his ally, Louis Brandeis, put forth political policies that offered arguments against and alternatives to opaque quarters of government and finance. In support of Wilson's antitrust reform proposed as part of his New Freedom, Brandeis in 1913 published a series of articles in *Harper's* in which he advocated publicity as a measure to curb monopolies and excessive commission for bankers. Both men extolled the virtues of "[opening] the doors and [letting] in the light on all affairs which the people have a right to know about" (Wilson [1913] 2018, 52). Such sentiments are familiar to us, repeated, adapted, and repurposed as they have been by various figures of the twentieth and twenty-first centuries, particularly American politicians and reformers. Take, for example, John F. Kennedy's pronouncement in a 1961 speech that "The very word 'secrecy' is repugnant in a free and open society"; or, more recently, Barack Obama's many invocations of transparency during his presidential campaign and time in office.

One of Wilson's speeches (and sections within *The New Freedom*) was called "Let There Be Light," making an unabashed reference to Genesis 1:3 while also referencing the Enlightenment appropriation of the metaphor. Of course, the evaluation of that light—"God saw the light and it was good" (1:4)—would have been well known by Wilson's audience. Wilson's rhetoric casts publicity and transparency, at risk of appearing to be dull, bureaucratic procedures, in a cosmic drama of good and evil. In positioning publicity and transparency as able to curtail the risks and worst excesses of both capital and politics—to hold back greedy bankers and dishonest politicians (or, more specifically for Brandeis, monopolies and big government)—the reformers presented light, and the publicity it represented, as part of a moral crusade. When Brandeis (1913) notes that "publicity is justly commended as a remedy for social and industrial diseases. Sunlight is said to be the best of disinfectants; electric light the most efficient policeman," he positions light as both the cure of cankerous secrecy and a guardian against reinfection.[9]

In the mid-1930s, Brandeis, by then a member of the Supreme Court, concentrated his enthusiasm for openness on establishing the *Federal Register* (Feinberg 2001). Some way of recording and communicating the plethora of regulations that arose from Roosevelt's New Deal was desperately needed. When it passed into law in 1935, the *Federal Register* ensured the daily publication of the growing number of executive agency rule and notice documents. Supplementing the *Federal Register* in a show of commitment to open government came a series of measures throughout the twentieth century, including the Administrative Procedure Act (1946), requiring agencies to publish notices of proposed rules for public comment. But none gave a clearer signal of in-principle transparency than the Freedom of Information Act (FOIA), even while classification would in practice place many limitations on access. The FOIA in the United States was implemented in 1966 and strengthened in the wake of the Watergate scandal and the fall of Richard Nixon. By making sure that all executive agencies made their operational documents available to the public in a timely manner, and by allowing for challenges against withheld information to be heard in court, it is clear that the FOIA, for all its limitations, "was a landmark development of a more open society" (Schudson 2015, 30).

Both Schudson and Fenster describe the cultural forces that coincided to make the FOIA possible in the 1960s and that eventually established transparency as "a consensual norm" (Schudson 2015, 18). At the beginning of his research, Schudson tells us, he had expected legislation supporting forms of openness to have originated in the cultural revolution of the 1960s; he was surprised to learn that the campaign for freedom of information and the right to know began decades earlier in response to increased government opacity that was in part simply due to the growth of the administrative state and in part due to sensitivity around weapons development during and after World War II.

Fenster explains how the movement for international press freedom in the postwar period fed into the calls for open government, sharing the same key phrases: "the right to know" and "freedom of information" (2017a, 27). Access to government information and the fight against executive secrecy animated both causes. Those members of the press concerned with freedom of information had a rousing activist in Harold Cross, author of *The People's Right to Know* (1953) and a government advocate in Democratic senator John Moss. Outraged by what Moss perceived as the arrogance displayed by an executive who refused to grant access to documents as it wished, he headed up a subcommittee of the House of Representatives' Government Operations Committee on government information (commonly referred to as the Moss Committee). He welcomed the support of media leaders, seeing his work as integral to their cause and vice versa. For over a decade, even as the presidency changed from Republican to Democrat, Moss chaired subcommittee hearings on government secrecy. The FOIA was unpopular with government agencies and his own party but lauded by a press concerned about the deleterious effects of government secrecy not only on the public's right to know but also on press freedom itself (Mellinger 2015). The legislation finally got enough votes with support from liberal Democrats and from Republicans wanting to aggravate the Johnson administration. Although it was far from unanimously supported at home, in time the act had far-reaching effects abroad. Currently, 119 countries, not all of which could be described as liberal democracies (including Russia and China), have adopted information access laws, most of them inspired by or modeled on the U.S. FOIA.

To gain support, Moss framed freedom of information in Cold War logic and rhetoric (Schudson 2015). As with so much Cold War discourse, this was as much a moral as a political argument. Moss intended freedom of information to stand as an emblem of the free world, in opposition to its communist enemies, who tightly controlled the dissemination of information. The phrase he repeatedly used in speeches and articles was the "paper curtain," which linked the obfuscating tactics of the government at home to the censorship used behind the "iron curtain"—Churchill's term for Soviet control. In the Cold War picture painted inside America, the Soviets stood for secrecy, suppression, and propaganda, and so Moss's rationale suggested that America could gain the moral high ground if it implemented legislation that aligned with openness, free speech, and a free press. Given that the press had campaigned hard to achieve access to information (including the work done by the American Society of

Newspaper Editors), it welcomed the FOIA and praised Johnson for, as a 1966 *Washington Post* op-ed put it, "signing it in the face of the adverse position toward it taken by a great many government spokesmen." The same article continues by claiming that the act has "morally armed" citizens with an "explicit assertion" of "the right to know."[10]

While sensibilities are difficult to chart, we can look to opinion polls to provide insight into public attitudes toward secrecy and openness, at least regarding the government. To commemorate the fiftieth anniversary of the passing of the FOIA, the Roper Center for Public Opinion Research published a report on changing public opinion on government transparency.[11] The report reveals that many postwar Americans thought that government was holding back important information that the public ought to have. In 1947, 59 percent of those polled thought this was the case, according to Gallup (as reported in Roper Center 2016). The FOIA might have passed without much notice from the pollsters and can be thought of as legislation that gained in public importance over time, but government secrecy was of concern to many midcentury Americans, at least when they were asked direct questions about it.

It would take the assassination of John F. Kennedy in 1963, the leaking and publication of the Pentagon Papers in 1971, and revelations about Watergate throughout 1972 to politicize government secrecy for, and place transparency on, the agenda of the wider population (as far as polls can indicate such things): "In 1977, a Harris poll found 76% thought it was very important for the new Congress to make government less secret and more open about what was going on" (Roper Center 2016). Although the 1980s saw Reagan roll back regulations with public support, "63% of the country opposed cutting the access people have to government records about themselves and public officials under the Freedom of Information Act" (Roper Center 2016). The Roper Center report rightly claims that in the following decade, the rise of the internet raised new concerns about the circulation of citizens' personal information held by government, sparking a debate that has only intensified with twenty-first-century digitization and datafication—and is the primary context of concern for much of this book.

Looking at citizen concerns with government practice only offers one element of the story about openness and its accrual of positive values. Any attempt to come to terms with the changing fortunes of openness and the rise of transparency in the latter half of the twentieth century must recognize that alongside legislation to make government more open (in theory, at least), a concurrent sociocultural, intrapersonal, and interpersonal change was taking place. These shifts are inextricably linked because both speak to forms of liberalization.

We can see a tolerance of and appetite for personal openness in evidence in twentieth-century practices and trends as varied as the validation of personal accounts by the implementation of oral history; the rise of support groups such as Alcoholics Anonymous and the importance of sharing one's story to recovery; experimentation with various drugs that encouraged greater communion and broke down boundaries; the frank discussions that accompanied the sexual revolution of the 1960s and feminist discourse of the 1970s; the coming-out narrative of the LGBT movement; and the uptake of psychotherapies based on the idea of a talking cure. Clearly some of these were produced within the cultural revolution of the 1960s; even those that preceded that period gained traction or validity during it. Of course, subjectivity and citizenship were reconstructed in the 1960s in a number of ways, and to reduce this to a shift in attitudes to secrecy and openness would be reductive. Nevertheless, it is fair to claim that while some cultural conservatives resisted, openness was becoming a positive signifier of modernity and progressiveness. It was praised in some influential quarters for being a mode of self-actualization capable of freeing the self, curing the self, making the self visible in the battle for recognition, or improving the quality of interpersonal intimacy.

The value of openness was reflected in and reinforced by twentieth-century media content. The 1960s saw certain figures contribute to a culture of confession, in particular celebrity evangelical preachers and therapists inviting the public to confess their sins and secrets on air (via radio and then television), and hailing the benefits of doing so (Wise Bauer 2008). From the psychoanalytic strand of this confessionary culture, Phil Donahue, and countless others after him, established the talk show genre, which relies on the currency of personal revelation. Reality television, which arguably began with MTV's *The Real World* in 1992, can also be seen as setting new standards for expectations of access and openness.[12]

The interplay of the personal and political would suggest that the more open people became about their own lives, the more open and available they expected their politicians and the government to become. This desire was answered first and foremost by the legislation detailed above, but also by (occasional) televised committee hearings (which began in 1948 but became popular with the hearings on interstate gambling in 1951); televised presidential debates (the first being that between Nixon and Kennedy in 1960); publication of detailed commission reports on matters of national speculation (such as the 888-page Warren Commission report investigating Kennedy's 1964 assassination, or, decades later, the Starr report in 1998, which provided an explicit account of relations between President Bill Clinton and Monica Lewinsky); a free press well trained in the art of muckraking; and, as a result of that investigative journalism, perennial political scandals and leaks.

The U.S. government had certainly committed enough sins of secrecy to warrant the repeated calls for transparency and fervor of belief in the powers of openness in postwar twentieth-century America. These include the following examples. Between 1953 and 1973, the CIA conducted experiments with mind control, information gathering, and psychological torture under the covert Project MK-Ultra. The activity came to light because of the efforts of the *New York Times'* Seymour Hersch in 1974 and prompted the Rockefeller Commission in 1975. Publication of the Pentagon Papers in 1971 revealed the extent to which government had shielded certain truths about the conflict in Vietnam from the public. As Powers summarizes it, "In a matter of days, the Pentagon Papers became the touchstone for a new view of American History: the decisions that shaped the Cold War were secret, and secrecy had protected these policies from a (virtuous) public that would have struck down the miscreants had the truth been known" (1998, 31). The break-in to and illegal wiretapping of the Democratic National Committee's Watergate headquarters sponsored by Nixon's reelection campaign committee, as well as Nixon's subsequent aggressive cover-up, were revealed by investigative reporters at the *Washington Post* and led to the president's resignation. Clandestine plots by the CIA to assassinate foreign leaders such as Fidel Castro and Patrice Lumumba, and surveillance and harassment of political radicals at home under the FBI's Counterintelligence Program (known as COINTELPRO) were investigated by the Church and Pike committees in 1975. An arms-for-hostages arrangement between America and Iran was revealed by a Lebanese newspaper in 1986. During the investigation into the deal, the secret and illegal funneling of funds from the sales of arms to the contras in Nicaragua emerged. Such revelations gave the impression that Congress and the Senate were symbolic bearers of power rather than real players, and that the levers of government were operated by forces beyond the glare of publicity that ignored the ties and responsibilities of representative democracy. In the post-Watergate climate, government secrecy was cast as admission of guilt and fed the public's antipathy toward it. Memorably, in his 1998 book, Patrick Moynihan, who as a senator experienced government secrecy firsthand, declared that "secrecy is for losers" (227). Far from proving that the twentieth century was "the secrecy era" (Schwarz 2015, 16), such revelations are evidence of the pressure placed on government secrecy by openness mechanisms including whistle-blowing, journalism, oversight committees, and the FOIA. Equally, with each morally questionable revelation, secrecy became increasingly difficult to defend.

Drawing on the way the health of democracy becomes entwined with the quality and extent of citizen oversight and access, government transparency in the twenty-first century has assumed new heights. Recent years have seen a shift in thinking about the role of citizens in democratic states and their relationship to those that govern. Representative democracy has been outmoded as an ideal in favor of participatory democracy as digital technologies make such participation more possible. In the process, transparency changes from a mechanism that improves the view citizens have of the state and the politicians representing their interests to an apparatus that stages a call to action—a demand on us to not only keep the state and politicians in our purview but to engage with the data on display in meaningful ways. I will turn to this in detail in chapters 2 and 4. In chapter 3, I will consider how contemporary open government advocates and lobbyists (those comprising the transparency movement) position transparency as a quasi-religious, universal good that reaches beyond partisan politics. Regardless of whether the dominant party happens to be Republican or Democrat, transparency is seen to bolster both democratic accountability and participation. I will consider how transparency is presented not only as bipartisan but also as postideological, while it is clear that increased digital storage and surveillance capacities have meant that our cultural proclivity for openness is being exploited by big tech and the security state.

Horn contends that "as a result of modern democracy's ideal of transparency and of the moralization of politics, secrecy has become precarious and problematic, something seen as both necessary and noxious, something constantly in need of legitimization yet never really legitimate" (2011, 105). Praise for openness, publicity, and transparency has meant that the value of secrets and secrecy, even while they continue to play a large role in statecraft and security, has been secreted away out of sight. Ambivalent about its commitment to openness from the start, the American state has always had a place for the dirty secret that secrecy became. One consequence of this cagey reliance on secrecy in the face of an increasingly moral register about the virtues of transparency is that the state has gained a monopoly on secrecy. Meanwhile, those to the left of centrist politics have often acquiesced to the moral lines inherited from Enlightenment thinking around these issues.[13] Much of this book is about the possibility of harnessing secrets and secrecy for progressive aims.

Fallen from grace yet still integral to the workings of the (everexpanding) security state, secrets in modern democracies represent sites of contestation; whenever they rear their heads, secrets prompt questions about the nature and health of democracy itself. Each administration handles "necessary" yet "noxious" secrets, as well as expectations of transparency, in different ways. The following chapter will consider the information imaginaries that have managed this relationship in twenty-first-century American politics. Doing so will allow us to unpack the relationship between secrecy and transparency beyond moralization.

# CHAPTER 2

# INFORMATION IMAGINARIES

The story of recent American politics can be told through the very different stances toward secrecy and transparency taken by the first three administrations of the twenty-first century. George W. Bush was overtly wedded to secrecy in the name of security, and it became a guiding modus operandi under the war on terror after the September 11, 2001, attacks. Barack Obama might have sanctioned many of the same covert security practices once in office, but he campaigned on the ticket of transparency and later implemented a number of open government measures. Obama's successor, Donald J. Trump, appeared indifferent to administrative transparency, but he presented himself as thoroughly unmediated and exposed invented secrets as conspiracy theories while being investigated himself for covert wrongdoing akin to conspiracy. (The analysis of Trump in this chapter concentrates on his presidential campaign and his term in office immediately before the Covid-19 pandemic.) The rise of transparency identified in the last chapter, then, veils a more complex relationship between rapidly multiplying and mutating forms of secrecy and transparency in contemporary mainstream politics. Paradoxically, however, openness can retain its moral position; it can remain an ideal even as actors practice secrecy. All kinds of maneuvers, contortions, and justifications are made in order to use secrecy while attempting to avoid being tarred by its brush. This chapter will examine some of the tensions and contradictions of each administration's attitude toward and implementation of secrecy and transparency, thereby challenging any reductive representation of a clear choice between secrecy and transparency. Such a representation may have political and cultural salience, but it fails to capture the complexity of twenty-first-century information-communication environments.

Political wrangles over the extent of government visibility tell us much about the priorities of each administration. Just as telling are the modes, mediums, and forms that transparency predominantly assumes at particular times. This chapter will therefore also place the different attitudes of Bush, Obama, and Trump toward secrecy and transparency within a shifting information-communication environment that sees the front line move from documents to digital data sets to social media feeds. In identifying these dominant forms, I am not suggesting that others have become defunct. Documents (paper or digital), for example, clearly remain a constant form of government communication for all three administrations. Rather, my focus is on how different dominant modes of transparency management are key components of information imaginaries. I use the term "information imaginaries" to capture the way in which fears, anxieties, and hopes about the uses to which information can be put, and about the subjects that might, nefariously or positively, act on information, inform otherwise prosaic regulatory or legal mechanisms that manage government information. If social imaginaries capture how a given people imagine their collective social life, then information imaginaries, in the context I am concerned with, offer insight into how certain state actors and formations implicitly and explicitly imagine and manage the different components involved in outward-facing communications and the flow of information. Each information imaginary relies on a particular form of communication. It also works on and with a specific idea of a citizen, the public, and the role and reach of oversight and access. Information imaginaries therefore shape the scope and tenor of accountability. This chapter reads political commitments and actions regarding secrecy and transparency in tandem with the communication forms used to manage competing claims on access and visibility.

## Bush, Secrecy, and Documents

Mary Graham, director of the Transparency Policy Project at Harvard, concerned with how emergency orders put in place during the war on terror were quickly becoming normalized, remarked, "We make policy by crisis, and we particularly make secrecy policy by crisis" (qtd. in Clymer 2003). The attacks on the World Trade Center in 2001 served as the crisis to justify increased secrecy. At the turn of 2006, Bush defended a recently exposed National Security Agency warrantless wiretapping program that he had authorized in 2002 in the following terms: "I think most Americans understand the need to find out what the enemy's thinking, and that's what we're doing" (qtd. in Lichtblau 2006). Indeed, the Bush administration appealed to intensified security needs during the war on terror to justify, enforce, and legitimize state secrecy—whether to the public, as in the example above; to newspaper editors when attempting to suppress a story about covert operations (Risen 2018); or to Congress when passing emergency securitizing measures, including extended surveillance capacity, such as those detailed in the Patriot Act (2001). In an attempt to release secrecy from its allotted place on the moral register in post–Church Committee, protransparency American politics, the Bush administration refashioned secrecy as being in defense, rather than to the detriment, of an American way of life.

As early as 2003, journalist Adam Clymer reported that "the Bush administration has put a much tighter lid than recent presidents on government proceedings and the public release of information, exhibiting a penchant for secrecy that has been striking to historians, legal experts and lawmakers of both parties." The title of a critical book by former Nixon counsel John Dean speaks to such an assessment: *Worse than Watergate: The Secret Presidency of George W. Bush* (2004). In practice, such secrecy had to be secured through the use of new measures and existing systems designed to stem the flow of information to the public and press. In terms of existing systems, I want to consider the Bush administration's use of the state secrets privilege and its attitude toward the classification system as emblematic of its information imaginary. This information imaginary centered on redacting and restricting access to documents, which were for so long the primary locus of government transparency, whether we think of the *Federal Register* or the FOIA.

The state secrets privilege is a common-law (nonconstitutional) evidentiary rule that prevents classified documents from being used as evidence in civil suits against the government. A "Secrecy Report Card" for 2008 makes for interesting reading: "Invoked only 6 times between 1953 and 1976, the privilege has been used a reported 48 times—an average of 6 times per year in 8 years (through 2008)—more than double the average (2.46) in the previous 24 years."[1] Other sources suggest that the evidence for greater frequency of use is inconclusive, but that "the Bush administration arguably invoked the privilege in a qualitatively different manner, advocating in a larger number of cases outright dismissal without considering any evidence" (Wittes 2009, 259).

The landmark case for the state secrets privilege was *United States v. Reynolds* in 1953. The widows of several civil engineers aboard a military plane that had crashed in 1948 sued the government for negligence. Their lawyers' requests for the accident report were met with a claim that doing so would compromise state security. The Supreme Court upheld the government's claim and "formally recognized and established the framework for the government's 'state secrets' privilege—a privilege that for decades [has] enabled federal agencies to conceal conduct, withhold documents, and block civil litigation, all in the name of national secrecy" (Siegel 2008, ix–x).

The state secrets privilege has long been a focus of criticism for liberals for the opportunities it provides for abuse of state power. Fears of abuse were only heightened when the accident report of the 1948 crash was finally declassified in 1996. The report did not reveal any sensitive information about the B-29's mission, but it did expose a compromised aircraft—information that would have supported the widows in their lawsuit. Given the checkered history of the privilege, it is not surprising that civil rights activists were (and still are) concerned by its use during the war on terror (Wittes 2009).

The most notorious invocation of the state secrets privilege under Bush was *El-Masri v. Tenet* in 2006. Khaled El-Masri, who was born in Kuwait but was of Lebanese heritage, became a German citizen in 1985. While crossing the border into Macedonia for a vacation in 2003, he was detained. Guards mistakenly identified him as a member of the Al-Qaeda Hamburg cell who had a similar name. CIA agents accompanied El-Masri to an Afghan secret prison where, according to El-Masri, he was held for five months without legal counsel and subjected to torture. When the CIA realized their mistake, El-Masri was unceremoniously released at an Albanian airfield. El-Masri sued George Tenet, the director of the CIA, but the administration invoked the state secrets privilege to block access to government documents. The case was dismissed by a district court, which was satisfied with the validity of the assertion of privilege—and satisfied as well that the national interest with regards to security outweighed what the court called El-Masri's private interests. When whole cases are dismissed like this, the fight over documentary evidence is shot through with the irony that a legal privilege can suspend legal process.

If the Bush administration on occasion used the state secrets privilege to divert legal scrutiny from covert operations and executive action, it relied on a tightening of the classification system in a more consistent manner in order to stem the flow of information. The Bush administration reversed a trend set by President Clinton and a 1995 executive order that "initiated one of the largest declassification efforts in modern history, releasing millions of formerly classified documents" (Bailey 2004, 188). Indeed, Bush was deeply invested (financially and ideologically) in the classification system: "In fiscal years 2001 to 2003, the average number of original decisions to classify information increased 50% over the average for the previous five fiscal years" (Barone 2006, xii–xiii). While defenders of Bush attribute this propensity toward secrecy to the increased pressures in post–September 11 America, even before the attacks, "the 260,978 classified documents in the executive branch represented an increase of 18 percent over the previous year" (Bailey 2004, 188). A memo, "in the works long before the terrorist attacks," according to Saskia Sassen (2006, 183), issued in October 2001 by Attorney General John D. Ashcroft informed agencies, "When you carefully consider FOIA requests and decide to withhold records . . . you can be assured that the Department of Justice will defend your decisions" (Department of Justice 2001). This markedly contrasts with the previous attorney general, Janet Reno, whose memorandum under Bill Clinton warned FOIA officers that they should presume that "the Justice Department would no longer defend an agency's withholding of information merely because there was a substantial legal basis for doing so. Rather, in determining whether or not to defend a nondisclosure decision, we will apply a presumption of disclosure" (Department of Justice 1993).

By 2004, J. William Leonard, the official responsible for oversight of classification, complained that war was being used "as an excuse to disregard the basics of the security classification system" (1). In line with this, the Bush administration classified material that had been previously public. Most controversially, they retroactively classified a former translator's accusation that the FBI had missed terrorist warnings concerning September 11 (Lichtblau 2004). In addition, the administration increased its use of the advantageously vague category "sensitive but unclassified" (SBU) to remove certain information that had been in the public domain from view. Crucially, "there is no federal agency charged with regulating the use of SBU or hearing appeals. It is therefore up to each federal agency, branch, office and official to decide where to draw the line between public accountability and security which allows near-infinite flexibility in standards and logic" (Masco 2014, 132). SBU speaks to an information imaginary that came to include fears about connected knowledge that positions individual documents as potentially dangerous when placed in relation to and in a network of others. Masco argues that this mosaic theory of information has "implicitly militarized" the public as "keeping basic governmental information from citizens is increasingly equated with antiterrorism and normalized as an administrative practice" (130).

While connectedness presented a danger in the public sphere, the Bush administration saw it as a solution to atomized intelligence in the security services. A proprietary attitude toward intelligence, reinforced by closed technological systems, was believed to have created the blind spot that permitted Al-Qaeda to orchestrate the September 11 attacks. As the military and security sectors increasingly utilized networked intelligence systems, the propensity toward nondisclosure in the classification system created obstacles for any citizen wishing to place the state under scrutiny. These conditions configured the FOIA as having the potential to weaken American democracy rather than strengthen it. The problem, as Steven Aftergood notes, is that legitimate and illegitimate uses of the classification system become hard to disentangle: "Genuine national security secrecy is diluted in an ocean of unnecessary bureaucratic secrets and defamed from time to time by abuse in the form of political secrecy" (2009, 404).

There are other notable attempts to curtail the flow of documents and information. These include Vice President Dick Cheney's closed meetings of the Energy Task Force and refusal for many years to disclose records of attendees; and the Bush administration's executive order of November 2001 that provided provisions for withholding presidential papers, even posthumously. This modified the Presidential Records Act of 1978, which was implemented, for salient reasons, in the wake of the Watergate scandal. In the FOIA, Bush inherited a document-based system of transparency that could only ever hope to offer imperfect accountability. By sequestering more and more information, and by implementing security measures via the classification system, the Bush information imaginary exploited the imperfect accountability built into the FOIA to its protagonist's advantage.

The secrecy of the Bush administration frustrated citizen oversight. In staging a battle over documents in this way, it inadvertently bolstered the argument for increased transparency, thus continuing the twentieth-century faith in transparency and publicity to secure (imperfect) accountability. That is to say, calls for access in the face of secrecy reinforce belief in the rewards that visibility will bring. For Jodi Dean, this process is what constitutes the very idea of the public: "The public as that subject with a right to know" is "an effect of the injunction to reveal" (2002, 11). She offers the following clarification, "A public isn't exactly called into being through publicity, through revelation or exposure; rather, publicity as a system or set of belief-materializing practices produces the sense of the public" (11). As long as there are secrets to be discovered and documents to clamor for, the promise and ideal of a liberal democratic public is sustained; freedom of information has been mistaken for real freedom. In the process, the subject is positioned by, but responds in myriad ways (depending on stratifying factors) to, "the paranoia, surveillance and compulsive will to know" that marks "the ideal of publicity" (53).

This model of the public as determined by an endless cycle of concealment and revelation is helpful, but we still need to pay attention to how publicity and transparency mechanisms evolve and also to the nature of the secrets being protected. Each new articulation of the information imaginary—the specific ways in which concealment and revelation are mediated and managed, and how the public is expected to engage with the information revealed—modifies the social contract concerning the scope of citizen's rights, freedoms, and agency. If, as Masco (2014) argues, the Bush era militarized the public, then the public sphere becomes laden with risk; knowledge and knowing are suspect; and networked information is rendered dangerous. The Obama administration inherited and reconfigured the components of this information imaginary with different results.

### Obama, Transparency, and Digital Data Sets

"For a long time now," Barack Obama remarked at a 2009 swearing-in ceremony for senior officials in Washington, D.C., "there's been too much secrecy in this city" (qtd. in Stolberg 2009a). This continued a long-running theme in Obama's presidential campaign concerning open government. He used transparency in his endeavor to restore domestic and international faith in the U.S. government. Obama's rhetoric and actions constituted an attempt to reinvigorate transparency as a position and practice superior to the preceding paradigm of secrecy. If Bush's administration seemed to be committed to a particularly resilient and excessive strain of secrecy, then Obama's administration deliberately sought to distinguish itself with the promise of financial, political, bureaucratic, and personal transparency. Press coverage of the incoming administration certainly focused on this shift in tone and strategy (Stolberg 2009a; Froomkin 2009).

Obama drew on the different Enlightenment traditions outlined in chapter 1, represented most clearly by Rousseau and Bentham. I will come to Obama's particular implementations of administrative utilitarian transparency later, but it is worth noting that transparency for Obama was more than simply an external goal to be achieved by policy. An aura of authenticity gleaned from self-transparency was integral to Obama's political persona and appeal. His prepresidential memoir, *Dreams from My Father* (1995), exemplifies this. Michelle Obama pointed to this book as evidence of her husband's lack of affectation and deceit: "Barack is who he says he is. . . . There is no mystery there. His life is an open book. . . . And unlike any candidate he has really exposed himself, pre-political ambition, so it's a book that is kind of free from intent" (qtd. in Remnick 2010). As a senator, Obama took opportunities to reinforce the impression that he was honest even when it might risk controversy. For example, whenever Obama was asked whether he had ever inhaled (in reference to Bill Clinton's infamous sophistry regarding smoking marijuana), Obama admitted that he had, adding, "That was the point" (qtd. in Anburajan 2007). The Obama campaign was one of the first to harness the reach of social media, which made Obama appear more available and accountable (Everett 2009). Mediation did not obstruct transparency, as it might have. Rather, it gave the illusion of bringing candidate Obama closer to the electorate. Of course, "this entire mechanism of visibility is . . . a much-mediated representation of unmediated access" (Spivak 2009, 191)—a feature that became even more pertinent in the case of Trump. This aesthetic (as well as ethic) of transparency resonated with those members of the electorate turning against the secretive and myth-investing Bush administration, guided for so long by the belief, as one Bush aide infamously put it, that "we are an empire now, and when we act, we create our own reality" (qtd. in Suskind 2004).

Obama's transparency of self offered a notable counterpoint to the negative stereotype of self-serving, obfuscating politicians from any party. But it was the immediate declaration of a commitment to government transparency that presented the starkest contrast to the inward-looking secrecy that Bush was associated with. The first minute of the Obama administration launched a new White House website, pledging to "provide a window for all Americans into the business of the government" (qtd. in Stolberg 2009b). On his first day in office, Obama released a memorandum on transparency, which committed him to an "unprecedented level of openness in Government," and he promised to make transparency one of "the touchstones of this presidency" (Executive Office of the President 2009a). The same memorandum pledged to develop recommendations concerning transparency; these became the Open Government Directive, issued on December 8, 2009. The directive required government departments to publish more information online, improve the quality of that information, and further "institutionalize a culture of open government" (Executive Office of the President 2009c, 4).

To understand the Obama information imaginary, we need to focus on the dominant form of administrative transparency at its heart. Obama certainly renewed commitment to the FOIA. He issued a memorandum that insisted, "In the face of doubt, openness prevails. . . . All agencies should adopt a presumption in favor of disclosure" (Executive Office of the President 2009b). He instigated an intra-agency review of classification procedures to remedy overclassification and to systematize procedures concerning SBU information, among other issues. However, his flagship transparency initiative was the digital data clearinghouse for the federal government: Data.gov. This signaled a shift from reactive and reticent disclosure to proactive disclosure.

Data.gov was greatly influenced by digital projects coming out of the transparency movement in the last years of the Bush administration. The Sunlight Foundation, for example, on its website notes that its aim is to "make government more accountable and transparent" through the use of "cutting-edge technologies and ideas." In practice, the transparency movement comprises a varied group of advocates, each with its own field of interest, whether aid and development in the global south, freedom of information, concerns about the influence of lobbyists on votes in Congress, or the nature of financial donations to American domestic political campaigns. Nevertheless, many of them work under the assumption that "publicity prevents the corruption that is almost inevitable in closed processes; . . . information allows citizens to participate in democratic decision-making; and this knowledge makes people better 'consumers' of both public and private goods and allows voters more effectively to hold politicians accountable" (Schmitt 2010). In their commitment to securing accountability, these projects are very much in keeping with ideas of publicity and openness from the past, but they include a new emphasis on the public as "consumers" of government information. As I will show, this marrying of accountability with market imperatives became a key characteristic of the Obama information imaginary.

Data.gov was intended, as the website claimed at its inception, to "increase public access to high value, machine readable datasets generated by the Executive Branch of the Federal Government."[2] It was launched in May 2009 with only 47,000 data sets, but now hosts more than six times this figure. The kind of data available has always been extremely varied. Users can find a data set published by the U.S. Census Bureau and the Department of Commerce charting national trade, including imports, exports, and balance of payments for goods and services; a data set containing disability claim information; and a data set providing demographic information on American nuclear facilities—to take just three examples. While the breadth of the catalog is impressive, the openness of all this data is obviously meaningless until it is witnessed. And it is the ideological call on citizens interpellated as data subjects that was key to the Obama information imaginary.

The big data released by Obama's government required particular skills from citizens and a new kind of (unelected and unregulated) mediator: those who could analyze data, and those who could create apps, data visualizations, and platforms to aid navigation and analysis. This form of transparency creates a "data public," which is imagined to be able to "analyse and do things with data" (Ruppert 2015, 135). Witnessing, as Evelyn Ruppert recognizes, "is thus turned into doing such that the literary technologies of auditor statements or government annual reports are displaced by myriad analyses conducted by imagined data publics" (2015, 129–30). In the process, the multiple agents that make up the data public produce rather than reveal (myriad versions of) the state. With the implementation of Data.gov, the burden of monitoring, regulating, and translating the transactions of the state moved from the state to the now-responsible citizen: in order to fully participate, citizens were asked to be auditors, analysts, translators, programmers. An experience of agency in this respect relies on digital competence, access, and leisure time. But there was an additional imperative at work here, for "do[ing] things with data" was not just a pastime of vigilant netizens wishing to keep the state in check; the data public included entrepreneurs and consumers because government posited data as a resource to mine and commodify.

The White House Office of Science and Technology Policy's remit for its Presidential Innovation Fellows in 2013, for example, was to "unleash data from the vaults of the government as fuel for innovation" (Chapman, Panchadsaram, and Farmer 2013). With this aim in mind, the Innovation Fellows organized a series of datapaloozas—gatherings of entrepreneurs, software developers, and policy makers to discuss new ways of harnessing the energy of different data streams—on health, energy, education, global development, and finance. Promoted at these events, open data streams give rise to downloadable applications intended to aid choices in the public and private sectors, such as choosing a school for one's child or assessing a surgeon's success rate.[3]

During Obama's time in office, the data economy was earmarked to stimulate and fuel economies, with some impressive potential figures cited. For example, a report by McKinsey Global Institute (Manyika et al. 2013) estimated that the global market in open data, measured in terms of job creation, profit margins, and efficiency savings, is worth up to $5 trillion a year. The World Bank ended its macroeconomic report on the value of open data by stating, "While sources differ in their precise estimates of the economic potential of Open Data, all are agreed that it is potentially very large" (2014, 20). These two reports, I should note, are not limited to open public sector data, but a report from Open Data Institute HQ analyzing research on the value of open data tells us that "those studies focused on the value of public sector open data alone found that it is worth between 0.4% and 1.5% of an economy's GDP" (ODIHQ 2015). It is not the case that the economic value of open data automatically casts suspicion on the rhetoric concerning its social value. But in the case of Data.gov, it certainly introduced market logics into government transparency mechanisms. This in turn carved out a particular position for citizens.

Data.gov's model of data-driven transparency addressed citizens in three stages. First, it positioned their vigilance as a form of civic duty that would enable them to realize the social value on offer and be fully engaged political subjects. Almost immediately, however, it excused citizens from their civic duty in this form, at least as mere citizens, because it acknowledged that vigilance was nearly impossible, necessitating skills and free time most ordinary citizens do not possess. The model thus outsourced vigilance to data entrepreneurs, with the implication being that citizens would consider becoming such entrepreneurs, or at least use applications produced by entrepreneurs. Finally, it asked citizens to buy back (or sell) the very data that was made available to (and for) them, now in a digestible, marketable form in order, as one Data.gov blog entry put it, to help citizen-consumers facing "increasingly complex choices in today's marketplace" (Gearen 2013). In order to be an ideal citizen within the Obama information imaginary, one had to be a consumer of mediated open government data and accept the responsibility therein implied. It becomes the citizen's responsibility to notice any anomalies, abuse, or corruption. Equally, citizens only have themselves to blame if they do not consume the data that can help them to navigate the system and the choices laid out before them.

As open data answered the dual demands of democratic accountability and economic growth, it configured the imaginary identity of the ideal data subject as at once citizen, auditor, consumer, and entrepreneur. Neoliberal ideology has long ensured the public acquiescence to and accommodation of the marketization of many aspects of social and political life, from education to health. What was new here was that the market (embodied by third-party data entrepreneurs) got to decide the very stakes of the political. Further, many apps made possible by Data.gov (and its British counterpart, Data.gov.uk) are concerned with things like real estate, finding the best school or surgeon, checking food-safety statistics, accessing transport information, and viewing the weather.[4] They help networked citizens navigate a variable field of provision rather than evening out that field—by, for example, implicitly encouraging people to avoid underperforming schools rather than ensuring that those schools receive more assistance.

In general, the government data sets that could be made to yield profits were those shared in such a format that the data could be received, understood, and rendered actionable. Profitability was also based on (public) demand, resulting in a paradox. The public already had to know what it wanted in order to receive the applications that could help it understand the data. Accountability was thus limited by the conditions of profitability.

The next two chapters will examine the implications of data-driven transparency from different perspectives. In chapter 3, I will turn to the ways in which data-driven transparency became a template to be exported around the globe in ways that are less than equitable. In chapter 4, I explore how such open government data, when considered in tandem with digital surveillance, shape a subjectivity for citizens that lacks, rather than gains, political agency. But at this juncture, the important point to recognize is that while transparency had been a buzzword for previous third-way approaches (including that associated with President Clinton and, in the United Kingdom, Prime Minister Tony Blair), Obama implemented transparency by harnessing the new capacities of data aggregation and storage in ways that reshaped the relationship between citizen and state. This new information imaginary transformed associations of government information from immanent security threat to entrepreneurial possibility and market form. However, it also transformed "ideal" citizens from subjects content with a social contract that trades reduced access to government information for increased safety into consumers responsible for individually accessing government data and services.

As I note above, the document-based systems of government transparency and reactive disclosure that offer flawed accountability were obviously still in operation during Obama's administration. However, it was data-driven transparency and the promise of disclosure by default that informed the information imaginary at that time. Real-time reporting and the perfect accountability it was supposed to enable remained a fantasy for the initially rudimentary public sector platform. Nevertheless, Obama's information imaginary certainly drew on these potential affordances; it also preferred to sidestep static documents—and the political contestation between citizens' rights and state security that they represent. Some research has shown that open government data reduces the need for Freedom of Information provision at the local level (Stern 2018). In theory, this could also work at the federal level. Access to accurate, timely, and granular data sets from every government agency in usable formats could circumvent the need to request information and data after the fact. Yet open data of federal agencies that help citizens navigate civic life is different from classified government documents that contain the decisions and actions that affect the parameters and underlying conditions of life in America and U.S. foreign policy. Open data cannot sate an appetite for classified (or even just buried) information. This asymmetric offering therefore did little to quell concerns over securitization and covert operations.

To address more overtly political concerns, Obama did try to rectify the most contentious aspects of Bush's secrecy policies. He announced the closure of the Guantánamo Bay facility—for so long an impenetrable detention center, its detainees beyond the Geneva Convention of Human Rights and public oversight—in Executive Order 13492 of January 22, 2009. (As we now know, Obama found the practicalities of closure insurmountable, and Guantánamo remained running at a reduced capacity through the end of his presidency.[5]) In another executive order issued on the same day (13491), Obama ordered the closure of CIA prisons known as black sites, authorized by a classified presidential directive six days after September 11 and containing "an untold number of 'ghost detainees' whose existence has never properly been confirmed" (Guardian 2009). Obama also outlawed the use of Bush-sanctioned "enhanced interrogation techniques" (Executive Office of the President 2009d), the use of which had come to light through detainee complaints and a subsequent FOIA lawsuit that the *New York Times* called "among the most successful in the history of public disclosure" (Shane 2009). Although Obama continued the practice of rendition, he promised to provide greater oversight of those detainees (Johnston 2009). Although reluctant, Obama even capitulated to pressure to publish the White House visitor's log on September 4, 2009. Obama made the most of this by claiming the moral high ground: "Americans have a right to know whose voices are being heard in the policymaking process" (qtd. in Associated Press 2009). Citizens for Responsibility and Ethics in Washington executive director Melanie Sloan said, "The Bush administration fought tooth and nail to keep secret the identities of those who visited the White House. In contrast, the Obama administration—by putting visitor records on the White House website—will have the most open White House in history" (qtd. in Associated Press 2009). Obama attempted to clear the deck of secrecy policies in order to start afresh.

However, the Obama administration leaned too heavily on the state architecture of secrecy and covert operations for his transparency measures to regain public trust. First, despite criticizing Bush's invocation of the state secrets privilege, initiating a policy review, and declaring that "we must not protect information merely because it reveals the violation of a law or embarrassment to the government" (Obama 2009), Obama's Department of Justice continued to invoke the state secrets privilege to block both civil cases and private lawsuits at an unprecedented rate. Under his watch, the Department of Justice failed to report to Congress regarding the government's use of the state secrets privilege since 2011, even though Attorney General Eric Holder committed to do so in 2009 (Department of Justice 2009).[6]

Transparency campaigners and press freedom advocates also criticized what they saw as the punitive approach to leakers and whistleblowers taken by the Obama administration, which prosecuted nine cases under the Espionage Act when it has only been used four other times in total since 1945. In addition to the repurposing of an act originally intended to prosecute spies rather than government employees who speak to the press, Obama's Department of Justice and the FBI used other methods to control the flow of information with respect to the press, including "[spying] on reporters by monitoring their phone records, [labeling] one journalist an unindicted co-conspirator in a criminal case for simply doing reporting and [issuing] subpoenas to other reporters to try to force them to reveal their sources and testify in criminal cases" (Risen 2016). Perhaps the clearest signal that Obama was willing to rely on and invest in comparable levels of legally questionable, secret activity to that of the Bush administration, however, was given by National Security Agency (NSA) contractor and whistle-blower Edward Snowden in 2013. Within the PowerPoint presentations explaining programs like XKeyscore, which allowed analysts with no prior authorization to search vast databases containing the communication and browsing histories of millions of users, the public was able to glimpse the extensive powers of a covert apparatus of mass data surveillance not subject to public oversight.[7]

Transparency always has its limits, both in practice and theory (about which I write more in the next chapter). Obama was the first to make it clear that advocating transparency did not mean he would be soft on security. Few transparency advocates campaign for total transparency, and national security is almost always seen as an exception (though the parameters of that exception are hotly debated). In this way, accusations of hypocrisy might not get us very far. They certainly keep us in a logic of either/or, in which practicing secrecy annuls any claims to transparency. Rather than the coexistence of secrecy and transparency prompting new appraisals of the concept and practice of transparency, conventional thinking maintains transparency as an ideal that few can achieve but that everyone must aspire to. We need to ask if the opposition between secrecy and transparency is sustainable. What is missing in this presentation of the political problem?

These questions animate this book, and I will attempt to answer them in several different stages that will involve challenging the efficacy of transparency, exploring the progressive potential of secrecy, and eventually deconstructing the opposition between secrecy and transparency to explore new political formations and frames. Before I begin that process in the chapters that follow, however, I want to devote the rest of this chapter to the Trump information imaginary as it evolved before the Covid-19 global pandemic. This is an important case for the deconstructive project I have just outlined because it represents a particularly cynical disruption of the opposition between secrecy and transparency. It also represents both a disregard for and disinterest in the model of imperfect accountability of document-based transparency and the implicit promise of perfect accountability embedded within the provision of open data. The Trump information imaginary has been characterized by the fragmentary, rapid, and adversarial nature of the Twitter feed. While I am interested in the progressive potential of a disruption to the opposition between secrecy and transparency, the case of Trump makes it clear that such a disruption can also be used in the service of regressive forces, inequality, and the arrogation of power. Rather than devalue or derail this book's attempt to reappraise the politics of secrecy and/or transparency, Trump's particular brand of populist untransparent transparency—which classed his opponents as remote and secretive, promised direct access through social media feeds, and utilized revelation as misdirection—makes such an endeavor all the more pressing.

### Trump, Immediacy, and Twitter

Mark Fenster writes: "The United States, whose 50-year-old Freedom of Information Act (FOIA) has served as a model for much of the activism that the age of transparency called forth, might be departing from the long arc of transparency's ascent under a Trump administration" (2017b, 173). Even during Bush's terms in office—which, as I have shown, are widely considered to have been shrouded in and supportive of secrecy—the way in which the ascent of transparency was tied to a grand narrative of progress was left largely intact. That is to say, even while Bush made the acquisition of government documents, and therefore oversight, more difficult, calls for and belief in the efficacy of publicity mechanisms like the FOIA intensified. The Obama administration tried to answer these calls. Trump's first few years in office raised a real question as to whether a belief in transparency's power could survive a climate in which revelation was so fetishized yet simultaneously rendered so impotent—that is, when transparency no longer acted as a corrective to corruption. Various factions clamored for Trump's tax returns, for example. Take Senator Elizabeth

Warren who, after taking a DNA test to rebut Trump's claim that she lied about her Native American heritage, took to Twitter to announce, "I took this test and released the results for anyone who cares to see because I've got nothing to hide. What are YOU hiding, @realDonaldTrump? Release your tax returns—or the Democratic-led House will do it for you soon enough" (Twitter, @elizabethforma, October 15, 2018). However, all kinds of sensational misdemeanors came to light, or half-light, without incurring, at least at the time of writing, power-diminishing consequences.[8] Revelations that at other times, with an alternative attention economy and political frame, might have turned casual supporters, if not the base, against a president, even served to bolster Trump's popularity.[9] Indeed, when details of how little Trump had paid in federal tax did leak out in the press, a majority of the rank-and-file Republican base said that they either did not believe the *Times* report or deemed Trump a good businessman for avoiding taxes (Reuters/Ipsos 2020). When revelation is not the prelude to justice, it becomes part of a rapid cycle of concealment and revelation that might mimic traditional liberal democratic processes, but in an increasingly exhausted form. This cycle is not new. Indeed, Jodi Dean's *Publicity's Secret* (2002), which I draw on above and at other points in this book, shows us the ways in which this cycle took on a particular identity through technocultures of the late twentieth century. However, as a result of the digital platforms and political configurations that ushered in Trump's presidency, the cycle was exacerbated far beyond what Dean observed at the beginning of the twenty-first century.

The Trump information imaginary mostly tolerated, but was largely disinterested in, existing administrative transparency mechanisms like the FOIA and open government data. Unlike the two preceding administrations, Trump was not quick to release a memorandum on how government agencies should handle public records requests, for example. With regards to open data, the transition period between the Obama and Trump administrations, then the early days of the latter, prompted concerns from open data activists, educators, environmentalists, and librarians regarding the continued availability of open data generated by government agencies.[10] Fears of data drying up abated once Trump signed the Open, Public, Electronic, and Necessary Government Data Act on January 14, 2019, committing federal agencies to publish machine-readable data sets. This was perhaps surprising—a win for transparency advocates in a hostile climate. However, the Trump administration's rhetoric made it clear that it was the economic potential of open government data, rather than opportunities to foster accountability, that was of most interest.[11] It also might reveal something about the limited scope of data-driven transparency's oversight if the Trump administration had nothing to fear from it.

While an investment in open data at home was justified for how it could create "American jobs" (White House 2017b), Trump did not show great enthusiasm for or commitment to international open government initiatives. For example, the United States delayed publishing its fourth National Action Plan for Open Government despite being a founding member of the Open Government Partnership (OGP). When the action plan was finally published in February 2019, it was criticized for its timid scope, announcing only eight commitments compared to the forty-five made in the previous action plan released in October 2015. Moreover, many of the eight initiatives were actually repurposed from existing legislation, not new ones.[12] Such a lukewarm attitude echoed Trump's distaste for other international alliances such as NATO.

In addition, concerns were raised about the presentation and use of certain open data sets under Trump. For example, there was evidence that some agency websites had removed links to key data sets, such as those concerning climate change, even while the data sets remained online (Environmental Data and Governance Initiative 2018). There was also consternation at the discrimination embedded in the Trump administration's requests for new "open" data. For instance, in January 2017, Trump issued an executive order that sought to tighten immigration law and included a section that directed the secretary of Homeland Security and the attorney general to collect data that would "promote the transparency and situational awareness of criminal aliens in the United States" (White House 2017a). Here transparency is used as an avatar for forms of surveillance that in practice fall on the most precarious communities. This is an example of "damage centered" research: "research that gathers data to reproduce damage" (Cifor et al. 2019).

With respect to other modes of administrative transparency, two of the most troubling reversals of Obama administration transparency protocols were the discontinuation of publication of the White House visitor logs and U.S. troop levels. The former meant that it was impossible to get a sense of which lobbyists and influential figures were meeting with the president. The latter meant that the public no longer had an accurate idea of where the United States was sending its troops, and consequently which military operations were priorities at any given time (Schulman and Friend 2018). Trump also pushed back on the new disclosure and reporting requirements that Congress adopted in the Further Consolidated Appropriations Act of 2020, claiming that that they "encroach on executive authority and that they may not be implemented as written" (Aftergood 2019). The importance of such targeted transparency black spots was heightened because there was little room for the oversight traditionally secured by the fourth estate within the Trump information imaginary. Daily press briefings dwindled under press secretary Sarah Sanders's watch (July 2017 to June 2019) and were only revived because of the Covid-19 pandemic; nondisclosure agreements among White House staffers were de rigueur; and Trump continually branded liberal legacy media the "enemy of the people" and, more commonly, "fake news."[13]

I want to consider the post-truth arsenal that characterized the Trump information imaginary in more detail. Doing so makes it easy to see where this indifference to administrative forms of transparency came from. In the Trump information imaginary, data and facts, when not produced in the service of or shaped according to Trump's populist agenda, were inconvenient but not insurmountable. Data and facts could be usurped by a deluge of other communicative content, including that which is best labeled conspiracist and post-truth.

### Conspiracy Theorist in Chief

The appearance of conspiracy theories in American political discourse is nothing new.[14] Historians including Bernard Bailyn (1967), David Brion Davis (1971), Gordon Wood (1982), and more recently Michael Butter (2014) have charted the influence and proliferation of conspiracy thinking at various points in American history, whether it be the belief in a systematic enslaving conspiracy against the American colonists conducted by the English that fueled the War of Independence, or the conspiracy rhetoric that followed in the wake of the 1820 Missouri Compromise and fed into the Civil War. In neither example were conspiracy theories the prerogative of the fringe. Rather, "they were obviously considered," Butter convincingly demonstrates, "a legitimate form of knowledge and not the kind of popular counterknowledge, ridiculed by experts, as which they are usually regarded today" (2014, 35).

While there may be nothing new about people in positions of power espousing conspiracy theories, the latter part of Butter's comment makes all the difference. Mainstream liberal political rationality (Bratich 2008) and scientific rationalism (Fiske 1993) have sought to stigmatize and delegitimize conspiracy theorizing in the contemporary era. When Trump expressed or repeated conspiracy theories, he spoke into an epistemological conjuncture that had expertise in place to disavow that sort of thinking. To contend with this, Trump's conspiracy theories had to not only arrive into that knowledgescape but also intervene in it. Accompanying conspiracy theories in the Trump information imaginary, therefore, was a mode of populist anti-intellectualism that marginalized expertise and undermined facts.

I will suspend a discussion of these until the next section to briefly outline some of the conspiracy theories for which Trump secured airtime. Conspiracy theories of course come in a variety of shapes and sizes, depending on the geopolitical site of production and the scope of circulation. There are many subgenres to this by now well-developed discourse: those that imagine alien involvement in earthly affairs; ironic and playful conspiracy theories that configure paranoia as performance rather than pathology; those that fear government collusion with other powerful agencies against its populace; theories about antigovernment plots that seek to undermine national values; conspiracy theories that chart a long historical trajectory for all-powerful clandestine organizations; and localized conspiracy theories about one particular event. Such categories are not necessarily mutually exclusive.

The conspiracy theories espoused and repeated by Trump mostly steered clear of extraterrestrials—but he did at one time or another make statements that could be described as belonging to the other categories listed above. His warning that a Clinton victory would be proof that "a small handful of global special interests [are] rigging the system" (Trump 2016) had much in common with antisemitic macro conspiracy theories that reach for enigmatic societies like the Bilderberg Group or the Illuminati to link the global elite and explain concentrations of power. Often, however, the Trump information imaginary introduced conspiracist skepticism not as the sustained narrative that Richard Hofstadter charts in his classic study of "the paranoid style in American politics," coherent until the "characteristic paranoid leap into fantasy" (1964, 78), but simply as a series of fragments that highlight gaps, doubts, and inconsistencies that dispense with the necessity of evidence. They seem to arrive in the middle of a leap, and never land.

Trump repeated conspiracy fragments he had encountered as if he were a mere conduit, never quite taking responsibility in order to clear the way for future deniability. Russell Muirhead and Nancy L. Rosenblum suggest that Trump's rhetoric offered "conspiracy without the theory" (2019, 2)—accusations without any lengthy explanation. In speeches, Trump uses disclaiming phrases like "some people say" and "many people think" to put out an unfounded conspiracy in a gesture that has been likened to retweeting (Johnson 2016). Other times, he repeats an accusation from a specific source. For example, Trump's claim that Government Communications Headquarters (GCHQ) assisted the Obama administration in wiretapping Trump Tower during the presidential campaign was gleaned from Andrew Napolitano, a retired New Jersey judge, who had made that claim in his role as an analyst on Fox News (Patel-Carstairs 2017). Crucially, the high volume of conspiracy statements and the stunning variety of channels used to disseminate them left little chance for fact checks to gain equal traction. Besides, "the virtual world far prefers the outrageous, the new, the controversial to the normal routine of reason and verification," which is one of the reasons why Trump's unverified claims were reposted and reported more than factual claims (Scherer 2017).

Trump's preferred conspiracy (without the) theories were those that featured and sought to delegitimize particular political opponents (Obama wasn't born in the United States; Ted Cruz's father was associated with John F. Kennedy's assassin, and by implication the assassination itself; "Hillary Clinton [met] in secret with international banks to plot the destruction of U.S. sovereignty in order to enrich these global financial powers, her special interest friends and her donors" [Trump 2016]); institutions (the "liberal media" failed to report Islamic terrorism and misrepresented Trump's achievements; the Federal Reserve artificially propped up the economy during Obama's time in office); or knowledge that threatened his interests (climate change science is a money-making hoax). They all represent the operation of power in terms of human motives and agency rather than structural forces. In Fredric Jameson's (1988) oft-quoted terms, this is perhaps a degraded form of cognitive mapping. It is degraded because it cannot adequately link "the most intimately local—our particular path through the world—and the most global—the crucial features of our political planet" (MacCabe 1995, xiv).

Elsewhere I have questioned delegitimizing gestures like Jameson's, arguing that conspiracy theories (as one example of popular knowledge) are best understood not as symptoms of a crippled epistemology or an inability to adequately express class relations, but rather as discursive phenomena that stage a confrontation with the undecidability of knowledge (Birchall 2006). Rather than leading us into the abyss of relativism, conspiracy theories thought in this way force on us ethical decisions about the nature of veracity, legitimacy, and knowledge. This will not be a simple task, not least because the concepts and criteria we usually depend on to help us assess knowledge have been under attack by what has been labeled post-truth, and related terms like "alternative facts," "postfacts," and "fake news." Such terms are important to the current inquiry because they represent a new distortion of transparency and authenticity.

### Post-truth Phenomena

The Trump information imaginary ensured that conspiracy theories were accompanied by a range of epistemologically disorientating phenomena that displaced the rationalist consensus that Butter (2014) sees as providing the ground from which conspiracy theories are judged as irrational. These post-truth phenomena, which preceded but were newly activated and licensed by Trump, have been the subject of many an op-ed. As such, I will only briefly chart this ground. My intention is to consolidate the connections between the different phenomena and the way in which they disrupt the epistemological assumptions and binary logic of visuality that have shaped the story of transparency, and its implicit faith in revelation, to date.

Hannah Arendt remarked over fifty years ago, "No one has ever doubted that truth and politics are on rather bad terms with each other, and no one, as far as I know, has ever counted truthfulness among the political virtues" ([1967] 2000, 545). While truth may always have had a weak hold on political discourse, christening Trump's early presidency as "post-truth" indicates the lack of common or firm ground from which judgments about statements in the public sphere could be evaluated. Vertigo-inducing layers of untruths, half-truths, lies, exaggerations, decontextualized facts, and propaganda have all allowed the Trump information imaginary to shape public opinion through "appeals to emotion and personal belief" rather than "objective facts" (as the Oxford Living Dictionary entry for "post-truth" would have it). For example, Trump's claim, announced on Twitter on November 27, 2016, that he "won the popular vote if you deduct the millions of people who voted illegally" (@realDonaldTrump), landed well with Republican voters; one poll suggested 52 percent of Republicans believed Trump on this point because it chimed with their partisan beliefs (Oliver and Wood 2016) and spoke to floating fears concerning legitimate citizenship and the subversion of democracy. In the Trump information imaginary, belief in the veracity of Trump's claims might even have been irrelevant to some supporters, as lying confirmed his self-professed antiestablishment status. After all, under extreme forms of individualist ideology, lying and cheating are wholly acceptable as part of the struggle for survival and supremacy. This is true even while Trump denounced the political system for being corrupt. Following this logic, the lone maverick can lie to beat a deceitful system. What is key here is that supporters might have offered allegiance to Trump because of what his claims, sound bites, and theories licensed them to feel rather than enabled them to know.

Much like Trump repeated and circulated conspiracy theories without fully owning those statements, he also used quotation marks to place a claim in the public sphere while creating some distance from it. For example, on March 4, 2017, Trump tweeted the following: "Terrible! Just found out that Obama had my 'wires tapped' in Trump Tower just before the victory" (@realDonaldTrump). Afterward, then press secretary Sean Spicer claimed that the use of the phrase "wires tapped" was not meant literally; rather, "the President used the word wiretaps in quotes to mean, broadly, surveillance and other activities" (qtd. in Diamond 2017). It is likely Spicer was not only using sophistry here but also acknowledging a fundamental feature of how Trump's communications were received by supporters. During the presidential campaign, Salena Zito (2016) suggested that Trump's supporters take him "seriously, not literally." For supporters, the liminal state between the figural and the literal, between something like wiretapping taking place in Trump Tower during Obama's presidency and actual wiretapping orchestrated by Obama challenged a consensus reality from which they might have felt excluded.[15] Eschewing normal procedures of knowledge production and verification, the liminal ground nurtured by the Trump information imaginary corroborated suspicions without necessitating facts.

As a way of defusing accusations of lying, questioning the neutrality of facts, and taking command of the public stage, the Trump information imaginary appropriated the term "fake news." This is an umbrella term that encompasses humorous stories that are circulated online and then consumed as if they were news; political propaganda and smear stories; and latterly any news item that did not support Trump's agenda. In using the term to refer to stories in the mainstream media that did not favorably represent his administration's goals, Trump shifted the parameters of truth from content to tenor. Indeed, in a press conference on February 16, 2017, Trump remarked, "The news is fake because so much of the news is fake." He went on to explain this tautology: It was not the facts that he had a problem with, but "the tone." "Fake" here designates critical pitch rather than forgery. Placed within the wider conjuncture, "'fake news' was but a single symptom of a far more massive destabilization, as people on every possible side of every possible political spectrum re-orient themselves to what feels like the new political" reality (Cohen 2017).

In "Truth and Politics," Arendt distinguishes between premodern and modern lying. Premodern lying constitutes the obfuscation of a known truth. Modern lying destabilizes the terms by which truth can be ascertained and instills its own reality. She puts it thus: "The difference between the traditional lie and the modern lie will more often than not amount to the difference between hiding and destroying" ([1967] 2000, 565). Writing primarily about totalitarian regimes, her comments still speak to the violence of simulation at work in the Trump information imaginary. While theorists such as Jean Baudrillard (1983) have long diagnosed these shifts, Trump harnessed this regime of simulacra in which the real is obscured in favor of the image, sign, or performance; or as Dean (1998) puts it, consensus reality is supplanted by virtual reality. Journalist Peter Pomerantsev (2017) argues that Trump was one of a number of politicians, including Vladimir Putin, who subverted "the idea that there is any knowable objective truth at all"—an operation that earned Trump the label "the postmodern president."

Despite their capacity for sharing knowledge, digital technologies provided few checks on the ascendance of post-truth phenomena. Indeed, the networked affordances of new and especially social media supported the circulation of post-truth's empty signifiers. Dean coined the phrase "communicative capitalism" in 2005 to capture the way in which communications technologies have harnessed and emptied out ideals of liberal democracy (such as access, inclusion, discussion, and participation) in ways that ensure political opportunity is obscured by "a deluge of screens and spectacles" (55). In the place of politics, citizens are offered access to a network that will never allow for strong oppositional voices to be registered in a meaningful way. Dean updated the concept after Trump's election: "In the affective networks of communicative capitalism, each communicative utterance or contribution is 'communicatively equivalent' in that it adds something to the communicative flow. . . . Whether an article is ill-conceived is unimportant, especially since a significant portion of what passes as an 'article' online was generated by an algorithm in order to improve its rank in search engine results. What matters is simply that something was expressed, that a comment was made, that an image was liked and shared" (2017, 38). In communicative capitalism, and perhaps even more so as it operated in the Trump information imaginary, revelations (of facts; of proof of malfeasance) are depoliticized and rendered ineffective by the volume of rival content that can be circulated without commitment (whether the process is automated or not). Post-truth communicative capitalism offers a poor substitute for political engagement; it is an emaciated incarnation of the ideal public sphere that demands attention, even affective investment, without conferring agency. At the same time, the privileged channel of the Trump information imaginary—Twitter—made Trump and his concerns visible, live, and immediate without rendering him accountable.

All of this has serious implications for a discussion of transparency. The story of transparency in the United States, in which transparency is intimately tied to the teleological trajectory of the democratic (and scientific) project of America, must now be revised. The link between the provision of information and accountability has always been fragile as a result of the possibility of misdirection and deception, but it came under great strain during Trump's early presidency. Fenster explains the break in the story of transparency imposed by Trump as a turning away not from transparency altogether but rather from a particular meaning of transparency. Whereas government transparency understood as a technocratic tool "focuses on the information a government must disclose—certain kinds of documents and certain types of meetings most prominently," when the case for transparency is articulated in moral terms, it "holds that the state must refrain from hiding itself and the truth from the public" (2017b, 173). In this mode, the Trump information imaginary began by lambasting Washington politics and politicians for being remote from the public gaze in a populist mode while promising a more visible alternative. "Trump promised to be morally transparent, if not technocratically so" (Fenster 2017b, 174). The stylization of Trump as a plain-talking, antiestablishment, anti-intellectual, off-script, and jargon-free populist and his reliance on a social media platform—Twitter—that creates the impression of real-time immediacy and access suggested "that [Trump hid] nothing," regardless of whether he spoke the truth or not (173).

Fenster writes, "Trump and his compatriots among right-wing populists have found political purchase and electoral success by decrying a lack of transparency. They claim that political and cultural elites have ignored the democratic will by secretly abandoning national traditions" (2017b, 173). Suspicion was thus cast on the intangible ideology of progressive multicultural liberalism itself; change was presented as a force that obfuscates "true" American values. Transparency in this scenario would be a mechanism that punctures ideology by exposing the way it presents cultural norms and values as natural. The revelation of progressive tenets as ideological is of course itself a deeply ideological maneuver in the way that it naturalizes a link between conservative values and Americanism. Just as American as conservative values are the notions of freedom and equality, which have been repurposed and reinvigorated to enable subjugated identities to gain visibility and legitimacy since the 1960s. Transparency, when called for from the edge of right-wing populism, is simply a call for a new regime of visibility built on different criteria and values. It appropriates the language of oppressed minorities by calling on more visibility for hitherto forgotten nonelite, less educated, lower-middle-class white voters.

The Trump information imaginary has derailed transparency in three main ways. First, by stressing moral transparency over administrative or technocratic transparency, the Trump information imaginary perverted the former and sidelined the latter. Second, in severing any residual links between visibility and truth and between visibility and accountability, the imaginary called into question claims made about transparency's efficacy. Third, by muddying the opposition between openness and occlusion, the imaginary's post-truth arsenal unsettled the binary logic on which transparency's legitimacy partly resides. Of note in this regard is the way the Trump information imaginary distanced the president from the traditional mechanisms of government secrecy as much as it did traditional and more recent modes of government transparency. For example, Trump was repeatedly at odds with U.S. intelligence agencies (Visser 2017) and seemed to give Fox News reports more weight than classified intelligence briefings when shaping policy, at least according to Michael Wolf in *Fire and Fury* (2018).

## Transparency Trumped

I do not want to downplay the risks posed by an administration that performed moral transparency to play with optics and paid little serious heed to administrative and technocratic transparency. The vertiginous obfuscating maneuvers in plain sight that characterized the Trump information imaginary left the public unsettled and disenfranchised. Indeed, the Trump information imaginary seemed designed to produce a public distracted by the flow of communication, not informed by it. The arrival of the Covid-19 pandemic, a global crisis that required clear communication, deference to science, and transparent criteria for decision making, modeling, and data gathering, revealed the real dangers of the Trump information imaginary.

Trump's presidency interrupted the trajectory of, and the story we have told ourselves about, the reach and purpose of government transparency in America. I also call for such an interruption here. Rather than lobby for a return to the narrative arc of transparency's goodness that we have inherited from the Enlightenment (and there were plenty of calls for increased transparency as a method to keep Trump in check), or slip back into a politics that can only oscillate between greater or lesser secrecy and transparency according to partisan allegiances, it may be that this disruption to the story of transparency can be used as an opportunity to rethink what kind of transparency best creates accountable and ethical government and offers real political scope for citizens. Ultimately, it may present an opening in which we can conceptualize a politics beyond the cycle of concealment and revelation—a cycle effectively weaponized by the Trump information imaginary.

The Trump information imaginary highlighted some important truths about transparency: it is a form of mediation, it is often performative, and it can obscure as much as it purports to reveal. The next chapter will concentrate on various critiques of transparency. These explore further such untransparent aspects of transparency. As well as thinking about forms of administrative or institutional transparency in practice, such an endeavor will also require a certain amount of abstraction in order to address the limits of transparency as an ontological or epistemological claim.

# CHAPTER 3

# OPAQUE OPENNESS
## The Problem with/of Transparency

In mainstream political, commercial, and also personal life, transparency has become the secular version of a born-again cleanliness that few can fail to praise. As Hans Krause Hansen, Lars Thøger Christensen, and Mikkel Flyverbom point out, "Expected outcomes range from increased visibility and efficiency to accountability, authenticity, participation, involvement, empowerment, emancipation, and trust" (2015, 118). It is hard to argue with such a panoply of positive effects. Whether CEO or consumer, politician or citizen, it is only acceptable within liberal democracy to be against transparency in exceptional circumstances. It is common to commend those in power who acquiesce to the transparent gaze. However, any commitment to openness today is undoubtedly championed not only for the public good that might come of it but also for what might be termed the transparency capital it bestows on the individual, organization, or politician advocating it. Transparency may open up data and information, but it also bequeaths moral distinction. Transparency has become a sign of cultural, political, and moral authenticity and authority. It is an identity as much as a mechanism, and even Trump, as we saw in the last chapter, tried it on for size, claiming in May 2019 to be the most transparent president in history (qtd. in Cohen and Lybrand 2019). Tied to economic, democratic, and moral gains as it is, transparency is offered as the solution to a whole host of social problems.

Such ascendancy has been achieved in spite of a sustained critique of epistemological, perceptual, self-relational, and ethical interpersonal transparency in twentieth-century thought, much of it French, for reasons that Geroulanos (2017) outlines. More recently, in response to transparency's staying power, there is a growing literature of critical transparency studies, produced by scholars working across a range of disciplines but who share a concern with what transparency practices occlude as much as make visible. Rather than offer an exhaustive overview of these traditions or fields, this chapter will consider only those critiques of transparency as a practice and a concept that have informed my thinking about the politics of transparency, and that will prove useful throughout the rest of this book.

After this selective review, the chapter will return to the technological manifestation of government transparency that offers the primary experience of transparency in governance today introduced in the previous chapter. As government transparency assumes the form of open data provision, and as this model is exported and assumes an ascendant position around the globe, it is imperative to ask what kind of publics, subjects, and indeed politics it determines. Given the implications of making citizens individually responsible, outsourcing, and commodification on the contract of representational democracy, I end this chapter by asking if there are other forms of transparency that might better resist neoliberal formations and repoliticize the public sphere. Given the number and range of critiques of transparency in practice and in theory, is a radical or even an ethical transparency possible? As a way into these issues, the chapter will assess the unregulated guerrilla transparency of WikiLeaks.

## Transparency's Limits

What all critiques of transparency share is the claim that there is a gap between transparency as an ideal and what actually happens in its name. In order to consider both the practical and conceptual limitations of transparency, I will look at two main critiques of transparency, which then have multiple subconcerns and applications. First, there are claims that transparency, when put into practice in social, commercial, and political life, has unintended consequences and does not deliver what it promises. Second, there are approaches from a range of disciplines that highlight the mediated, nontransparent nature of transparency. For those with their eye on politics and society, this means that transparency is an idea and practice that is open to ideological articulations. In philosophical terms, this recognition, when applied to the idea of intersubjective transparency or transparency of self, necessitates nothing less than a reexamination of identity and subjectivity.

### Transparency in Practice

Organizations implement transparency measures for a number of different reasons. They might want to appear responsive and responsible, to have a share of that transparency capital. They may see transparency as a way to promote greater trust in the organization from investors, consumers, and staff. Organizations may turn to transparency measures for the role they can play in optimization and efficiency. There are just as many reasons why in practice transparency measures fall short of the hopes placed in them. Critical transparency scholars point out these failures. Christopher Hood (2006b), adapting Albert Hirschman (1991), helps to break down the critiques of transparency in organizations into three subsets: futility, jeopardy, and perversity. The first point out all the ways in which a perfectly reasonable transparency policy in theory may in practice be circumvented and rendered redundant (take, for example, a government that counteracts a Freedom of Information Act with overzealous classification). The second focus on the unintended consequences of certain transparency measures (such as the self-censorship of committees whose members are aware that proceedings will be published). The third extend the second to claim that transparency policies can in fact result in the very opposite of their intended goals (so, for example, the idea that the sheer quantity of information and data made available by transparency might create "data smog" and render citizens less, rather than more, informed).

Exemplary of this first line of critique is Archon Fung, Mary Graham, and David Weil's *Full Disclosure: The Perils and Promise of Transparency* (2007).[1] The authors consider various case studies in which transparency has failed, despite good intentions, to improve public safety.[2] Within the "futility" category, they write about the collapse of Enron in 2001, which "signaled a failure of the nation's oldest and most trusted transparency system—the detailed federal requirements that publicly traded companies disclose their profits and losses" (xii). The disclosure policies in the financial sector were simply not robust enough to prevent deceptive bookkeeping and off-balance sheet financing.

Fung, Graham, and Weil (2007) also include criticism of transparency that would fall into the perversity category. They examine, for example, the Bush administration's attempt to use transparency to reduce the risk of death and injury from terrorist attacks—namely the color-coded ranking system used to indicate the terrorist threat level implemented in 2002. They write: "Announced increases in the threat level created confusion, leaving millions of Americans uncertain what they should do to protect themselves. Before long, terrorism threat ranking degenerated into fodder for late-night comedians" (xii). They evaluate this measure according to its own stated purpose—to "encourage government agencies, the private sector and . . . the public to take steps at each threat level to minimize attacks and their consequences" (xii)—and find it a failure. The apparent desire for increased awareness and safety led to confusion and then apathy.

Fung, Graham, and Weil conclude that targeted transparency works best: "Effective policies did not simply increase information. They increased knowledge that informed choice" (2007, xiv). They call for policies that engage the public in participation. The problem, in this view, is that transparency is not being implemented in a way that shapes the public to whom it is transparent. It does not guide the public in how to view, understand, and participate in its own disclosures. Even Lawrence Lessig (2009), whose controversial critique of transparency was far more damning ("I fear that the inevitable success of [the transparency movement]—if pursued alone, without any sensitivity to the full complexity of the idea of perfect openness—will inspire not reform, but disgust") concludes that "if the transparency movement could be tied to [a] movement for reform . . . then its consequence could be salutary and constructive." Rather than there being something awry in the concept of transparency itself, commentators tend to call on action, reform, and engagement to valorize and renew it.

Mark Fenster (2017a) thinks this continued belief in transparency's power in the face of its internal and external limits is due to the lure of the legal, institutional, and technological solutions that together make up the "transparency fix." All we need, under this illusory promise, is the right leader and more institutional will. According to Fenster, this leads transparency advocates to "fetishize means without fully considering the ends they are intended to reach and without attempting to grapple with the question of why these means always prove unsatisfactory" (9). In practice, he notes, government transparency becomes a line-drawing exercise between defensible and indefensible secrecy, and thus just "one among many values vying for legal and administrative predominance" (10). When exceptions to the transparency rule are entertained and given credence, as they must and should, "transparency" becomes "a term of concealment and opacity that promises more than it can deliver" (11). He advises relinquishing "impossibly high expectations and abandon[ing] the quest for a magical solution to a complex endeavor of governance" (16).

Extending the argument beyond governance, Evgeny Morozov (2013) is concerned with the way in which digital transparency is pitched as an easy technical solution to a whole host of complex social problems. To illustrate, he offers a number of case studies in which open data initiatives have had unjust outcomes. He cites the recent digitization and publication of land records in India. On examining the open records, investors could see where poorer families lacked official documentation to prove ownership. Those investors then hired legal teams to claim rights over the land. The ostensibly open system to regulate land ownership could only recognize certain forms of land ownership. Within the system, there was no place for oral business agreements or other less formal claims on the land. It was open, but not inclusive. The issue of land ownership in India required a more nuanced approach and a more rigorous contextualization that could allow for heterogeneous relationships to and indigenous ways of understanding property. In a book about the dangers of relying on the internet to save us, Morozov ends his chapter on open data by warning, "The tyranny of openness—the result of our infatuation with Internet-centrism—must be resisted" (99).

Public philosopher Onora O'Neill (2002) questions the turn to transparency in practice by dismantling the assumption that more transparency leads to greater trust. This issue of public trust is crucial because it is often cited as a reason for the implementation of transparency practices. On its website in 2011, for example, the Sunlight Foundation claimed its origin has to be understood in the context of the many political scandals in 2005: "Trust in government was falling to another all-time low. Multiple corruption scandals engulfed Washington." Elsewhere, the founders wrote, "Improved transparency is not a threat to public trust; it is the very basis for restoring that trust" (Miller and Klein 2009). O'Neill resists this logic: "Transparency certainly destroys secrecy: but it may not limit the deception and deliberate misinformation that undermine relations of trust. If we want to restore trust, we need to reduce deception and lies rather than secrecy. Some sorts of secrecy indeed support deception, others do not. Transparency and openness may not be the unconditional goods that they are fashionably supposed to be. By the same token, secrecy and lack of transparency may not be the enemies of trust." In suggesting that secrecy need not be in the service of deception, O'Neill's comments question the working principles of the transparency movement. No longer, she claims, can the "goodness" of transparency be taken for granted.[3]

I will consider these contextualizing critiques, which all focus on the effects of transparency practices, alongside meditations on the ideological character of transparency in a bid to question both transparency's efficacy and its accumulated moral and social value. A focus on ideology helps us to answer a question left hanging by contextualizing critiques: if transparency does not deliver the benefits its proponents promise, what other agendas might it support?

### Transparency as Ideological Form

Although his focus was not on the myriad practices we associate with transparency today but rather on social transparency, Theodor Adorno offered an important early critique. In *Minima Moralia* ([1951] 1974), Adorno attempts to train his reader to seek truth through the opacity rather than transparency of language. In *Dialectic of Enlightenment,* this time with Max Horkheimer, Adorno equates "false clarity" with "myth" and undermines the promise of immediacy ([1944] 2002, xvii). "For Adorno," Eric Jarosinski explains, "society's crystal clear order offers a promise of insight that fails to deliver anything more than ready-made enlightenment, blocking out a more engaging vision of change that is still to come" (2009, 160). Belief in the transparency of socioeconomic relations under the conditions of capitalism is only ever false consciousness. What we take as transparency in fact can only reveal modes of knowledge, reason, and logic that are conducive to maintaining the status quo: modes that can be received in already prescribed ways. Matthew Fluck examines Adorno and Horkheimer's thinking, noting that the assertion of clarity "is not only a matter of moulding cognition into a form conducive to technical success, but also of creating communities and individuals who present no obstacle to the pursuit of that same goal. The experience of those subjects and their interaction with one another becomes impoverished as a result" (2016, 69). Transparency's part to play in any utopian or revolutionary project is foreclosed. Critique is privileged over transparency. Despite the different context, what I find useful in Adorno and Horkheimer's formulation for the concerns of this book is the way in which it problematizes the idea that transparency, when implemented within and secured by nonprogressive contexts, can facilitate radical knowledge as well as, I would contend, radical relations, networks, and subjectivities.

Henri Lefebvre was also pessimistic about the possibility of genuine transparency, dreams of which he consigned to the past—to Marx's thought, which contained the promise of a world free of mediation (Geroulanos 2017). While Marx thought that "the religious reflections of the real world can, in any case, vanish only when the practical relations of everyday life between man and man, and man and nature, generally present themselves to him in a transparent and rational form" ([1887] 1976, 173), Lefebvre thought that alienation extends beyond and is more generalized than that embedded in capitalist conditions of production, preventing the possibility of "ethical transparency" in the event of changes to the economic base ([1962] 1995, 69). Illustrative of Lefebvre's understanding of the ideological deployment of "transparency" as an idea can be found in his work on space. The idea that space is "innocent," pure, and unmediated is an illusion obscuring its socially constructed and stratified conditions ([1974] 1991, 28–29). Space is not transparent but produced by labor and conditioned by ideology.

What we see again and again is that the problem with transparency (in the form of the fantasy of unmediated space, relations, and communication, but which can also extend to the practices I focus on in relation to open government and other institutions) is that it is always itself a form of mediation. As such, its apparent neutrality is an effect of its ideological form. In material terms, the provision of open data, for example, can reproduce inequalities by giving advantages to those citizens who already have the cultural, political, and social capital that enable them to engage meaningfully with data and policy makers, just as fiscal transparency can simply make inequitable markets more efficient.

Many contemporary critics of transparency seek to expose the fallacy of such neutrality by attacking transparency's complicity with "a neoliberal ethos of governance that promotes individualism, entrepreneurship, voluntary forms of regulation and formalized types of accountability," as Christina Garsten and Monica Lindh de Montoya put it (2008, 3). For them, transparency aids free market late capitalism, facilitating global fiscal transactions by increasing the legibility of local regulations (or offered in lieu of regulation altogether), and also shapes our understanding of the individual in line with neoliberal ideology. That is, transparency fits in with "a certain way of organizing society that emphasizes the individual as the basic constitutive active agent in the construction of his or her fate and of society-at-large. In such a vision of social life, the transactions between citizens and the state and within the economy must be open and observable in the interests of maintaining a level playing field for all concerned" (4). Also contributing to the production of this neoliberal subjectivity is the very real link between transparency and contemporary audit culture (Garsten and Lindh de Montoya 2008; Strathern 2000). That is, rationalization and restructuring legitimized through the project of transparency might make ways of doing business that privilege the market over other markers of success (such as workers' safety or well-being, ecological footprint, or community involvement) easier to implement.

Given dominant associations of transparency with greater accountability in the public sector, it is important to note this compatibility with an ideology that champions private control of public services, creating shadowy spaces that fall beyond accountability (Hood 2006a; Roberts 2006). Transparency can be mobilized in the service of a variety of desires that cannot always be openly advocated. It therefore gives an apolitical sheen to highly political visions. This is particularly evident in the way in which transparency, in the guise of open government data, is offered as a democratic good while making smaller government and looser regulation possible because it serves as a self-regulatory mechanism in lieu of centralized monitoring and policy making. We can add this neoliberal feature of open government data to those already identified in the previous chapter.

Texts such as Garsten and Lindh de Montoya's (2008) account for a general correspondence between transparency and neoliberal conditions. This offers an important starting point for thinking about the politics of contemporary transparency. But I also want to look beyond effects to take on board the interest in transparency's mediating qualities that we see, for example, in the work of Adorno and Lefebvre. Both approaches are useful when considering the specific subjectivity activated, communicated, and supported by transparency technologies, as well as looking for ways to interrupt a politics of transparency. My consideration of Data.gov in chapter 2 extends the observation that transparency has neoliberal characteristics, to understand it as instrumental in modifying the democratic contract and producing subjects invested in the continuance of that modified contract. Chapter 4 will take this further. In a familiar move, transparency changes the rules of the game and the players' engagement and expectations—or, as Maurizio Lazzarato puts it with reference to neoliberalism more generally, it "ensures the conditions for power to exercise a hold over conduct" (2009, 111).

Byung-Chul Han names transparency a "neoliberal dispositive" because it "forces everything inward in order to transform it into information" in an attempt to optimize "communication without borders" (2015, viii).[4] Han extends the critique of transparency as ideological form to paint a totalizing vision of contemporary life. Eschewing the kind of case studies offered by a volume like Fung, Graham, and Weil's *Full Disclosure* (2007), Han's book is a speculative polemic against "the transparency society," drawing on arguments not dissimilar to those of Baudrillard (1990). For Han, transparency is not only an inhibitor of long-term political planning but also a pernicious cultural dominant that promotes a tyranny of homogenous positivity and maintains the status quo. Under its logic, "smooth streams of hypercommunication" and "hypervisibility" produce obscenity (2015, 12); ideological conviction gives way to "postpolitical" opinion (7); desire is no longer possible without "the secret, the veil, and concealment" (15); and surveillance has proliferated to become "aperspectival," ensuring surveillance "of everyone from everywhere" (45). Han moves seamlessly between the critique of transparency as ideological form and the critique of transparency's promise of legibility and knowledge—the illusion of immediacy—to be found in continental theory of the twentieth century. This type of critique problematizes transparency's moral high ground (and in turn modifies the relationship it has with secrecy). It troubles the foundations on which the very idea of transparency rests.

### Transparency in Theory

Theoretical critiques of transparency changed the direction of a whole host of academic disciplines in the twentieth century, but they did not derail the rise of transparency in the public and political discourse of many liberal democracies.[5] These critiques do not primarily engage with transparency practices but rather with the impossibility of unmediated, pure knowledge (of oneself, others, and the world). In exploring alterity, absence, difference, and the unconscious, for example, postwar French thought systematically dismantled the idea that a self-transparent subject is possible or desirable (Geroulanos 2017). Such an opaque subject also meant that an ethics based on intersubjective transparency was in need of reconceptualization, for what hope do two or more subjects have to be transparent to each other if a single subject necessarily keeps secrets from herself? In addition, various thinkers, aware of the gap between mind and world, challenged epistemological transparency, dismissing it as "a fantasy of scientific positivism and idealism" (Geroulanos 2017, 9).

In his intellectual and conceptual history, Geroulanos (2017) discusses the obstacles that interrupt the possibility of transparency in perception—obstacles, that is, between self and world—in Jean-Paul Sartre's existentialism; the opacity in Maurice Merleau-Ponty's phenomenology that forecloses the possibility of a human consciousness transparent to itself or others; the impossibility of human knowledge and science "to grasp the totality of life in the transparent manner that the Cartesian cogito promised" (80) in Georges Canguilhem's work; "the failure of wholeness, homogeneity, homogenization" (197) guaranteed by the other and the Other in Jacques Lacan's psychoanalytic framework; and various critiques of social transparency to be found in thinkers like Foucault and Lefebvre. This multidisciplinary and far-reaching turn against transparency in many manifestations offers important context for the current inquiry. Any one of the thinkers Geroulanos considers would present useful opportunities for parsing contemporary transparency and for better understanding the relationship between transparency and its others. But for the concerns of this book, it is Jacques Derrida's work that I implicitly and explicitly draw on most because although it begins with a critique of Rousseauist ideals of self-transparency and the metaphysics of presence (in *Of Grammatology*, [1967] 1997), it also speaks to the political context I am primarily concerned with in this book.⁶

Derrida's work on the absolute or unconditional secret can help us think through the problems of a democracy committed to an idea of total transparency. During an interview with Maurizio Ferraris, Derrida remarks, "If a right to the secret is not maintained, we are in a totalitarian space" (2001a, 59). What can we take from this? Transparency cannot easily accommodate those who want to be exempt from its project—those who want to not merely remain private but be recognized as singular. Because of this intolerance for singularity, because of an insistence to belong and agree, transparency risks looking less like an agent of democracy and freedom and more like a tool of totalitarianism. Han attributes this condition to the very ideologization of the term: "Like all ideologies," transparency "has a positive core that has been mystified and made absolute.... If totalized, it yields terror" (2015, viii).

In practical terms, a regime that embraces a logic of and requires acquiescence to transparency will only ever be able to go so far before it tips over into totalitarianism because of its proximity to surveillance, particularly when extended to citizens. Resisting the call to be transparent to the state is automatically registered as a sign of guilt rather than as an acknowledgment of singularity. If the regime does not go far enough, if it shrinks back from applying transparency to its own actions, then the regime meets the charge of totalitarianism coming the other way (for acting covertly, autonomously, and without an explicit mandate)—hence an infinite hesitation, a radical undecidability, within any democracy that counts transparency among its operating principles, and hence too the prospect of a debate between transparency and secrecy that will never be concluded, because far from being inimical to each other, they are symbiotic.

This is why the stakes of that debate are so routinely misunderstood. It is not a question of reframing the supposed opposition between transparency and secrecy in ever wider perspectives, because such reframing assumes that the terms can be made to yield to interpretative mastery. The undecidability might be unbearable, might tempt us to come down on the side of secrecy or on the side of transparency, yet the best response is not to seek to resolve the tension so much as to inhabit it strategically. We need to find different ways of staying with the aporia of transparency as secrecy.

The same goes for secrecy as transparency. The aporia becomes clear if we restate the condition of the democratic subject outlined above. Without a right to secrecy, the subject in a democracy—a liberal democracy committed to transparency—will find itself deprived of that which confers its singularity on the subject, where the singularity of the subject constitutes democracy's primary unit. Yet the subject who in its singularity regards its right to secrecy as absolute—as it should—will thereby jeopardize its right to belong to the social bond construed now as the *democracy* of individual subjects rather than the democracy of *individual subjects*. The right to be counted among democracy's subjects involves a minimal coming into the transparent light of that social bond, even as every step toward it marks a step away from the singularity, the singular possession of the singular secret, which licensed that very movement. The singular, democratic subject is charged with maintaining an absolute secret that is incorruptible while holding it out for it to be corrupted, to have its secrecy dissolved in the light of the common forum—this being the price to pay for belonging to the democracy that recognized its singularity in the first place. The subject of democracy is fated to vacillate endlessly between the shadow and the light.

The ways in which secrecy and transparency, conceptually and practically, are co-constitutive is central to my approach, and I will return to it explicitly in the Conclusion, where I explore the possibility of deconstructive postsecrecy. The aporia does not mean that all instances of implementing transparency in government systems and settings are ipso facto redundant; it may still be the case that greater openness is preferable to greater secrecy in any given circumstance.

But it does render problematic any claim to or conception of transparency that denies its relationship to secrecy.

Keeping this discussion of the aporia in view while also drawing on the contextualized readings and the ideology critiques above, I return to the open data platform introduced in chapter 2 during my discussion of the Obama information imaginary. This example of a technocratic offering, particularly when replicated in other geopolitical contexts, demonstrates how the secret as singularity is forcefully sidelined by the universalism inherent within the drive toward transparency.

## Transparency Imperialism

During the early days of open data advocacy, the U.S. open government data portal, Data.gov, provided a blueprint for other countries looking for a platform to provide public access to different data sets produced by government agencies. There are many reasons to applaud transparency measures such as this, especially compared to closed regimes with endemic and extreme forms of corruption. Yet this comparison might foreclose important questions, for within ostensibly open liberal democracies, it is important to ask which forms of openness take precedence in any particular era, and what kind of subjectivities they promote. Regions wishing to make the move toward more open forms of society and governance often look to those *dispositifs* already in operation elsewhere; thus, forms of openness, and the political settlements they compound, travel through what I refer to (with plenty of caveats given the contentious nature of the latter term) as transparency imperialism.[7]

From 2012, the United States, in collaboration with Canada and India, developed the open source Open Government Platform (OGPL, also described as "Data.gov in a box"), which was based on Data.gov and which was intended to be exported around the globe. The status of OGPL is currently in doubt, as the project has been left unattended under Trump's watch. However, the United States and other members of the OGPL team helped to develop its more user-friendly successor, the open source platform from the Open Knowledge Foundation called CKAN, now used by Data.gov and its Canadian and Indian counterparts, as well as an increasing number of governments and municipalities around the globe.[8] Although OGPL has given way to CKAN, I want to consider this early bid to establish a transparency prototype for what it can tell us about the operation of hegemony today. My aim is not to prove that transparency illustrates, reflects, or reinforces a fixed, singular ideology as Garsten and Lindh de Montoya (2008) attempt. Rather, I want to show how, through the latest technological model of government transparency, we can see neoliberalism and its subjects, as a lived and living set of relations or network, adapting. This offers a more hopeful view, for it is possible that in the process of adaptation, the conditions for or material forms of resistance are unwittingly produced.

In order to think about which ideas and relations might have been exported along with OGPL, I want to recall the argument of the previous chapter. Data.gov imagines an ideal subject who is at once made responsible through watching data and expected to outsource that vigilance. I suggested that the rationality and desires of the market, embodied by data entrepreneurs, determine the dominant articulation of openness in political life (data-driven transparency) and therefore the scope of the political, of visibility, itself. We could say that platforms like Data.gov and its open source offspring, OGPL, offer data in place of politics. We might be tempted to describe open government data as a postpolitical solution, an asymmetric offering that needs to be thought of as related to communicative capitalism (Dean 2005, 2009). Communicative capitalism, to recall the discussion in chapter 2, is characterized by "the circulation of content in the dense, intensive networks of global communications" that "relieves top-level actors (corporate, institutional and governmental) from the obligation to respond" (Dean 2005, 53). Instead of responding to antagonists, actors simply contribute to the flow of communication, "hoping that sufficient volume (whether in terms of number of contributions or the spectacular nature of a contribution) will give their contributions dominance or stickiness." This is disabling to politicization proper, Dean insists, because the multiplication of positions "hinders the formation of strong counterhegemonies" (53).

Yet providing data as a proxy for accountability, asking data to speak for itself, diverges from these other postpolitical communications. Its contribution to the flow is positioned differently. While the proliferating contributions from top-level actors at least seem as if they are engaging in politics and are positioned as being within the political debate, even if by Dean's standards they fall short, data provision gains its force from evading the pall of politics, just as transparency in general is presented as nonpartisan or pan-ideological (Triplett 2010). While it is easy to demonstrate the fallacy of such a position, the provision of data is presented as above the flow of both real and simulated politics: it is made available rather than communicated; it trumps communication. Transparency's postpolitical status is claimed not because it leaves ideology behind, but in reference to its presentation as apolitical and nonideological. This recalls the common configuration of data as information rather than knowledge or interpretation: transparent, pure, raw. Ironically, it is our very enthusiasm for and belief in the efficacy of more and more data that "become a faith in their neutrality and autonomy, their objectivity" (Gitelman and Jackson 2013, 3). Public confidence in data provision makes us complicit in the current trend to provide data in lieu of politics. In fact, in the next chapter I will argue that open data–driven transparency contributes to an antipolitical settlement. Postpolitics is thus an ideological move that produces antipolitical effects.

When operational, the OGPL website informed readers that its digital project was "an example of a new era of diplomatic collaborations that benefit the global community that promote government transparency, citizen-focused applications, and enrich humanity." By 2013, Ghana and Canada had launched open government portals using this platform, with others lining up to implement Data.gov in a box. Given such rhetoric, the charge of a transparency imperialism that encourages different nation-states to offer data instead of politics seems uncharitable. The provision of open source software and platforms that would take considerable time and investment to create from scratch is, of course, laudable—on a par, perhaps, with the distribution of generic medicines in the developing world. But such a comparison would be misleading. On the one hand, the circulation of goods and services at a reduced cost or for free certainly levels a rocky playing field. On the other hand, in the case of the provision of the OGPL at least, a particular formulation of the relationship between citizen and government, and the role of data in that relationship, a whole discursive regime, risks being exported alongside the technology. It could be argued that all imports are aligned with particular power relations, but that the positive outcomes outweigh the burden of inheritance. The pull or desire from transparency advocates in the global south for platforms and tools also perhaps renders the label "imperialism" problematic. In any case, the neoliberal relations fostered by the protocols of Data.gov in a box would not be perceived as a negative in the first place, given the reach of what Mark Fisher (2009) calls "capitalist realism" around the globe. Capitalist realism is not the acceptance of neoliberal policies but the acceptance that there is no alternative. Such acceptance is often always already present, canceling out the need for debate over seemingly apolitical imports like technology (and, I might add, medicine).

While the flow from center to periphery is neither ubiquitous (applicable to all technocultural productions) nor monolithic (the same in any and every exchange), and while the multiple trajectories of networked globalization are rarely discussed in this way, I nevertheless think it is useful to conceive of data-driven transparency in terms of imperialism.[9] While developing the open source version of Data.gov was a partnership between the United States, Canada, and India, and local content or data would appear on each site, the particular combination of an ideoscape and technoscape (Appadurai 1996) of interest here, *this* neoliberal form, risks harming as much as emboldening democratic impulses and structures by replicating the cycle of antipoliticization outlined above.[10] Some effects and affects of data-driven transparency will be wholly singular to a given context, but because the economic imperative of open data is reinforced by important institutions like the World Bank, the force of neoliberal logic is a constant. In this way, it is not that the United States per se acts as an imperialist agent but rather that a fluctuating network of control via technological protocols produces imperialist effects. Dominant concepts of and expectations for subjectivity, agency, and democracy travel with the exported model. Writing about the World Trade Organization, Felix Stalder writes, "The result is structural coercion under conditions of formal freedom" (2011, 20). While the positioning of fiscal transparency as a prerequisite for assistance evident in the agreements of the WTO and other organizations is not the same as the implementation of a digital platform intended to make such transparencies possible, the point is pertinent for how it makes clear that alignment with protocols and practices involves acquiescence to soft forms of power and control. I concur with Rachel Adams, who, drawing on an impressive range of examples in her thesis about the ascendance of transparency norms within a neocolonial context, argues that the "proselytisation of transparency" (2017, 85) on the global south through the Open Government Partnership and various forms of aid agreements marginalize other forms of governance and delegitimize modes of information and knowledge that are not easily accommodated by transparency measures of the bureaucratic state.

## Radical Transparency

I fully understand resistance to this line of argument that comes from practitioners and campaigners from the developing global south who say they can only hope for transparency mechanisms and tools as sophisticated and well funded as those in developed countries. Such advocates are often battling chronic and destabilizing corruption through transparency initiatives. I am not suggesting that accountability is outmoded or that transparency is always and in every circumstance a bad idea. However, for anyone concerned about the limited or perhaps interrupted political agency produced by neoliberal formations, there is a real question here about what form transparency should take and the kinds of social and political relations technologies of transparency imply, imagine, and engender.

It is therefore the responsibility of advocates, developers, exporters, and importers of transparency models to ask themselves the following questions:

1. Does this model of transparency (mis)read social problems as information problems?
2. Does this model of transparency offer data as a proxy for accountability?
3. Is this model of transparency being mobilized in the service of desires that cannot be openly advocated?
4. Does this model of transparency facilitate a political response rather than a contribution to the flow of communicative capitalism?

5. Is this model of transparency the one that will best serve the interests of politics understood as an arena of dissensus and agonism?

6. Will this model of transparency enable the formation of subjectivities that have meaningful political agency or will it simply make inequitable structures and distributions more efficient?

7. Does this model promote an engagement with the state that collectivizes rather than individualizes human experience?

If asking these questions is considered a luxury pertaining only to those who already have ostensibly open and accountable systems, consider this: Those states that do not yet have data-driven transparency but that are looking for models have a strategic advantage over those that already do. The economic and ideological investment in data-driven transparency has meant that no real alternatives have been entertained in the contemporary global north. If one wants accountable, trustworthy government, then there might be other forms of transparency to achieve that. (Indeed, there might be other methods to achieve that altogether, given the multiple problems with transparency highlighted in this chapter.) If dataphilic technological solutionism has yet to determine the scope of the political and terms of the democratic contract, there is still hope that other models can be implemented—models that give subjects a better chance of resisting neoliberal formations, perhaps. This should not be mistaken for encouraging conservatism, like asking developing nations to stick to homegrown forms of governance and politics. Rather, it is a call to be open about and to openness. What would this look like?

Radical transparency—what I am calling an openness to openness—should be a mode that not only avoids the reinforcement of neoliberal subjects and relations but also interrupts the self as a surveilled data object, about which I shall write more in the following chapter. It would need to understand the mediated nature of and ascribe alternative cultural values to data and transparency; it would also acknowledge the unconditional secret with which it is grafted. It would need to politicize data, transparency, and openness in general—to ask what role revelation can and should play in democracy. This would not necessarily involve a move away from data technologies; neither data as such nor the technological infrastructure that makes the storage and circulation of it are ipso facto the problem here. Rather, it is the delimitation of their position and role within a network by political, technological, and economic protocols with which I take issue.

According to Alexander Galloway and Eugene Thacker, hypertrophy, "the desire for pushing beyond," is more politically effective than resistance with the latter's implicit "desire for stasis or retrograde motion." Hypertrophy involves pushing technology "further than it is meant to go" (2007, 98). While Galloway and Thacker are thinking about the technological exploit that computer viruses and hackers seek, I want to ask what it would mean to push transparency "further than it is meant to go." It might involve platforms that are programmed to explicitly state the value of open data (to whom or what). It might require, as Stalder (2011) suggests, communication technologies that enable large-scale sociality to ensure that transparency is horizontal rather than top down. It might demand, as Frank Pasquale suggests, that surveillance technology be used not against citizens but deployed on their behalf "to monitor and contain corporate greed and waste" (2015, 218). It would obviously entail a commitment to the kind of structural shifts that would enable equal access to technology and the skills to navigate it rather than merely an in-principle democratization of data. In addition, this hypertrophy might make a commitment to not ever more data but instead data that is radically contextualized, with the word "radical" pointing toward an account of the conditions, assumptions, and politics that informed the production and gathering of the data in the first place, rather than the provision of metadata (which merely makes data searchable) or the packaging of data within apps (which might decontextualize as much as contextualize). After all, a data set provided to us through transparency tools is not itself transparent. Not only has it been gathered with a particular agenda in mind and according to a certain methodology, but also statistics that indicate a success story can belie other goals or values that have been sacrificed in the process (Morozov 2013).

All of these suggestions or principles require speculation, experimentation, and imagination. Whatever form this hypertrophy takes with respect to transparency, "during the passage of technology into this injured, engorged, and unguarded condition, it will be sculpted anew into something better, something in closer agreement with the real wants and desires of its users" (Galloway and Thacker 2007, 98–99). Might the rogue transparency of WikiLeaks, which often exposed those government operations and communications that fall out of the purview of open data transparency measures, have constituted a form of hypertrophy?

## WikiLeaks

At first sight, the ways in which WikiLeaks' disclosures were framed seem to be fully aligned with the liberal conception of transparency inherited from Enlightenment thinking. High-profile Julian Assange defender Jemima Khan certainly described the project in these terms when she considered WikiLeaks as offering "a new type of investigative journalism" (qtd. in Giri 2010). As Saroj Giri (2010) points out, the print media outlets Assange collaborated with on the publication of the U.S. diplomatic cables in November 2010 justified their relationship with WikiLeaks according to traditional liberal thinking concerned with the public's right to know. Assange (2010) himself placed WikiLeaks within the liberal tradition of free speech and a free press, with remarks like, "The swirling storm around WikiLeaks today reinforces the need to defend the right of all media to reveal the truth." Such language was invoked by Assange for legal reasons, seeking the protections afforded to journalists. Indeed, defenders of Assange turned to the First Amendment when the charge sheet accusing him of the theft of American state secrets was released in April 2019. Despite this liberal framing, I think there is something about WikiLeaks that resists being reduced to Enlightenment language concerning the public's right to know and, more importantly for me, that challenges the neoliberal logic underpinning centralized transparency.

Assange's whole vision of transparency, for example, was fueled by a conspiracy theory of power. Assange (2006) professes to want to break the communicative links between, and therefore curb the powers of, what he terms the conspiratorial nation-states by creating distrust through leaked information. We might suppose that this is dangerously close to the disruptive tactics of Trump—and in hinting that

murdered junior Democratic National Committee worker Seth Rich
was the WikiLeaks source for the DNC e-mails rather than Russian
hackers, Assange was certainly not above Trumpist tricks (Merlan
2019). Yet while Trump misdirected attention through the flow of
outrage, disinformation, and rumor, WikiLeaks (rather than Assange,
to separate the two for a moment) published inconvenient data and
information.[11] Transparency in this guise is positioned as the tool not
of liberal democracy but of anarchism. It is not in the service of optimization; rather, it introduces disruptive friction. If seamless transactions are the key component of a globalized economic market that
presents itself as an even playing field, and if international diplomacy
is based on carefully managed communication, then what could be
more subversive than revealing the often unpalatable or embarrassing
undercurrent of the shiny surface of official transparency?

Since Assange's fall from favor—due in large part to accusations of
sexual misconduct in Sweden, the way in which the leaked e-mails of
John Podesta and Hillary Clinton supported the rise of Trump, and
the fact that the anonymous information drops left the WikiLeaks
system open to abuse by antidemocratic entities—it is easy to forget the astonishing scale and content of the leaked documents made
available on the WikiLeaks platform. With over a decade of material available, now presented on an easily navigable interface, there
appears to be a tighter rationale behind the leaks than might have
been apparent during the early years after WikiLeaks was founded
in 2006. The targets might seem indiscriminate at a national level (in
the United States, WikiLeaks has embarrassed both Republican and
Democrat administrations, for example), but the content is not apolitical. Rather, the self-professed remit to analyze and publish "large
datasets of censored or otherwise restricted official materials involv-
ing war, spying and corruption"[12] suggested an antistatist, pacifist,
perhaps libertarian agenda not easily reducible to partisan politics. It
was certainly an agenda against concentrations or abuses of power.

Yet the importance of WikiLeaks for anyone interested in exploring "an alternative vision of the good" (Brown 2005, 59) beyond the
tenets of liberal democracy does not necessarily only or predominantly lie in the content and politics of the leaks. Of greater importance is the fact that WikiLeaks offered a model of transparency
that was decentralized and beyond state control. To some degree,

WikiLeaks modified the dominant understanding of transparency that, although not synonymous with neoliberalism, certainly supports it in a number of ways, as I have shown. WikiLeaks' transparency simply did not subscribe to the well-behaved, containable, regulatory, seemingly apolitical and neutral manifestation of transparency compatible with neoliberalism today. This is one of the reasons why many factions of the mainstream transparency movement castigated WikiLeaks (as well as the controversies that surrounded Assange).

In organizational theory, "radical transparency" signifies an organization that implements total openness at all levels of operation, but I want to think of "radical" in terms of politics rather than scale. "Radical transparency" might thus be envisaged as a mechanism able to challenge the circumscribed role allotted data transparency. "Radical" here means changing not only the kind of information that is made visible but also, and more crucially, the conditions of visibility in general. Some of WikiLeaks' projects would certainly fulfill those criteria.

What might have been most radical about WikiLeaks, despite having a founder who appeared to be as enamored with power as any of those heads of state WikiLeaks went after, was simply that it reminded us that there are other possible models of transparency out there. There are models not dedicated to optimizing inequitable systems, that are not easily harnessed for profit, that genuinely add to public knowledge about covert government activity, that perhaps offer data and documents not in lieu of agency but as the first step toward meaningful political contestations.

Of course, the WikiLeaks model, replicated in part by platforms such as GlobaLeaks and SecureDrop, is not the only alternative formation. Elements of the global activist left have also chosen to invest in versions of transparency as an anticapitalist tool. Consider, for example, the "sousveillance" tactics of anticapitalist protesters; the World Social Forum's charter (2002), which declares itself "a movement of ideas that prompts reflection" and promises "the transparent circulation of the results of that reflection"; or the Green New Deal, a radical proposal for noncorporate green energy from the New Economics Foundation that relies heavily on transparency as a way to deliver its ideals. Or we might turn to projects connected with Black Lives Matter, such as Data for Black Lives, which as part of its work calls for counterdata to fill in data gaps that leave minoritized people at risk at the same time as pushing back against the harms that can be caused by overrepresentation of those same communities in existing government data sets.

These attempts to take more control over the conditions and scope of transparency measures are echoed by particular artists and digital activists. Julian Oliver, for example, developed his "Transparency Grenade" (2012)—a tiny computer, microphone, and powerful wireless antenna that together can capture network traffic and audio—as a way to mirror and make transparent the asymmetric surveillance capacities of big tech and intelligence services. James Bridle developed Citizen Ex, a browser extension that calculates what he calls "algorithmic citizenship," a constantly revised identity based on the sites a user browses online.[13] Graph Commons is a collaborative platform founded by Burak Arikan for mapping, analyzing, and publishing data networks that reveal flows of power and influence.[14] With the aim of rendering consumer data surveillance more transparent, the Data Calculator produced by the *Financial Times* allows users to calculate the worth of their personal data and browsing habits via a data broker (Steel et al. 2013). With similar concerns, the Facebook Data Invoice calculates digital labor on Facebook and playfully generates an invoice to Mark Zuckerberg on behalf of a user.[15] Finally, while it is more associated with anonymous cryptocurrencies at present, blockchain has the potential to aid forms of transparency given that it is a technique to create a massive distributed tamper-proof database.

None of these interventions sets a new model of transparency, but each one raises questions about the limits of established transparency norms. Collectively, they challenge us to think about the role nonhegemonic transparency might play in targeted acts of structural transformation. The term "radical transparency" might be a holding space for something yet to come, an unsettling of what it means to "see through" and the relationship between data, narrative, information, interpretation, and understanding. Radical transparency would involve workers and citizens making decisions about what kind of disclosure is the most effective in a given situation and about the scope of sociopolitical change that disclosure can precipitate. After all, far too often, disclosures are used to renew rather than disrupt the economic or political system. It might even involve the counterintuitive measure of withholding information in certain circumstances, like when we are called on to respond to an auditing exercise that we suspect is being implemented for less than transparent reasons, thus effectively investing in secrecy over disclosure.[16] Then radical transparency comes to look very different from the ascendant vision of transparency we are currently being asked to ascribe to. "Radical" indicates not more (of the same) transparency but instead transparency rethought through a resistant, critical methodology. It requires us to be open about what forms openness might take. Radical transparency might, in fact, be another name for, or a particular working through within, postsecrecy.

I will examine the radical potential of secrecy and opacity in later chapters, but first I turn to a particular form of subjectivity that is shaped by an experience of open and closed forms of data.

# CHAPTER 4

# SHAREVEILLANCE
## Open and Covert Government Data Practices

Two questions dominate debates at the intersection of privacy, governance, security, and transparency: How much and what kind of data should citizens have to share with surveillance states? And how much data from government departments should states share with citizens? Yet these issues are rarely expressed in terms of sharing in the way that I will be in this chapter. More often, when thought in tandem with the digital, the word "sharing" is used in reference to either free trials of software (shareware); the practice of peer-to-peer file sharing; platforms that facilitate the pooling, borrowing, swapping, renting, or selling of resources, skills, and assets that have come to be known as the sharing economy; or the business of linking and liking on social media, which invites us to share our feelings, preferences, thoughts, interests, photographs, articles, and Web links. Sharing in the digital context has been framed as a form of exchange but also as communication and distribution (John 2013; Wittel 2011).

In order to understand the politics of open and covert government data practices that share data with citizens or require citizens to share their data, I will extend existing commentaries on the distributive qualities of sharing by drawing on Jacques Rancière's (2004b) notion of the "distribution of the sensible": a settlement that determines what is visible, audible, sayable, and knowable, and what share or role we each have within it. In the process, I articulate "sharing" with "veillance" (*veiller*, "to watch," is from the Latin *vigilare*, from *vigil*, "watchful") to turn the focus from prevalent ways of understanding digital sharing toward a form of contemporary subjectivity. What I call shareveillance—a settlement in which we are always already sharing; indeed, in which any relationship with data is only made possible through a conditional idea of sharing—produces antipolitical positions for subjects who are caught between the affects and demands of different data practices. Shareveillant subjects are shaped by the data practices and digital infrastructure under scrutiny here, but that access to and the impact of those practices and infrastructure will vary. That is to say, experiences of shareveillance are inflected by markers of identity and what Patricia Hill Collins calls matrices of oppression (1990).[1]

While it is tempting to use the term "depoliticized" here, I prefer "antipolitical" because it better captures the way that the open and covert data practices that constitute shareveillance invoke political agency while greatly delimiting it, not least by the way in which some encourage actions framed by the notion of choice and the citizen qua consumer. Moreover, "depoliticized" might imply nostalgia for a once fully agential autonomous subject, but political agency has always been limited by structural and relational conditions as well as the fluidity, fragmentation, absences, blind spots, endless divisibility, or fracture of psyches and subjectivities diagnosed by psychoanalysis, (post-)Marxism, and poststructuralism, among other discourses. Nevertheless, the particular discursive material conditions that curtail agency alongside those other inescapable metaphysical limitations matter, for it is from here that we can more fully understand the singularity of the particular distribution we are faced with. I am therefore interested in the precise ways in which open and covert government data practices (and the open and closed data they deal in) foreclose politics while simultaneously seeming to foster forms of democratic engagement with governance through open data.

Open and covert government data initiatives both involve forms of sharing and veillance, though they are differently pitched. Government practices that share data with citizens involve veillance because, as I have shown in chapter 2 and will expand on below, they call on citizens to monitor and act on that data. Information imaginaries reliant on open government data envisage, watch, and hail subjects as auditing and entrepreneurial. Citizens have to monitor the state's data, or they are expected to innovate with it and make it profitable. But watchful citizens are watched in turn, and data is also the currency in covert state data practices (practices that we cannot see through and that are not readily knowable), such as those revealed by Edward Snowden. Such programs produce closed data. The main point about closed data in relation to the state (the details would be different for commercial enterprises) is that it is withheld from general access and circulation for reasons concerned with diplomacy, stability, power play, or security.[2] Covert government data practices involve sharing because they require citizens to (often unknowingly) share data with the veillant state in a way that renders them visible and trackable.

However, we should not think of the positions carved out for citizens in each configuration as an oscillation between agency and impotence. Nor is it quite right to think of this as the "equiveillance" diagnosed by Steve Mann (2013): an evenly poised balance between surveillance and sousveillant forces. Rather, shareveillance feeds into the way in which the datafied neoliberal security state shapes an antipolitical role for its public. The latter is configured as either a flat data set or a series of individual auditor-entrepreneurs rather than as a force with political potential. For those of us unhappy with politics being delimited and disavowed like this, we will need to experiment with ways to interrupt shareveillance that do not play into or endorse the post-truth disavowal (or even disappearance) of facts and data under populist figures like Trump.

A radical critique of ubiquitous and default sharing in the digital context is clearly necessary, but I also want to seek out opportunities to salvage the concept of "sharing" in order to imagine a collective politics that could emerge from within this sociotechnological moment (rather than pitching one against it). I will begin this work in the current chapter, but I will return to it in earnest in chapter 6, where I propose that we can interrupt shareveillance by claiming not a right to access more and more data or a right to privacy, but rather, following Glissant (1997), a right to opacity.[3] In the context of shareveillance, I am imagining this right as the demand not to be legible as, reducible to, and responsible for the demands of data, and to resist the terms of engagement set by the two faces of shareveillance (that is, sharing data with the state and monitoring shared data). The formulation of such an argument rests on an appropriation of the term "sharing" by calling on the etymological roots of "to share," particularly the Old English for "portion" *(scearu)*, which points toward a cutting, shearing, a part or division. With this in mind, we can imagine a right to opacity that cuts into, and apart, veillant formations and data distributions through various tactics such as hacking, data obfuscation, decentralization, encryption, and anarchic algorithms. Accepting shareveillance means accepting a "distribution of the sensible" that is not based on equality, necessitating a different, more ethical distribution, cut, or share by way of a response on our part. Exploring a right to opacity in the face of shareveillance can politicize the concept of sharing by envisioning it as an equitable, ethical cut. If, as Jose Van Dijck has suggested, online sharing is a networked and negotiated "evolving norm" (2013, 46), might it then evolve away from the meanings and roles it has been allotted by neoliberal and/or security states and surveillance capitalists?

## Digital Shares

Commercial excitement about the rise of the sharing economy as facilitated by digital technologies is tempered by concern in the academy. If the dominant discourse celebrates this economy for its entrepreneurial ability to utilize spare capacity (usually with regards to for-profits like Uber and Airbnb rather than nonprofits like Freecycle), skeptics focus on the neoliberal erosion of labor rights and safeguards and the commercialization of communitarianism. Gary Hall, for example, points out that "even if this form of economy is presented as a revival of community spirit, it actually has very little to do with sharing access to goods, activities and services, and everything to do with selling this access. . . . It thus does hardly anything to challenge economic inequality and injustice" (2016, 17). What Mike Bulajewski (2014) finds unpalatable is the way in which the utopianism expressed in populist studies like Yochai Benkler's *The Wealth of Networks* (2006) and Clay Shirky's *Here Comes Everybody* (2008), as well as rhetoric accompanying the sharing economy more generally, "conflates political action and market transaction."

The use of the term to refer to a range of platforms and apps that facilitate the harnessing of surplus time, skills, goods, and capacities is only the latest incarnation of sharing's articulation within the digital context.[4] Nicholas A. John (2013) lobbied for sharing to be considered as a keyword for understanding digital culture in the tradition of Raymond Williams (1976). Subsequently, "sharing" was included in Culture Digitally's "Digital Keywords."⁵ John's (2014) contribution to that project discusses sharing in terms of three examples. First, he calls on computer time sharing, which was developed during the late 1950s and early 1960s to make efficient use of expensive processor time. Second, file sharing, which informed the U.S. Department of Defense's development of ARPAnet, and which was strengthened by the introduction of transmission control protocol (TCP)/internet protocol (IP) in 1973, which offered computers a common language and enabled packets to be routed to the right destination. Subsequent protocols such as hypertext transfer protocol (HTTP) and simple mail transfer protocol (SMTP) develop the concept that networks can facilitate direct connections and transfers between hosts. Recent peer-to-peer file-sharing techniques present the latest evolution of such logic (Johnson, McGuire, and Willey 2008). Third is "data sharing," the term that has come to denote the simple transportation of data. Though all three of these make an appearance, John chooses to focus on a fourth instance—one embedded in the logic of Web 2.0. Here he turns to the way in which social networking sites have appropriated the term "sharing" to refer to the imperative and logic of communication and distribution. Because posting, linking, and liking are all termed "sharing" on social networking sites, in effect, "sharing is the fundamental and constitutive activity of Web 2.0" (John 2013, 176).

In addition to acting in the service of communication, sharing data also has to be understood as a form of distribution. Human and nonhuman actors are involved in the dissemination of data, documents, photos, Web links, feelings, opinions, and news across space and time. Such an obvious point is worth making because it allows us to think beyond the dominant, morally inflected imperative to share, connect, and be open with others in a network through a confessional communicative style, toward circulation in a purely spatial sense (albeit one with ethical and political implications). It might be useful here to think about such a process as one of spatial differentiation, a term borrowed from economics that refers to the uneven dispersal of resources, goods, and services. Differences in natural and human resources lead to inequitable access to inputs and outputs. I want to retain this inflection—of inequality, of disparity—with the intention that it will open the way for a broader discussion of the politics or ethics of (data)veillance, distribution, and sharing in the context of the state rather than private platforms.

## Distribution of the (Digital) Sensible

Whereas John's use of the term "distribution" points toward the act of disseminating photos, files, videos, and so forth (2013, 176), I will draw on the way it is invoked and used by Rancière. *Le Partage du sensible* is translated as a sharing, partition, division, and, more commonly, distribution of the sensible. This distribution of the sensible is a political-aesthetic settlement. It is, in Rancière's words, "a delimitation of spaces and times, of the visible and the invisible, of speech and noise, that simultaneously determines the place and the stakes of politics as a form of experience. Politics revolves around what is seen and what can be said about it, around who has the ability to see and the talent to speak, around the properties of spaces and the possibilities of time" (2004b, 12–13). Aesthetics for Rancière is a distributive regime determining what action, reaction, and thought is possible in any given situation. It is political precisely because in every "distribution of the sensible," equality is either undermined or affirmed as what is common and what is exclusive become apparent. A distribution determines "those who have a part in the community of citizens" (7); it "reveals who can have a share in what is common to the community based on what they do and on the time and space in which this activity is performed" (8). Equality is enacted or verified when those without part, the unrepresented, come to take part; those without a share have a share. In a process of subjectivization, this involves refuting the subject position allocated by the system and finding a position, as well as a name or identity in relation that will enable full participation and recognition, akin to the work the term "proletariat" once might have performed (Rancière 1992). An instantiation of politics, which for Rancière has to verify a presupposed equality, is when demands for a new division and sharing of the social whole are granted to those rendered invisible and unheard.

Such a conception can be helpful in the context of open and covert government digital data practices and the settlement of shareveillance that connects them. It makes sense today to include digital data in an understanding of "the sensible" (that which can be seen, heard, touched, thought). Its availability to a subject's veillant capacities or range, and the conditions of its visibility (to whom, in which circumstances, to what ends) are usefully thought as part of a particular distribution. In any encounter we can ask: "Who has a share of the data?" and "What kind of subjectivity is presupposed, imagined and made more likely as a result of that division and/or access?" Before turning to discuss these questions in terms of open and covert government data practices in more detail, I want to pause to consider the logic of sharing as it pertains to the digital in general in order to demonstrate a technological underpinning to the rise of shareveillance.

## Protocols of Sharing

John notes that it is possible to argue that "the entire internet is fundamentally a sharing technology" (2013, 179), citing the importance of open source software and programming languages, as well as sharing economies of production in the development of websites based on user-generated content. Likewise, Engin Isin and Evelyn Ruppert claim, "the ubiquity of various uses of digital traces has made data sharing the norm" (2015, 89). While I am also interested in sharing configured in this way, I want to slightly rephrase and shift the emphasis of these assertions to suggest that sharing can be conceived as the constitutive logic of the internet. Rather than thinking about sharing primarily as something that users do on the internet, I want to focus more on the idea that sharing operates at the level of protocol. My use of this term draws on Alexander Galloway's exposition of computer protocols as standards that "govern how specific technologies are agreed to, adopted, implemented, and ultimately used by people around the world" (2004, 7).

In arguing this point, I am not supporting a utopian celebration of the internet's open or free origins. Galloway (2004), among others, makes the error of such an assumption clear, as he characterizes the internet as a technology marked by control and hierarchies of enclosure. Rather, in thinking through sharing protocols and protocols of sharing, I imply that the internet's grain is, first and foremost, stateless in the sense that programming intends: as a lack of stored inputs. In other words, the basic architecture of the internet does not automatically keep a record of previous interactions, so each interaction request is handled only on the basis of the information that accompanies it. For example, the internet's fundamental method for sending data between computers, IP, works by sending small chunks of data known as packets, which travel independently of each other. These discrete packets are put together at an upper layer by TCP, yet the IP itself operates without state. We can also look to how the Web's HTTP serves up requested pages but does not "remember" those requests. Such discrete communications mean that no continuity is recorded.

As Tom Armitage points out, because the internet's default architecture is open or stateless, it is very good at sharing, but it is not so good at privacy and ownership.[6] By this, he means simply that "implementing state, or privacy, or ownership, or a paywall, is effort" (Tom Armitage, e-mail to author, February 9, 2016). State is a secondary level, patched onto a stateless system. This is not to say that the development and design of the internet was free from a proprietary impetus, or that "default" architecture is anything but conscious and intentional. Rather, at a technical level, to limit connection and sharing on the internet must be introduced in secondary layers and mechanisms. It also follows that tracking a user's activity has to be imposed at that secondary level. The Netscape Web browser, for example, introduced the cookie, a text file that stores small amounts of data associated with a domain. As long as the cookie has not expired, it will track the pages a user visits and help build a user profile (Elmer 2003). In its stateless formations, before the effort to impose statefulness, the internet can be conceptualized as a technology of stateless, borderless, always already sharing. Sharing (without tracking or remembering) in this instance is a rule conditioning the possibility of computers communicating with each other at all.

However, introducing state—tracking users' online movements, say—foregrounds a different kind of sharing, but one no longer concerned with open and nonaccumulative peer-to-peer communication. Rather, it is a sharing of the journey, searches, and data transfers from one IP address or an individual user with the Web publisher, and often third parties. Indeed, tech companies like Facebook and Google use the word "sharing" when referring to the monetization of users' data (John 2013). In Instagram's 2018 privacy policy, for example, there is a section titled "How is this information shared?"[7]

   \* This links protocol and profits. Legal and illegal entities want a share of our data and to share data with (that is, sell it to) those that can monetize it. The prime commercial "data dealers" are big tech search and social media platforms, of course. Other interested parties include hackers (should our data be interesting or profitable enough) able to overcome any data loss prevention (DLP) software and systems from firewalls to encryption. Web publishers such as Doubleclick use trackers that log the data we create through our online activity to customize service and advertising and sell it to third parties. Such trackers do not often announce themselves; we must seek them out through antitracking browser extensions (like Ghostery) or conduct forensic examinations of user agreements (which still do not list specific trackers). Many websites have multiple trackers (cookies and beacons). Ironically, even website publishers that use trackers are themselves subject to "data leakage," which "occurs when a brand, agency or ad tech company collects data about a website's audience and subsequently uses that data without the initial publisher's permission" (McDermott 2015). Such secretions, the unintentional sharing of already shared data, also highlight the difficulties of not-sharing from a different perspective.

    I posit the idea of sharing as a protocol here to emphasize the fact that specific modes of sharing and not-sharing, as well as the particular distribution of the (data) sensible, are determined by ideologically charged *dispositifs*. As Galloway puts it, "Protocol is how technological control exists after decentralization" (2004, 8). Crucially, the conditions of sharing/not-sharing today inflect different experiences of subjectivity by imposing limits on veillant and agential capacities.

### The Sharing Assemblage

Depending on our politics, we will be more or less resistant to the sharing of our data in exchange for security; depending on our willingness and time to read the clauses in different privacy policies, we might be more or less cognizant of what it is exactly we are sharing with private corporations. Depending on how much attention we paid to the details of the Snowden revelations, we will have greater or lesser understanding of the ways in which our communications and movements can be monitored by the state. While we should take into account these variables in knowledge and politics, as well as the stratified and uneven reach of and reliance on the digital, sharing today should be understood not as a conscious and conscientious act but as a default component of contemporary data subjectivity.

Although data is etymologically derived from *dare*—Latin for "to give"—it often feels as if data has been taken. This recalls Rob Kitchin's observation that data might be better referred to as *capta* (from Latin *capere*, "to take") (2014, 2). Kitchin invokes this alternative etymology to drive home the fact that data is never raw, transparent, or objective; that it never gives itself over without the intervention of a subjective interpreter or scientist. Data has to be extracted, selected, or taken. Kitchin is thinking about the mediated, "cooked" nature of data, but we can also see this tension between giving and taking in terms of subjectivity. Is the relation between subjects and data better encapsulated by giving or taking?

Neither verb quite encompasses the experience of shareveillance to which I am referring. It is not clear that data belongs to subjects in the first place, for it then to be given or taken. Rather, subjects are within a dynamic sharing assemblage; they are always already sharing, relinquishing data with human or nonhuman agents. I want to identify a subjectivity that is shaped by the play between openness and enclosure. The term "shareveillance" is intended to capture the conditions in which subjects are asked to consume shared data and produce data to be shared, are required to be surveillant and surveilled, as elements of control. To phrase it with a different emphasis: The subject of shareveillance is one who simultaneously works with data and on whom the data works. Of course, these general conditions are experienced in heterogeneous ways according to "matrices of oppression," as I point out above.

Sharing prevails as a standard of the system because of the difficulties of unsharing data and the effort of safeguarding data or rendering it proprietary. To take the first of these, the ease and speed of copying digital data means that data already in circulation cannot be revoked. This has led to some farcical situations in the United Kingdom in which information freely available on the internet has been repressed by injunction of the regular press. Or consider the move in 2016 by PinkNews to publish stories removed from search engines through Google's right to be forgotten policy in the European Union that came into operation in 2014 (Duffy 2016). While these examples pertain to information rather than data per se, the principle of digital reproduction and dissemination is the same. Moreover, in the case of cloud storage, or even backups to hard drives, replication of data is the default. More than one copy of files often exists on a hard drive, let alone in different storage facilities. It is also pertinent to point out that it makes little sense to talk about an original when it comes to digital data, the consequence of which is that data is nonrivalrous and sharing nondepleting. We could also look to the way in which the use and reuse of different data sets for various applications makes it non-sensical to talk about the unsharing of data. Once it is the lifeblood of various apps, bringing oxygen to a new economy, it is being shared in multiple directions through various media. We can thus detect a propensity toward duplication, secretion, circulation, and sharing.

Sharing in commercial contexts is clearly a central part of experiences of shareveillance. Much has been written about the commodification of users' browsing habits and metadata in the context of social media, online gaming, and the trend toward quantified self, particularly as it pertains to surveillance capitalism (Zuboff 2015, 2019). The political economy of commercial data surveillance ensures that the activity of watching (in this case watching not the state or the commercial entity itself but rather the posts, newsfeeds, and products that have been curated by friends or algorithms) is closely aligned with sharing (of linking and liking while simultaneously leaving a trail to be shared with brokers, analysts, and political consultants like the now defunct Cambridge Analytica that harness and trade in big data). While I have pointed toward a distribution of the digital sensible that would encompass private and public, national, and transnational entities, in what follows I want to focus on the ways in which state forms of open and closed data feed into such a distribution. Because of the level of collaboration between the state and big tech revealed by Snowden, as well as the ways those companies can sometimes challenge, exceed, transcend, or evade nation-state legislation and taxation, distinguishing between government and commercial data sharing is somewhat artificial. As a consequence, while I will focus on state practices in what follows, this will also have ramifications for the private commercial sector.

## Open and Closed Government Data

The labels "open" and "closed" are not essential but relational, adhering to particular moments in space and time. When articulated to data, the identity of each, and the binary opposition itself, are contingent on the political climate, the market, the security complex, and technological and veillant capacities. The tendency toward secretion identified above should be enough to indicate the provisional nature of any identification of data as closed. Likewise, because of the inherently opaque nature of much open data (which leaves many questions unanswered, such as for whom was this data collected? To what end?), it is never simply open or transparent.

Open government data is generally understood as the provision of big and small digital data on the part of government agencies of the kind on which I focus in the previous two chapters. Alongside a few critical voices, such as those of Morozov (2013), open government data is celebrated in the mainstream for democratizing knowledge distribution and research, invigorating economies, increasing efficiency, ensuring accountability, and operating as a key element in digital democracy, or Democracy 2.0 (Goldstein and Dyson 2013). Open government data is data shared with no depletion—sharing not in the sense of division but in giving multiple citizens access to the same thing.

By contrast, we can understand closed government data as data that is withheld from public view, whether in the interests of privacy, diplomacy, or national security. "Close" comes from Old French *clore,* "to shut, to cut off from," an etymology that permits us to see how citizens are cut off from the state's data—even data they have (perhaps unknowingly) shared. In sharing this kind of data, we have in effect given it away. Our share can never yield. That is to say, without the interventions of whistle-blowers or hackers, closed government data will never be given the opportunity to be put to uses other than those that the state deems appropriate.

In its open formation, government data is deliberately and strategically shared by the collecting agent; in its closed formation, data is deliberately and strategically not shared. With respect to closed data, citizens perhaps acquiesce to the surveillance imperative to share data with a proprietary agent in exchange for certain protections and privileges.[8] Some might consciously or unconsciously, explicitly or implicitly consider the collection of their GPS data or phone meta-data a fair price to pay for the freedoms and benefits that come with holding certain passports. Again, the way citizens feel about this so-cial contract will depend on the way they experience the apparatus of the state. This pragmatic attitude to sharing with respect to closed government data, the transmission of citizens' activity to a veillant other, is echoed in the experience of digital consumers in general. Users of social media and search engines are familiar with making trade-offs between services they want and acquiescence to data col-lection. As well as protocological in a technological sense, then, shar-ing also needs to be thought as a political, cultural and industry stan-dard; it "frame[s] the terms and parameters by which elements of a system interact and behave" (McStay 2014, 5).

Sharing is not something we do after possessing data; rather, it is the basis on which having any relation with that data can be possible at all—which does not necessarily indicate that the data we have shared is digested and immediately put to work by any surveillant. Rather, to borrow the words of Gus Hunt, the CIA's chief technology officer, it indicates that "collect[ing] everything and hang[ing] on to it forever" (Ingram 2013) relies on the idea that the archive is "structurally spec-ulative" (Andrejevic and Gates 2014). The uses to which collected data will be put and the meanings it will be given are dependent on future algorithms and political concerns. This means that in a networked era, we are always already sharing without any actor in the system necessarily knowing precisely why. The principle of sharing overrides any uncertainty over the uses to which shared data can be put. Such a condition is obviously in the interests of commercial and state sur-veillance that, in general, currently have monopolies on accruing eco-nomic or security value from big, aggregated archives of data.[9]

By looking at the national security data surveillance revealed by Snowden and revisiting the open government data initiatives of the Obama administration and implemented in other geographical con-texts, I will consider how shareveillant subjectivity is closely tied to the securitized neoliberal state.

### Closed Data, Securitized Veillance

The data collected by the National Security Agency (NSA) in the United States, the Government Communications Headquarters (GCHQ) in the United Kingdom, and other security agencies around the globe is mostly experienced as closed; the data is inaccessible to those without security clearance. Before Snowden revealed the programs implemented to collect communications data and metadata—programs such as Prism, which since 2007 permitted the NSA to access data from service providers, and Tempora, which saw GCHQ place interceptors on fiber-optic cables that handle internet traffic in and out of the United Kingdom—the programs were also closed, covert, and opaque. This is not to deny that there were all kinds of secretions regarding those practices; details or speculations erupted now and again into the public sphere through reportage, whistle-blowing, or popular cultural representation—what Tim Melley (2012) refers to as the "covert sphere": the representation of and cultural counterpart to the covert sector. Rather than focus on the content of the revelations and to what extent such news was new, however, I am interested in the conceptual apparatus that was available to those who wanted to resist or challenge this aspect of the shareveillant assemblage.

Though domestic protests were subdued, calls to end the NSA's activities, as evidenced on the banners held at the march on Washington, D.C., in October 2013, were expressed as an "end to mass spying" (Reuters 2013). Exercising protesters' imaginations and offending their constitutional rights was the suggestion that the security agencies of their own government had the ability to view their communications data and metadata without their knowledge or explicit consent. While many would agree that this move toward ubiquitous communications surveillance is indeed something to resist, the appeal to privacy falls flat. Privacy is like the light we see from an already dead star. We cling to it even though we live in what our digital conjuncture has essentially rendered a postprivacy paradigm. This does not mean that the concept of privacy is no longer important; it still organizes legal processes, rights-based debate, and common understandings of our own sense of self. In some ways, as Andrew McStay points out, "many social changes since the industrial revolution involve a net increase in privacy, be this less familiarity with our neighbours, more geographically dispersed family arrangements, working away from home, weakening of religious authority, . . . greater possibility of children having their own bedrooms, increase in car ownership (versus public transport)" (2014, 2). Yet the risk of still appealing to privacy as protection in an era of surveillance capitalism with closed data that it wishes to market, and ubiquitous state data surveillance with its closed data that it wishes to use in the service of security, is that it reduces rather than increases political agency precisely because it misunderstands the subjectivity in question and because privacy claims are particularly weak when it comes to collective politics. In Rancièrean terms, it cannot redistribute the digital sensible.

To take the first of these issues, the appeal to privacy in the wake of the Snowden revelations misreads the deindividualizing character of mass covert data mining. The fear expressed on the banners and placards of the protests is that the state sees the crowd as individuals, a mass that is made up of many "I"s, each with infringed privacy. The concept of privacy imagines a state violating the rights of a fully self-present sovereign citizen. However, the way data mining works means that the security services are not particularly interested in the actions of individual citizens except inasmuch as those citizens are relational data points; they are interested in how each data point contributes to a larger background pattern on which an algorithm can work to recognize minority anomalies. As Clough et al. write, "In the case of personal data, it is not the details of that data or a single digital trail that is important, but rather the relationship of the emergent attributes of digital trails en masse that allows for both the broadly sweeping and the particularized modes of affective measure and control. Big data doesn't care about 'you' so much as the bits of seemingly random info that bodies generate or that they leave as a data trail" (2014, 154). Nova Spivack (2013), in an article infused with technological utopianism, puts it slightly differently: "We are noise, not signal." Spivack problematically invokes this argument to excuse the NSA's data scraping (echoing the common mantra that if you have done nothing wrong, you have nothing to fear from surveillance). But we can also come to a different conclusion. The configuration of citizens as "noise, not signal" points toward our delimited role within the shareveillant assemblage read from the perspective of closed data.

The offense, I suggest, is less the intrusion into private space and more the disavowal of the public as potentially political. The surveillance state imagines its citizens in this configuration as primarily an aggregated data set. It is not that citizens are being spied on that is of most concern in this view, but that unless their actions are flagged as extreme outliers, they are not considered fully formed political agents worthy of anything more than bolstering an algorithm for data analysis. The data set neutralizes any potential such aggregations might have of acting like a multitude, Michael Hardt and Antonio Negri's term for an internally differentiated social multiplicity that can nevertheless act in common (Hardt and Negri 2000; Hardt 2004).[10] The multitude does not resemble traditional configurations; rather, as Jeremy Gilbert suggests, it is "a field of collectivity which is composed of singularities: unique points of intersection and potential self-invention which cannot be subsumed into any simple totality nor reduced to the status of individuals" (2008, 164). This is important because it points to an idea of political agency beyond individualism toward a distributed or networked agency. Hardt (2003) claims that

> it is important to distinguish the multitude from a series of other concepts—the masses, the crowd, the rabble. All of these are social multiplicities, are pluralities. But they are passive, they cannot act on their own. The mob and the masses not only can be guided, they have to be guided, they need an external force that leads. By contrast, the multitude acts on its own, it is able to act in its own name, it refuses leadership. For me the definition of the multitude is the social multiplicity that is able to act in common. It is able to be active, so that these various differences can act together, can act in common.

When the collective singularities of the multitude are captured as a data set, a hopeful reconfiguration of the political is, it would seem, foreclosed. Rather than being of comfort, the fact that citizens only count in terms of their role as flat data influences the scope of (a networked or distributed) political agency to alter the distribution of the sensible, and the possibilities therein that this implies for effective, counterhegemonic collective action. All of the data points we compulsorily contribute to the data set are used to identify outliers in ways we may not agree with.

The second limitation of privacy is that it is a poor foundation on which to build collective action. This limitation is not tied to the big data turn, but it is nevertheless a critique that has been given a new inflection in that context. While it is not within the scope of this book to provide an extensive survey of work on privacy, it is worth recalling the ways in which privacy has been subject to critique from the left for its connections with individualism, the perpetuation of oppression, and property. To call on the right to privacy is to frame the debate in terms of an individual's right to limit the access other people, the state, or commercial entities might have to the individual's content (data, thoughts, feelings, information, communications) at any time. It reinforces a sense of a self that lives in political isolation. Therefore, even when people coalesce around privacy concerns, when they step into the light of the demos, they do so in order to insist on their right to step back into the apolitical shadows of individualism, away from the possibility of collective creativity or an identity in common. Equally, feminists like Catharine MacKinnon (1989) have challenged privacy for allowing gendered inequality, including domestic violence, to exist beyond the purview of society. The private sphere potentially offers respite and refuge, but might be experienced more like a prison for some oppressed women. Moreover, as a notion used most adeptly to protect property, privacy has been an uneasy bedfellow for collectivist leftist politics more interested in the redistribution of wealth.

In short, privacy claims are ill equipped to fundamentally challenge the data surveillance being conducted that contributes to the experiences of shareveillance I am outlining. In an era of total data surveillance and digital protocols rooted in the ideal of sharing, anyone not wanting to be fully transparent to the state is forced to treat anything private as if it were secret. But closed data and covert data practices are only half the story.

### Open Data Redux

Previous chapters have shown that the provision of open data is a professed concern and commitment for many liberal democracies today. In sharing its data sets with citizens, the state adds to the interpellation of shareveillant subjects. Althusser's vivid and oft-quoted scenario depicting the process of becoming a subject sees a figure that responds to being hailed by a "Hey, you there!" (1971, 174). The calling police sees the subject who turns to acknowledge the ideological call. While it is clear that interpellation is experienced according to social stratifications, Althusser's model is still useful. We could say that shareveillant subjects (who may not share much apart from this determined relation with data sharing) are hailed with an added imperative—"Hey, you there! Come closer and watch." Being made a subject involves being seen and becoming vigilant. Of course, because of all I have said about data surveillance, the presubject who turns to be seen is in fact always already seen (as data), and therefore is a datafied, relational, technological-human assemblage that comes into being through the act of looking as much as being looked at. The subject must acquiesce to being surveilled, but the subject also has to be seen to be seeing. More accurately the subject is asked to see through; the transparency of the state is the interface that hails citizens, and they cannot but occupy the position (whether they feel technically capable or not, whether they perform the function or not) of auditor, analyst, witness.

For example, an early incarnation of Data.gov included an array of data sets and documents that contained statistics of varying importance in a variety of formats (CSV files, Word documents, PDFs, and so on). Watching and seeing through (and acquiring and refreshing the technological competence required to do so) become forms of immaterial labor. As Isin and Ruppert recognize, "acts of sharing place unique demands on citizen subjects of cyberspace" (2015, 88). As my discussion of this in chapters 2 and 3 makes clear, in the process, a characteristic of neoliberal logic is performed: the subject is bequeathed responsibility without power. Citizens are given the responsibility to watch without the expertise to know what to look for, nor the power to act in a meaningful way on what might be found. Echoing Max Horkheimer's conclusion that the cultural industries "constantly profess their adherence to the individual's ultimate value and his inalienable freedom, but . . . operate in such a way that they tend to foreswear such values by fettering the individual to prescribed attitudes, thoughts, and buying habits" ([1941] 1989, 265), open data offers the promise of agency and freedom (of information), yet it shapes the scope and manifestation of those ideals to entrench the logic of shareveillance.

As I have shown, the act of looking, of being asked to look, is more complicated still, for even while this call to be vigilant is made, the reach widens to draw in unelected mediators: third-party application developers and data visualizers. Data entrepreneurs step into the ideological void to help fulfill the demand to watch, to see (through) the state. The so-called datapreneurs willingly perform this function, taking the data sets made available by the government on websites like Data.gov and turning them into user-friendly interfaces. In doing so, those datapreneurs are also themselves responding to a hailing: a call to help operationalize the new data economy. The datapreneur is the key figure in the success of the (open) data economy, the actor who must harness the potential of the data to create value from raw data sets. To illustrate, consider the team behind Zocdoc, an app that uses data from the U.S. Census Bureau and the Centers for Medicare and Medicaid Services to assist patients as they manage the complex system of U.S. health insurance and provision, or the datapreneurs behind Spotcrime, an app that again uses census data, but this time to produce a searchable map that contains crime statistics for each area. In the United Kingdom, the Findthebest website uses the open census and Department of Education data on Data.gov.uk to produce searchable league tables on primary and secondary schools, with information as detailed as average teacher salaries and how school budgets are spent. For the state and datapreneur alike, data is configured as a resource ripe for mining and commodification.

Where does this leave shareveillant subjects? At once asked to watch the newly transparent state, with all its data organs on display, and to rely on the mediating and translating functions of datapreneurs to do so, the relationship of these subjects to the state is shaped by the market. The veillance called for in this instance is watchfulness not of the fully transparent state but of selected mediations brought forth. Transparency is obscured by its own impossible glare; only the data that the market has primed us to want (usually data that can help us make apparently informed choices in a complex public–private landscape) assumes the face of state transparency in the data economy. The risk is that it becomes increasingly difficult to participate in and navigate the state outside of these commodified, edited, and algorithmically governed forms of aggregated data. How best to describe the contours of the soft power at play here?

Gilles Deleuze's short but influential essay, "Postscript on the Societies of Control" (1992), offers a helpful reading of how capital is organized and control exercised in postdisciplinary societies. Deleuze recalls the discrete and autonomous units of confinement characteristic of Foucauldian disciplinary societies to show what is distinct about the dispersed, mutating mechanisms of control that characterize the dominant socioeconomic logic of contemporary capitalism. He describes this logic as a "modulation" (4). As opposed to enclosures, which are molds or castings, a modulation is "like a self-deforming cast that will continuously change from one moment to the other" (4). Data-driven government transparency, which as a move from administrative to democratic accountability might seem like an unequivocal good, can be problematized through Deleuze's text to give a clear sense of why techniques of emancipation can be harnessed by the logic of capital and therefore serve the purpose of control for entities, including governments, invested in the furtherance of that economic mode.

While Deleuze's piece predates by several decades the open government data practices that I focus on in this book, it can help us understand this phenomenon in several ways. First, just as Deleuze identifies the way in which environments of enclosures (the prison, the hospital, the school) are now subject to forms of free-floating control, we can see how in opening up government, making selected boundaries porous through open data, outsourcing, and making citizens individually responsible, data-driven transparency ensures that the business of governance (and citizenship) is without boundaries or end. So while government becomes "smaller" to allow the market to do much of the work previously accorded the state, government simultaneously has a ubiquitous presence in the form of raw data—or, perhaps more importantly, digital tools to help navigate the state in its market form. If the factory has been replaced by the corporation as "a spirit, a gas" (Deleuze 1992, 4), then data-driven government transparency shows how the state does less while requiring citizens to engage more.

Second, through Deleuze's observation that control mechanisms are inseparable variations, we can see open data and the data economy in relation to other elements within the network or modulation that is the control society. Open data is imbricated with the way in which wages are "in states of perpetual metastability that operate through challenges, contests" (1992, 4). The data economy as an entrepreneurial enterprise, in which open data plays a crucial role, necessarily requires such metastability to become profitable. Moreover, datapaloozas and hackathons are clear examples of the challenges and contests that drive remuneration and profit and that endlessly address workers through their entrepreneurial capacities. Crucially, the logic of control means that each experience of governmentality is a continuity. Open data is thus one feature within a "continuous network" (6) that demands perpetual vigilance and innovation.

Third, in a formulation that helps us to assess what is at stake in the technological conditions of open data, Deleuze shows that we can be controlled through the conditions of access as well as confinement. He cites Félix Guattari's example of an electronic card that can open barriers in a city, but that "could just as easily be rejected on a given day or between certain hours; what counts is not the barrier but the computer that tracks each person's position—licit or illicit—and effects a universal modulation" (1992, 7). The emancipatory qualities of open data involve control because of the entrepreneurial metastasis required to convert a previously extraeconomic form into capital, the continuous vigilance of data subjects, submission to market logic as a form that can determine the scope of the political, and forms of data sharing that make life susceptible to value extraction and data surveillance that render life trackable. It is within this logic of control that the two faces of shareveillance make sense.

It would be an exaggeration to claim that Deleuze is nostalgic about the certainties of disciplinary societies, but it is fair to say that environments of enclosure with their clear borders offer more opportunities for distinctive, oppositional subject positions or the creation of counterpublics. Although she does not use disciplinary societies as her reference point, Jodi Dean writes, "Whereas the Keynesian welfare state interpellated subjects into specific symbolic identities (such as the worker, the housewife, the student or the citizen), neoliberalism relies on imaginary identities. Not only do the multiplicity and variability of such identities prevent them from serving as loci of political action but their inseparability from the injunctions of consumerism reinforces capitalism's grip" (2009, 51). In general, the atomized, neoliberal subject is "one who strategizes for her- or himself among various social, political and economic options, not one who strives with others to alter or organize these options" (Brown 2005, 43). Even armed with the information provided through open data, shareveillant subjects in particular occupy a precarious position from which to enact or coalesce counterhegemonies because they are reliant on continuing the forms of control to which they are exposed. That is to say, shareveillant subjects have learned to experience and accept agency and subjectivity via the forms of veillance and sharing that I have described here.

### Fresh Cuts

The shareveillant subject is thus rendered politically impotent from (at least) two not necessarily distinct directions. In the face of state and commercial data surveillance, the subject's choices (whether that be with whom to communicate, what to circulate, or what to buy) are compulsorily shared to contribute to an evolving algorithm to optimize advertising, say, or governmentality, to make them more efficient, targeted, precise. The public is configured as rich big data rather than a network of singularities with resistant potential. Open government portals share the state's data with citizens, and in doing so, they make them responsible for it while isolating them, thereby eroding the legitimacy and possibility of collective power. In addition, this form of accountability produces a limited relation with the information provided. In monitoring the granular transactions of government, armchair auditors are only permitted to spot anomalies or aberrations in a system they have to otherwise acknowledge as fair. This form of sharing, of openness, anticipates a limited form of engagement and response. As I have already suggested, even this armchair auditor able to engage with raw data is largely a fiction produced by information imaginaries in which open data plays a key part; the crucial role that datapreneurs and app developers play in mediating data means that the state's sharing and the citizen's share of the state are subject to market forces.

Of course, it is one thing to diagnose a condition and quite another to prescribe a remedy. If one accepts that shareveillance is a political settlement not conducive to radical equality, and that a more equitable distribution is something to strive for, how might shareveillance be interrupted? Chapter 3 considered some interruptions in the form of radical transparency. In later chapters, I will recognize, and offer ideas concerning, tactics and strategies of secrecy and opacity. The conceptual framework for my interruptions is inspired by the etymology of "share." "Cutting," from the Old English *scearu*—"a cutting, shearing, tonsure; a part or division"—the root of the meaning of "share" apropos "portion," to the term *scear* with respect to plowshare, meaning simply "that which cuts," clearly resonates within the concept and practice of sharing.

This focus is certainly supported by Rancière's framing of the distribution of the sensible, at least in certain translations: "I understand by this phrase the cutting up [decoupage] of the perceptual world that anticipates, through its sensible evidence, the distribution of shares and social parties. . . . And this redistribution itself presupposes a cutting up of what is visible and what is not, of what can be heard and what cannot, of what is noise and what is speech" (2004a, 225). What share we have of resources, as well as the mode of sharing, fall along the lines of a particular distribution or cut. The way we share, the conditions and decisions underlying how and what we share, what I am calling the cut, create a certain distribution. My focus on the term "cut" here is, as I have confessed, inspired by the etymological roots of "share," but I am also mindful of Sarah Kember and Joanna Zylinska's productive use of it in *Life after New Media* (2012). Thinking about mediation as a "complex and hybrid process" that is "all-encompassing and indivisible" (xv), the authors draw on a range of thinkers from Henri Bergson to Karen Barad, Jacques Derrida to Emmanuel Levinas, to imagine cuts (into the temporality of mediation) as creative, ethical incisions and decisions. Thus, photography, to take their most potent example, is "understood here as a process of cutting through the flow of mediation on a number of levels: perceptive, material, technical, and conceptual. The recurrent moment of the cut—one we are familiar with not just via photography but also via film making, sculpture, writing, or, indeed, any other technical practice that involves transforming matter—is posited here as both a technique (an ontological entity encapsulating something that is, or something that is taking place) and an ethical imperative (the command: 'Cut!')" (xvii–xix). This leads Kember and Zylinska to ask what it means to "cut well" (xix). It is a question that all artists must ask themselves and practice, they argue. This imperative to cut well extends to all acts of mediation (any technical practice that involves transforming matter), including the kinds of practices that mediate data that I engage with in this book. Obviously, not everyone who works with data is an artist in the way we would traditionally understand that term. But if we draw on aesthetics in the Rancièrean sense—as a distributive regime that determines political possibilities (a formulation I will draw on in the next chapter)—then we can begin to see different decisions being made as to how and when to cut into data, and what to reveal or conceal about that decision-making process itself as ethical or unethical.

When we are cut off from our data (as is the case with closed data), we are not given the opportunity to make our own cuts *into* it. Equally, if the cut *of* data is such that we can only engage with it in ways that support a political settlement we might not agree with—if what might appear as an ethical provision of data (through transparency measures, for example) in fact supports or makes more efficient an unethical and discriminatory system—then our cuts are determined by strict parameters. To cut (and therefore share) differently, to cut against the grain, we have to interrupt the strictures of shareveillance.

There are many interruptive cuts that deserve to be mentioned. First, by not abiding by the rules of privatized and securitized access and copyright laws, some acts of hacking can highlight the unidirectional sharing of closed data and systems. Setting aside hackers recruited by intelligence agencies and cybersecurity firms, independent hackers could be characterized as performing guerrilla sharing (of source code, access, software, recovered data), taking a share where none was offered.[11] Second, decentralized data storage facilities like Storj and SAFE offer distributed object storage across the network, utilizing excess hard drive space, as an alternative to traditional cloud storage solutions, or what Geert Lovink calls "centralized data silos" (2016, 11). By using peer-to-peer technologies to distribute data across nodal points, this alternative formulation of cloud computing shares out encrypted data in a way that interrupts the flow of data upstream to surveillant third parties. Third, and this follows from the previous example, encryption technologies delimit sharing communities by requiring keys for decryption; sharing is therefore more controlled. Far from being an unconscious default, sharing becomes a purposeful and targeted action. Take, for example, the "Off-the-Record" encryption used by the free and open source instant messaging application Adium, a tool favored by journalists and NGO workers. According to the Off-the-Record Development Team, this technology offers not only encryption of instant messaging and authentication of a correspondent's identity but also deniability, because the sent messages do not have digital signatures that can be checked by a third party. It also offers what the team calls forward secrecy, which means that if users lose control of their private keys, no previous conversation is compromised.

Alone, such cuts may be limited in scope. However, when we think about them alongside the instances of radical transparency of the previous chapter, the artistic interventions of the next, and the various experiments that I gather under the banner "secrecy of the left" in chapter 6, they begin to realign a politics of visibility.

# CHAPTER 5

# AESTHETICS OF THE SECRET

The Secret itself is much more beautiful than its revelation.
—Jill Magid, *Becoming Tarden*

I will now turn to the secret more fully. This may only be a tactical, temporary turn before a radical, meaningful, equitable form of transparency can take hold, but it is one that might allow some respite from the demands and discourses of shareveillance. Such a turn, however, is far from simple. By definition, secrets are that which resist representation and dissolve under the glare, however minimal or tentative, of revelation. Who better to seek help from, then, than artists who have long tasked themselves with representing the unrepresentable? Today there are a number of artists addressing issues of secrecy.[1] The resulting body of work is important not because it offers solutions to the complex problems of closed data, state surveillance, and securitization, but because it invites and allows us to stay with the secret as secret rather than foregrounding the more individualistic notion of privacy or moving too quickly toward revelation and reform. It allows us to privilege an aesthetics of the secret over a hermeneutics of the secret. Considered as a "distribution of the sensible," a formulation introduced via Rancière (2004b) in the previous chapter to understand asymmetric encounters with data, this aesthetics can help us to imagine a politics of the secret not bound to policy and legalities. By looking at secrecy beyond the realm of politics proper, we find, somewhat counterintuitively, the secret politicized.

As a way to make clear the kinds of opportunities an aesthetics of the secret can provide, I will recall reactions to the Snowden revelations that began in 2013. In reigniting a familiar debate about the balance between state security and individual privacy, the revelations of the former NSA contractor quickly became stalled on matters of regulation and reform, which treat secrecy, security, and surveillance largely in procedural terms (whether a warrant is needed; the difference between data and metadata; whether U.S. citizens as well as foreign nationals can be spied on; how long data can be retained; and so forth). Suggested government reform missed the mark; far from curtailing mass surveillance, it might very well have been "permanently entrenching it in American law" (Timm 2014), and the mainstream pushback on data surveillance never managed to prompt enough public outrage.

This chapter seeks to interrupt the containment strategies of communicative capitalism/democracy evident in these debates by configuring secrets as both subject to and the subject of radical politics rather than regulation. Its premise is that we might be better able to form a radical political response to revelations like those revealed by Snowden, and to symptoms of shareveillance more broadly, by situating the secret within a distributive regime and imagining what collectivities and subjectivities the secret might make available—an inquiry that will shape the following chapter also. While in chapter 6 I will consider the secret through experiments with digital and political formations, in the current chapter I explore work by Trevor Paglen and Jill Magid because of the way it so clearly invites onlookers to experience the limits of secrecy.

I will conclude this chapter by arguing that in order to mount an enduring political response, we need to consider collective formations available to us after Snowden. I will propose the possibility of thinking and identifying horizontally under the banner of the "data multitude," or a non-self-identical, decentralized network linked by the imperative to make use of, and be used as, data, connected through data access, production, accumulation, and exploitation. Of course, this network is one stratified by "algorithms of oppression" (Noble 2018), racial formations of surveillance that precede but are intensified by the digital (Browne 2015), and uneven digital access. Despite these internal differentiations and struggles, data is the prime currency, vector, commodity, lifeblood. It is the means used by third parties to evaluate the worth of any data subject. However, data can also serve as the basis for a politics that puts first not privacy but rather a secrecy that interferes with the dominant distribution of the sensible.

## Hashtag Choices: #Patriot or #Traitor

We are still living in the wake of the revelations made by Snowden about the reach and capacities of the NSA, GCHQ, and other members of the intelligence alliance knows as the Five Eyes. The leaked classified material made it clear that these agencies enjoyed access to the servers of tech giants such as Google, Microsoft, and Apple; monitored social media applications in real time; intercepted, and for a time stored, data and metadata relayed over fiber-optic cables; collected the phone records of American nationals; and worked with the telecommunications industry to undermine internet encryption. It is not only the content of the files that is of note; the scale of the leak was also remarkable. The Pentagon announced in early 2014 that Snowden had committed the biggest theft of American secrets in history; it estimated that the leaked intelligence files numbered as many as 1.7 million (Strohm and Wilber 2014).

By now, details of the Snowden revelations—through high-profile newspaper features and subsequently Laura Poitras's film, *Citizenfour* (2014)—are well known, and I have offered a brief overview in chapter 4, so I will not recount them here. However, because my argument rests on the claim that the revelations were configured as objects of regulation rather than radical politics, I will give an account of the discursive ground as it developed in the months after the initial revelations of June 2013.

The debate quickly polarized. Champions of civil liberties decried governments' warrantless access to private data; their opponents defended the necessity of mass surveillance in a post–September 11 security landscape, especially in an era of digital and mobile communication. To the former, Snowden was a patriotic whistle-blower in need of protection; to the latter, he was a traitor who should be punished. Civil rights advocacy groups such as Amnesty International, Transparency International, and Human Rights Watch all defended Snowden as a champion of privacy rights, while former U.S. ambassador to the United Nations John Bolton (de Nesnera 2013), Australia's foreign minister, Julie Bishop (Murphy 2014), House speaker John Boehner (Phillip 2013), and Senator Dianne Feinstein (Herb and Sink 2013) are among those who presented the Snowden leaks as an act of treason that seriously jeopardized the security of the United States. This oppositional framing of the Snowden event has shaped public discourse. Public opinion polls in the weeks after the story broke, for example, asked either/or questions that implied a clear choice between opposing positions.[2] Even in May 2014, almost a year after the first revelations, NBC (2014) asked viewers to take a stand after airing its exclusive interview with Snowden: "Do you view former NSA contractor Edward Snowden as a #Patriot or a #Traitor? Post your message on Twitter using the appropriate hashtag."

Moral inflection aside, at the heart of all this is the perennial debate about the trade-off between national security and individual privacy. In the absence of any way of resolving the issue, political discourse focused on questions of definition, regulation, and reform. To take one prominent example, the Obama administration took great pains to establish a distinction between data and metadata in the hope that the NSA's primary interest in the latter would appease critics. On June 7, 2013, Obama made the following statement: "Nobody is listening to your telephone calls. That's not what this program's about. . . . What the intelligence community is doing is looking at phone numbers and durations of calls. They are not looking at people's names, and they're not looking at content. But by sifting through this so-called metadata, they may identify potential leads with respect to folks who might engage in terrorism." The distinctions between data and metadata and between American and non-American targets were central in discussion of the legal question as to whether or not a warrant is needed for monitoring and surveillance.

These debates treated the Snowden event either in macro conceptual terms (privacy versus security) or in terms of micro legal and procedural issues (such as the data/metadata distinction). Both approaches involve assumptions that prevent the Snowden event from becoming a resource for radical politics. The opposition between privacy and security, for example, positions the citizen as an individual first and foremost, for whom collectivity is envisaged and imagined by the security state (as a nation in need of protection). Privacy is, as I discuss in chapter 4, problematic as a mobilizing concept for the left for a number of reasons. Just as limiting, the micro legal and procedural questions reduce the problem to one of scope rather than ethics or politics. For example, an Obama administration fact sheet called "Proposal for Ending the Section 215 Bulk Telephony Metadata Program" states that the then president was recommending restricting NSA queries regarding metadata to "within two hops of the selection term being used, instead of three" (White House Office of the Press Secretary 2014). (Two hops, as Trevor Timm [2014] points out, still means tens of thousands of people.) There ensued much discussion of how intelligence operations should be regulated and reformed—and some actual reform, such as the added legal authorization needed by the NSA to access bulk phone data stipulated by the U.S. Freedom Act of 2015.[3] But beyond the concern about privacy, little has been said in mainstream discourse about the effect of data surveillance on agency and subjectivity, and even less regarding ways we might think differently about the geopolitical value currently ascribed to intelligence.

For those interested in configuring secrets as a properly political subject, it is necessary to sidestep the debate as constructed by mainstream discourse. It is more productive to stay with the secret, to interrupt the way in which the secret is configured as a rhetorical problem subject to legal tweaking or as an entrenched component of the security industrial complex. It is the secret, prior to any appropriation by the state, that can aid the subjectivization necessary for a radical political response to the state's treatment of its citizens as data objects of only algorithmic import. If secrets are left to the security state, or if they are passed over in favor of privacy, the left will have missed an opportunity.

### Aesthetics and the Secret

In an attempt to stay with the secret and interrupt the dominant discourse surrounding secrecy, I will seek help from certain artworks and an aesthetics of the secret. Such an endeavor requires a few more preliminary remarks about aesthetics and secrets when approached together. Can aesthetic experiences and judgments be brought to bear on that which does not present itself, that which is intended to be neither seen nor heard? What kind of judgment, affective response, or sensory contemplation can be elicited by a formless, unrepresentable entity like the secret? In Louis Marin's words, "The secret seems quite unable to be—to be a thing, a being, a word, a thought, a discourse, a 'what' set apart. It is only an appearance or apparition, a light, incorporeal envelope that floats over things" (1998, 196). Can a secret be an aesthetic object at all?

In some ways, the secret is the ideal aesthetic object; in being by definition that which is unknown, it resists cognitive judgment. This turn from knowledge arguably opens the way for a purely aesthetic response. The secret, as the epigraph from Magid with which I opened this chapter suggests, is more "beautiful"—perhaps beautiful only; subject to aesthetic judgment and affect only—when it is concealed. Once revealed, the secret is translated into knowledge, confession, evidence, or statement and becomes subject to cognitive judgment, particularly questions of veracity. As the aesthetic is usually associated with the visible, presentable, or audible, the secret tests its very limits.

Artworks by Paglen and Magid offer an alternative to traditional framings of the secret. By asking us to stay with and encounter the secret rather than positioning it as a problem to be solved—a wound to be sutured through moral discourse, say, or legislation—these works shift us from a concern with meaning to an affective register: from a hermeneutics of the secret to an aesthetics of the secret. When knowledge is lacking and cognition is interrupted, as it must be in the case of a secret (even an open secret), an aesthetic response or field opens up. As I have shown in the previous chapter, Rancière demonstrates that this aesthetic turn does not have to involve a retreat from political concerns. Rather, "aesthetics" is the ground that "[determines] what presents itself to sense experience" (2004b, 8).

If in principle the sensible is common and available to all, in practice, access is distributed or determined by stratifying factors of labor and identity. Though not considered by Rancière, secrets seem central to these discussions; in their own way, they operate as regulatory mechanisms that manage *aisthēta:* perceptible things, people, histories, data, and voices. We could say that this art helps us focus less on a distribution of knowledge and more on a distribution of the sensible. Crucially, Rancière's understanding of politics as an equitable distribution governed by certain conditions of possibility for that which can be perceived essentially renders politics an aesthetic order. For

Rancière, aesthetics and politics are conjoined because in every distribution of the sensible, equality is either undermined or affirmed.

The shift from the cognitive toward the aesthetic prompted by certain artworks, and Rancière's reading of aesthetics as a political and ethical distribution of the sensible, offers a different vantage point from which to consider a contemporary politics of the secret. Reading the artworks and Rancière together produces the potential for a more substantial politicization of the secret. First, however, I want to introduce a schema that will help with navigating this terrain.

### Mapping the Aesthetic

I am aware of the limitations and risks inherent in cartographic and taxonomic impulses. Despite the obvious pitfalls, Figure 1 helps show how relationships between secrecy, knowledge, and aesthetics are configured as well as where particular artworks might fit in. While the aesthetic and the conceptual are traditionally seen as incommensurable in Kantian philosophy, both will be required here if we are to grasp the challenge any move from a distribution of knowledge to a distribution of the sensible poses to the status of the secret.

### Category A

The far-left column in Figure 1 is the category in which perceivable things reveal themselves to the human senses and so become subject to both cognitive and aesthetic judgment. This is the traditional

**DISTRIBUTION OF KNOWLEDGE**

| A | B | C | D |
|---|---|---|---|
| Known Known | Unknown Known | Known Unknown | Unknown Unknown |
| Revelation / Presentation | Lost / Rendered Invisible | Open Secret / Half Secret | Secret |
| Aesthetics / Antiaesthetics | Anaesthesia | Aestheticized | Non-aesthetic |

**DISTRIBUTION OF THE SENSIBLE**

FIGURE 1. Mapping an aesthetics of the secret.

arena for aesthetics because it is here that objects, people, things, art, music, representations, acts, and nature present themselves; once perceptible, they can then be judged according to certain aesthetic criteria and elicit particular feelings and responses. While the aesthetic must resist becoming subject to knowledge, in cognitive terms this category is best indicated as the "known known."[4] This is not an uncontroversial category in either cognitive or aesthetic terms. In what sense the revealed is fully present or known has been a matter of contention for a range of thinkers.

Some artworks themselves problematize the idea of the presentable. Conceptual art enacts "a dematerialization of the art object" (Lippard 1973), resulting in art that privileges ideas or process over materiality. Jean-François Lyotard has described modern art as that which challenges the sublime "to make visible that there is something which can be conceived and which can neither be seen nor made visible," that which "enable[s] us to see only by making it impossible to see" (1984, 78). That as much is held back as given forth in artifacts here leads us to see that even this category is always in a relation with the unpresentable and the secret. Nevertheless, even conceptual art and nonfigurative art present something—the work of art as process to be witnessed, an idea communicated through medium, an abstraction, a study in form—that engages with particular senses and prompts affect. Even art that challenges certain aesthetic criteria (beauty in particular), or art that resists an aesthetic experience like the sublime, can be productively placed in this category. This is because even antiaesthetic art relies heavily on the sense perceptions, judgments, and criteria against which it reacts.

### Category B

Moving from left to right in Figure 1, the next column pertains to all things that were at some point perceivable and therefore subject to cognitive judgment as well as aesthetic criteria and experience, but that are now gone from view. These things are not hidden as such but rather lost or rendered invisible. Knowledge of these things has been, and may still be, available, but the things have perhaps been forgotten or un-known; knowledge and perception have been disabled or deactivated through a drive that retreats from presence to nonpresentability. In cognitive terms, they are the unknown known. The trace of aesthetic affect lingers; absence elicits new feelings about the freshly vacated space.

Specific examples of artworks that fall into this category were included in two exhibitions from 2012: *Invisible: Art About the Unseen, 1957–2012* (London, Hayward Gallery, June 12 to August 5, 2012) and *Gallery of Lost Art* (online exhibition curated by Tate, July 2, 2012, to July 2, 2013). One piece that appeared in both exhibitions was Robert Rauschenberg's *Erased de Kooning Drawing* (1953). The scuffed surface leaves tantalizing hints of the de Kooning that Rauschenberg took three months to erase.[5] The title, author, and date, inscribed in the border by Jasper Johns, seal the status of the piece as an unknown known: We know what is now unavailable to perception. We are invited to speculate or dream about the drawing that has been usurped by stubborn remnants. Our experience of this artwork is guided by and reliant on knowledge regarding the artwork's history; it only works if we value what has been lost. Rauschenberg understood this; his early experiments with erasing his own drawings had little of the impact he was after. "It had to begin as art," he explains in a 2007 filmed interview; it had to be "an important piece." It had to have been present and perceptible as an aesthetic object and have accumulated value within the art market in order to be able to resonate as a loss.

As well as erased or disappeared art, the Tate's *Gallery of Lost Art* project gathered stories of artworks that were destroyed (including Tracy Emin's *Everyone I Have Ever Slept With, 1963–1995*, which burned in a fire at Charles Saatchi's warehouse), stolen (Lucian Freud's *Portrait of Francis Bacon* [1952], taken while on exhibition in Germany), discarded (paintings by Francis Bacon, who carefully controlled his public oeuvre), transient (such as Rachel Whiteread's concrete cast of the interior of a Victorian terraced *House* [1993], which was always intended to be demolished), and of course lost (all record of Frida Kahlo's *The Wounded Table* [1940], lent to the Russian ambassador to Mexico, has vanished).

We might also want to include in category B (or C) suppressed or censored art: art that is not given a legitimate public stage on which to circulate. The status of suppressed or censored art is wholly contingent on a political-aesthetic regime and is subject to change, thereby enabling an artwork to move from B to category A, becoming present and potentially knowable. There is nothing intrinsically imperceptible or unknowable about these works when given the right climate for reception. These works are rendered secret by authorities, but because of interest accumulated through political resistance, martyrdom, or cult status, such works are rarely entirely secret, particularly in an internet age that enables easy dissemination beyond national borders. Often the artworks themselves or knowledge of them circulate via underground or anonymous viral networks.

I have linked this category with the term "anaesthesia": loss of sensation. In the examples above, sight is the sense most clearly denied or lost. Yet the loss does not eradicate the sensation altogether because of the nature of imagination and memory. We might experience a real or imagined memory of a lost artwork; mourning or loss might "reconstruct" the artwork until it is all but materialized. In light of this, we could say that Rauschenberg's erasing is haunted by the de Kooning drawing, and that what we experience here is a revenant, a visible ghost. Anaesthesia, then, might entail a loss of sensation but also instigate the sensation of loss.

### Category C

The third category in Figure 1 is that of the open secret, or, in cognitive terms, the known unknown. It is in this category that the work of Paglen and Magid most easily sits. Its engagement with and exploration of the open secret can assist a move from reading secrets as a distribution of the cognizable to seeing them in terms of a distribution of the sensible. This has important implications for a politics of the secret.

The work of both Paglen and Magid addresses the material shifts that occur not through revelation but through concealment itself. Paglen (2014) has claimed that for him, secrecy is not an "abstract idea" but "a series of physical, legal, social, cultural, economic institutions, and as such it is made out of the same stuff as the rest of the world." That is, secrecy has a materiality, leaving traces that can consequently become the focus of artistic practice. In different ways, the art of both Paglen and Magid speaks to an aesthetics of the secret by bringing the secret, systems of secrecy, withholding, obfuscation, and opacity into the realm of the sensible, finding what Paglen calls indirect ways of seeing and showing the secret and secrecy in the same way that astronomers have found ways to see and show dark matter. These artworks are not only in relation to the unpresentable in the way that all representations are, but they also take unpresentability in the form of the secret as their explicit subject.

If the principal trajectory of the lost art to be found in category B is from presence and revelation toward nonpresentability/perceptibility, then the material in category C moves in the opposite direction, from nonpresentability/perceptibility toward (though stopping way short of full) presence or revelation. Category C thus refers to the open or half secret. There are at least four kinds of open secret, not wholly distinct. First, an open secret is that which "paradoxically announces its clandestine quality by virtue of its public appearance" (Lee 2011). We might at some level know that the secret exists, but we do not have access to its content. Second, an open secret could be that which everybody unofficially knows or suspects, but proof (and therefore knowledge) of it remains elusive. The "secret" sexual orientation of certain officially heterosexual Hollywood stars would constitute one example. Another would be the understanding that the U.S. government conducted data surveillance on its own people before the Snowden revelations. Snowden simply provided the proof and detail, turning the open secret into a revelation.[6] The third kind of open secret is one that has been revealed, but the revelation has had no discernible effects in the world; it does not behave or resonate as a revelation. Revelations can be rendered ineffectual for all kinds of reasons: lack of media coverage; media coverage that does not allow for a real response; political whitewashing; dearth of public interest. They can also be muted because the difference between a secret and a revelation can be derailed in psychosocial terms. In other words, when faced with a revelation about political malfeasance, a cognizant public might act as if it did not know. This acting "as if" resonates with Slavoj Žižek's well-known reformulation of ideology, which he configures not as a lie taken for truth but as a lie we readily accommodate: "The emperor is naked and the media trumpet forth the fact, yet no one seems really to mind—that is, people continue to act as if the emperor were not naked" (1995, 18). Last, and this open secret is in fact an extension of the third, we can think of things that we somehow all know but do not articulate: Michael Taussig's constitutive "public secret" (1999, 5). Taussig's work is insightful for the way that it recognizes how the promulgation and exercise of a kind of agnotological capital—knowing what not to know—is a crucial form of social and self-discipline.

All forms of the open secret challenge standard assumptions about the cognitive process and template: An open secret requires us to know and not know at the same time. This chink in the armor of cognition, this acknowledgment of knowledge's fallibility and accommodation of its lack, leaves space that can be filled by the aesthetic. This is important because it offers an alternative experience of the politics of secrecy to that which has dominated the debate thus far.

Certain artworks can instigate or negotiate this turn by moving us from a hermeneutic concern with the meaning or content of a secret to an affective response to form. My first example is the work of Paglen, which focuses on what Pamela Lee (2011) archly describes as the military-aesthetic complex. Paglen's art is very much engaged with the open secret, particularly, but not exclusively, the sort I place in category A: known form, the content of which is classified. From his work on extraordinary rendition (*Torture Taxi,* 2006) to his collection of military patches "for programs, units, and activities that are officially secret" (Paglen 2008, 9), Paglen repeatedly invites us to encounter the limits of visibility and experience secrecy's form rather than find meaning or content through total revelation.

The lettering on one of the military patches collected by Paglen gave him the title of the print version of the project: I could tell you, but then you would have to be destroyed by me—a passive phrasing of an intelligence cliché used in many popular cultural representations of clandestine work. Emblazoned with the Latin version, "Si ego certiorem faciam mihi tu delenous eris," the patch (Figure 2) invites interpretation only to exclude the linguistically initiated on translation. The meaning, in other words, leads us nowhere. There are no visual clues; indeed, the patch is unusual in its lack of figurative imagery. A black background seems to absorb the possibility of representation (and interpretation), save the red Latin text, the meaning of which prohibits further knowing. The patch, Paglen informs readers in accompanying text, "was designed as a generic insignia for 'black' projects conducted by the Navy's Air Test and Evaluation

**FIGURE 2.** Trevor Paglen, *I Could Tell You but Then You Would Have to Be Destroyed by Me*, 2006. Fabric patch. Courtesy of the artist, Altman Seigel, Metro Pictures, and Galerie Thomas Zander.

Squadron Four (VX-4) based at Point Mugu, California" (2008, 155). We can look at the patch, feel the exclusion, and witness secretion from the dark side, but we cannot know the nature of these black projects.

The patch is a holding space for a secret that cannot be told; it is a visual marker of clandestine activity that wants to be commended and commemorated without being known. These patches are signifiers that bar access to the signified. In a performative gesture, it announces the secret's form but not content. Interpretation and cognition are stalled by the open secret.

There is a similar logic at work in *NOYFB* (Figure 3), an insignia from the 22nd Military Airlift Squadron, "which flew C-5 cargo aircraft out of Travis Air Force Base in Northern California" (Paglen 2008, 109). Rubbing against the warning, NOYFB (an initialism for "none of your fucking business"), the punctuation in the center posits the secret operation as a mystery. The question mark invites us to approach the patch as a hermeneutic problem, but the patch as a whole points to the limits of interpretation.

**FIGURE 3.** Trevor Paglen, *NOYFB*, 2006. Fabric patch. Courtesy of the artist, Altman Seigel, Metro Pictures, and Galerie Thomas Zander.

The crescent moon, an inverted version of the image that appears on many Islamic flags, suggests an operation that takes place under cover of darkness, rather than in daylight. If "sunlight is said to be the best of disinfectants" (Brandeis 1913, 191), then the moon is a poor substitute, only able to weakly reflect rather than produce light. The moon provides only enough light for us to know that there is something here we cannot know, to understand that we are in the presence of an open secret. In chapter 4, I referred to Althusserian interpellation in order to conceptualize the imperative to share and watch under shareveillance. Rancière also invokes and updates the formulation; the subject of ideology previously hailed into being by a "Hey, you there!" is now told, "Move along! There's nothing to see here" (2010, 37). It is none of our fucking business, as Paglen's found covert ops patch tells us. The patch communicates the subtext of Rancière's formulation: "Move along! There is indeed something to see here, but only by those with security clearance." As Nicholas Mirzoeff puts it in his study of visuality and authority, "there is [something to see], and we know it and so do they" (2011, 1). In other words, it is, after all, precisely our business.

In terms of the open secret, these military patches seem exemplary. In a visual culture, the act of marking classified military operations presents a paradox. The patches capitulate to the temptation to recognize, belong, mark, and take pride in, even while confidentiality is written into the code of practice and the entire logic of clandestine work. They speak to a desire for the secret to be known as secret—that is, to be an open secret, and therefore providing no real knowledge at all. We can therefore say that no knowledge, and consequently no catharsis, is on offer here. The patch *NOYFB* implies a question that cannot be uttered. "Don't ask!," it tells us. We are requested, or rather instructed, not to question or interpret. In a poignant mirroring of the animating logic here, Paglen's re-presentation of these patches itself transforms a refusal of knowledge into an aesthetic object.

Paglen's work here is curatorial. He carefully yet artlessly or blankly presents us with both images of original patches and images scanned from reproductions. In this act of assembling, Paglen makes the images resonate in their official muteness. They become collectively interesting for how they do not communicate rather than for what they do. They might initially demand our attention as a hermeneutic problem, but they ultimately refuse to cooperate under such an approach. The onlooker is excluded from knowledge and knowing, left with the affective intensity of a refusal.

The series Limit Telephotography (2005–) also presents us with an open secret, and therefore a cognitive fissure that opens the way for aesthetic and affective concerns. This set of photographs of secret military bases shows us Paglen asking himself how he can make visible that which institutionally and physically resists technologies of representation. This is both a practical technological question and an aesthetic one.

The spaces Paglen is interested in are classified bases so remote that they cannot be seen by the naked eye. He tackles the technical difficulty of photographing matter across miles of thick atmosphere by repurposing lenses intended for astrophotography. Henrik Gustafsson describes them as "images of the limits of what we are capable of seeing, of a place where seeing ends, where the law is blind" (2013, 157). They are also, as John Beck (2014) remarks, "images of

**FIGURE 4.** Trevor Paglen, *Open Hangar, Cactus Flats, NV, Distance 18 Miles, 10.04am,* 2007. C-print. Courtesy of the artist, Altman Seigel, Metro Pictures, and Galerie Thomas Zander.

absent content." The results, including *Open Hangar, Cactus Flats, NV* (Figure 4), are suggestive and abstract rather than evidential. They appear less like fixed images and more like processes; the interference of dust and heat makes them seem as though they are coming in or out of focus, leaving onlookers in a suspended state of curiosity and expectation, teetering on the edge of fear, disappointment, or frustration.

Lee (2011) writes, "To call them strikingly hazy is to identify their animating contradiction. Paglen's efforts are as occult and abstract as they are revelatory and as beautiful as they are terrifying." Lee's invocation of the language of the sublime hints at the ironic resonance between these landscapes and the photography of Ansel Adams, which Paglen himself cites as a source of inspiration (Paglen 2009; Potolsky 2019). The landscapes of both photographers invoke the pleasure of pain that results from being unable to present the absolute (Lyotard 1991), but by using very different registers of representation (Adams's high-resolution images and Paglen's abstraction), and in reference to different ideas of the absolute (Adams's nature/God as opposed to Paglen's all-powerful state and the secret as such). Unlike Adams's iconic photographs of America's national parks, Paglen's pictures point to nonpublic spaces, clandestine national parks—a covert state within a state. The spaces that Paglen photographs belong to the state, but not to the collection of people known as "the nation." The landscapes were "purloined," as Beck (2014) puts it, for military-industrial interests. "The appropriation of millions of acres of Western land for military purposes after the attack on Pearl Harbor in December 1941 (under the principle of eminent domain whereby the federal or state government is able to claim private land for its own use), removed huge areas of one of the most photographed landscapes in the world from public scrutiny."

Paglen's images unsettle and dismantle the national pride and identity that Adams's photographs are often said to instill. Bridging this gap between state and nation requires trust; black operations and sites are justified as being for the good of the nation. But *Open Hangar, Cactus Flats, NV* (Figure 4), as well as other photographs in the series, register Paglen's unwillingness to leave the secret state untouched, to trust it to operate out of view. As a civilian, Paglen has no rights or access to the secret, but as an artist, he can bring the secret (at least halfway) to himself and to us. In aestheticizing the secret, rendering it as a visual if abstract phenomenon, the photographs of his Limit Telephotography series both resist a purely hermeneutic approach to secrets and register distrust in the state's monopoly over the organization, presentation, and uses of the secret and secrecy.

Jill Magid's work is a more performative response to the question of how to visualize, curate, or exhibit the open secret in a way that does not limit the viewer's experience to hermeneutic concerns of interpreting content and revealing meaning. Magid declares that much of her work is "an experiential investigation of secrecy and government institutions" (2009a, ii). Even later work, which departs from earlier themes of surveillance and secrecy, shares a desire to tease and tease out the relationship—formal, bureaucratic, and affective—between institutions and individuals. For one project, Magid embedded herself within the Dutch secret service, the AIVD. In a somewhat comic dance, which goes beyond standard institutional critique to speak to the wider contradictions of open but securitized liberal democracies, Magid's commission by the AIVD was characterized by an oscillation between intervals of granted and refused access. That is, the AIVD invited her in (after Magid had applied and won the commission), only to resist when she touched on its limit point of visibility and secrecy.

As Magid tests the rigidity of the security "distribution," she repeatedly encounters (and asks the onlooker to encounter) this tension between concealment and revelation, access and denial. For example, after interviewing and compiling notebooks on the agents she met, Magid's knowledge of their appearance was declared "dangerous." Magid was told by an agent that she was in a position to burn the agent's face—a phrase agents used to refer to the act of disclosing the identity of a source. Magid improvises on the phrase for one of the installations (Figures 5 and 6) in her exhibition *Article 12* at Stroom in the Hague in 2008 (shown again at Yvonne Lambert in 2009). It resonates ironically with the AIVD's stated intention for commissioning the artwork in the first place: "to provide the AIVD with a human face," as the press release for Magid's exhibition puts it (Yvon Lambert 2009).

The agents, Magid (2012) claims, liked being interviewed. They enjoyed talking about and revealing themselves. But the agency found it difficult to accommodate Magid's accumulation of information. The artist and her work came to represent a security risk, although it would be more accurate to describe the agents' desire to be a part of the work as the security risk. In *I Can Burn Your Face: Miranda III* (Figure 6) (all the female agents were known to Magid as Miranda and all the male agents as Vincent), we can see some of the suggestive descriptions of Miranda III taken from Magid's notebooks. Magid's observations are transcribed in neon, scorching the darkened gallery: "deep wrinkles," "pointy nose," "dedicated photographer," "loud squeaky voice." It is possible that these fragments could be used to identify an agent among, say, ten other people, but it is difficult to imagine how they could be used to single out an agent in a large population. We see here not only the limits of the AIVD and the secret identities of its agents—the limits of the secret—but also the failure of language to be commensurate with identity. Magid was given knowledge, granted access, only to be warned that such knowledge

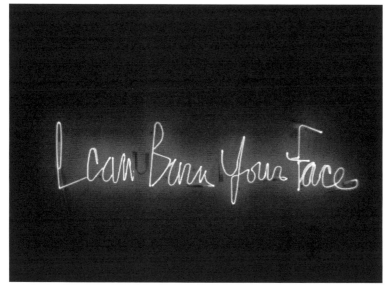

**FIGURE 5.** Jill Magid, *I Can Burn Your Face,* 2008. 7mm neon and transformer, 12 × 38 inches. Courtesy of the artist and LABOR, Mexico City.

**FIGURE 6.** Jill Magid, *I Can Burn Your Face: Miranda III,* 2008. 7mm neon, transformers, and wires, dimensions variable. Installed at Yvon Lambert Paris, 2009. Courtesy of the artist and LABOR, Mexico City.

could not become part of the artwork. In order to be included, her knowledge had to be transformed into aesthetic material. Frustrated by the hermeneutic dead ends offered by the work, the onlooker's response follows this aesthetic cue.

Another example of this animating imperative can be seen in the fact that Magid was commissioned to make art, yet large portions of that art—the novel component of the Becoming Tarden project—had to be redacted. In deciding to exhibit *Becoming Tarden* complete with these obscuring marks, Magid forces the viewer to face the aesthetics of concealment. Redaction as the subject of art has precursors, of course, notably Jenny Holzer's 2006 Redaction Painting series. In Magid's novel, the redactions (which efface 40 percent of the text) are in white rather than the iconic black blocks we have come to know from the American system, and which Holzer reproduces in her silk screens. In a further play on the limits of visibility, the hand of the active agent "sanitizing" the text is difficult to detect. In *Becoming Tarden,* it is as if the text were erasing itself, disappearing into the page at inopportune moments. Censorship itself wears a mask; agency is whitewashed. Redaction forces us to look and feel rather than to know.

In a further instance of the transformation of knowledge into aesthetics, the AIVD granted permission to Magid to exhibit the novel at the Tate Modern in London in 2009 (in the *Authority to Remove* exhibition), but, as agreed, confiscated it at the exhibition's close (Magid 2009b). The planned removal gave the exhibition its title and has to be considered very much a part of the artwork. Bureaucratic attempts to control the circulation of knowledge add new layers to Magid's performative engagement and provide the context in which the art operates. Because art—even art such as Magid's notebooks and the resulting novel, the production of which mirrors the act of intelligence gathering—always exceeds (and falls short of) definitions of information and knowledge, it resonates beyond the content that activated the AIVD's concern. Equally, Magid's operation shows that intelligence work itself is never only the transmission of neutral information or data: it always draws on imagination, aesthetics, and art.

Magid places herself at the center of this drama of concealment and revelation. Consequently, it becomes a story about the limits of agency as much as the reach of secret agencies. She is interested in how the individual—here the artist herself, but also by implication the onlooker—is positioned in relation to and by the secret (whether as system or master signifier). Within this distribution of bodies, institutions, and capacities, Magid explores the affective register of the secret—its seductive draw, the structure of desire it operates within. She is the one who asks to be subjected to a full vetting procedure. At one point she considers becoming an agent herself (Magid 2012). Such confessions playfully evoke the link between knowledge and power. Yet despite the detail amassed about individual agents and the workings of the AIVD, Magid's agency, like that of Paglen, is largely aesthetic. Magid sets herself the task of drawing out the beauty of the secret. What we see at work here is the power to bring aesthetics to bear on the secret rather than the power to expose or reveal secrets, and to give us knowledge in an uncomplicated manner. The political register of these works is to be found in their aesthetic process and choices rather than at the evidentiary level. That is to say, they reveal more about the act of looking at, our response to, and the limits of open secrets than they do about individual intelligence operations. For Gustafsson, writing about Paglen's images, "the politics of producing the photographs outweighs the significance of whatever information they contain" (2013, 156). The same is true of Magid's performative process. Though Gustafsson is referring to a system that bars citizens from seeing and knowing about military sites, his statement can also help us to focus on the form rather than content of secrets as aesthetic objects.

Because the art I have discussed is clearly situated within the contemporary tension between secrecy and transparency (and the contradictions and compromises embedded within liberal democracies that stem from this tension), its ability to point toward a different way of thinking about the relationship between politics and art (or rather aesthetics), its place within a "meta-politics" (Rancière 2004b, 56), always risks being overlooked. By pushing secrets at least halfway into the light, the work risks being subsumed and fixed by the discursive production of the political issues as they are commonly understood. To put it a different way, it always risks remaining within a hermeneutics rather than an aesthetics of the secret. Many commentators are indeed quick to align the art discussed in this chapter with an overtly political position, claiming it as art that challenges the reach of the national security state. Indeed, the artists themselves, particularly Paglen, are often outspoken critics of surveillance, secrecy, and securitization. The political valence of the art in this category is therefore at risk of being decided in advance. Inasmuch as these works present ideas—secrecy is detrimental to democracy, for example—and inasmuch as they lean toward secretion as revelation, perhaps they are not so different from the art in category A, in which we placed dematerialized conceptual art.

We have to recognize, then, that the explicit and contextual politics of this art puts it at risk of being contained by existing debates. But although it may begin from and signify within the same ground as familiar political debate—the kind that has arguably delimited our reception and analysis of the Snowden revelations—this work can also trouble its parameters and unsettle procedural responses. Work such as that by Paglen and Magid resists treating the secret as a blockage preventing the truth from coming out, whether it be in terms of a decision regarding the politics of secrecy or the implementation of bureaucratic mechanisms to process secrets.

Crucially, the proximity of these works to the next category in the schema in Figure 1, category D, means that they are also being drawn in the other direction, away from knowability, revelation, reduction, containment, and the sensible. The hold of the secret as secret—an unconditional secret, as Derrida (1992) would have it—is never quite quashed in these artworks by the hermeneutic drive or routine political debate, so it remains possible for them to resonate beyond the empty circulation of content characteristic of communicative capitalism. In their liminal state between revelation and concealment, the artworks certainly pose questions concerning regimes of looking, the rights and responsibilities that accompany visibility and invisibility, and the circulation of sensible matter and knowable knowledge. But rather than bringing us to knowledge, these concerns align with a view of secrets as part of a distributive regime.

This returns us to Rancière's positioning of aesthetics as, in the words of his translator, "an implicit law governing the sensible order that parcels out places and forms of participation in a common world by first establishing the modes of perception within which these are inscribed. The distribution of the sensible thus produces a system of self-evident facts of perception based on the set horizons and modalities of what is visible and audible as well as what can be said, thought, made or done" (Rockhill 2004, 89). With this in mind, we should perhaps concern ourselves less with an aesthetics of the secret and more with an aesthetics that enacts itself through the limits of the secret. We could rephrase Rancièrean aesthetics as a system of distribution and organization of that which is and is not secret, those who are and are not secret. For Rancière, the key question is whether the world defined by any distribution of the sensible is compatible with equality, with equality understood here not as "a value to which one appeals" but "a universal that must be supposed, verified, and demonstrated in each case" (1992, 60). On the basis of this "primary aesthetics," we can then consider individual artistic practices, "'ways of doing and making' that intervene in the general distribution of ways of doing and making as well as in the relationships they maintain to modes of being and forms of visibility" (2004a, 8).

The art of Paglen and Magid indicates that the contemporary distribution shaped in part by the securitized state is not compatible with equality; it tells us that there are plenty of people who play no part in establishing "the perceptual coordinates of the community" (Rockhill 2004, xiii). Paglen's presentation of military black sites as well as Magid's neon allusions to certain secret agents constitute playful, testing, and teasing articulations of and interventions in a certain distributive regime that reveals "who can have a share in what is common to the community based on what they do and on the time and space in which this activity is performed" (Rancière 2004b, 8). Moreover, it forces us to encounter the intensities of the relationships (between animate and inanimate entities) within that distribution.

The Snowden event could also be considered less a bestowing of knowledge (though it was certainly that) and more a reminder that "politics . . . is an intervention in the visible and the sayable" (Rancière 2010, 37), that it "revolves around what is seen and what can be said about it, around who has the ability to see and the talent to speak, around the properties of spaces and the possibilities of time" (2004b, 8). Hegemonic structures and discourses, akin to the "symbolic constitution of the social" (Rancière 2010, 36) that Rancière early on names "policy" (1992), and later "police" (1999), determine scopic possibilities; limit who is able to take part in what is common; and prevent the formation of effective political subjectivities. But when a (re)distribution is compatible with equality, an instantiation of Rancièrean politics occurs. In reorganizing the realm of the perceivable to disrupt limits on who or what can be heard or seen, and therefore on what is thinkable and possible, real politics affirms equality.

After circumventing classification and confidentiality protocols, effectively evading the policing of the sensible and the secret, Snowden revealed details of the NSA's mass surveillance programs. In doing so, he not only shifted the horizon of perception with regards to intelligence operations but also showed America's surveillance capability to be more extensive, and classified data far more vulnerable, than previously thought. The horizon of visibility was itself made visible. The systemic inequality of access to information and data (and to knowledge about that access) was challenged by Snowden's act—for a moment, many more people had a share in the secret and were able to take part—government secrets became a shared or common element.

When viewed this way, the Snowden event might serve as an occasion to posit a collective, albeit internally differentiated, political subjectivity that is based on a commonality of data labor and experiences of datafication. The term "data multitude" will serve as a placeholder here because it is general enough to allow equal identification while acknowledging that intersectional stratification produces variable experiences. This is a process that Rancière (1992) calls subjectivization. That is, because Snowden reminds the public of its status as data subjects in the eyes of the security state, it can begin to think about the relatively collective identities data makes possible when imagined outside of the parameters set by Rancière's "policy/police." For Rancière, political subjectivization "is the enactment of equality—or the handling of a wrong—by people who are together to the extent that they are between. It is a crossing of identities, relying on a crossing of names: names that link the name of a group or class to the name of no group or no class, a being to a nonbeing or a not-yet-being" (1992, 61). "Proletariat" is Rancière's prime example because it was the name given to those who are "between several names, statuses, and identities; between humanity and inhumanity, citizenship and its denial; between the status of a man of tools and the status of a speaking and thinking being" (61). The data multitude too can be thought of as between "humanity and inhumanity, citizenship and its denial"—and, I want to add, secrecy and transparency, the material and immaterial, the quantifiable and the unquantifiable. Crucially, however, whereas "proletariat" is supposed to supplant and subsume other identities, I invoke "multitude" to recognize the identifications and stratifications that render experiences different and singular under conditions of shareveillance.

There is a utopian strand at work here. Rancière is interested in "impossible identifications" that can raise individuals above the identities bequeathed to them by "policy/police." Subjectivization is thus never just the assertion of an identity; rather, it is the refutation of an identity given by the ruling order (1992, 62). The data multitude would be an identity that refutes shareveillant subjectivities—citizens who on the one hand are subject to data surveillance and on the other are asked to interact with data only when this contributes to the entrepreneurial economy ("Come and join our datapalooza!") or makes them individually responsible for acting ("Look at pollution data by area code and then choose where you want to live!"). Shareveillant subjects are not allowed to interact with data in the creation or exploration of radical collective politics. In contrast, in an endeavor to find names or identities-in-relation that can allow those without part to "take part" (Rancière 1992, 62) in an equitable distribution of the visible and sayable, "data multitude" might very well "create political subjects and redraw the sensible parameters" (Tanke 2011, 68). It might constitute a collectivity between otherwise differentiated subjects that are "together inasmuch as they are between" (Rancière 1992, 61)—subjects capable of putting forth the demand that data accumulation serves horizontal, community-forming, and above all radical transparency rather than its hierarchical manifestation.

Yet the risk of containment outlined above—the risk of a redistribution being reduced to a mere reshuffling of the sensible (a risk that I am arguing has been realized in the case of the Snowden event)—is never far away. Emancipatory potential, the chance of politics taking place instead of policing, is only potential. If interventions into the sayable and visible through the open secret or the possibility of networks coalescing around the collective identity of the data multitude become readily contained, perhaps the secret as secret might offer itself as an unexpected resource. Both Paglen and Magid put secrecy rather than privacy in the foreground. In doing so, they move us away from the perennial debate between privacy and security, which tends to emphasize individualism rather than collectivity (and which arises whenever the surveillance powers of the state are revealed), and force us to consider the secret on its own terms. It may be that the most radical response to the Snowden event would be a secrecy to rival that of the state.

## Category D

Category D in Figure 1 takes the secret seriously in its own right, rather than as a temporary state that precedes revelation. It is the category of the absolute, unconditional secret rather than common, contextual secret. The unconditional secret is "a more ancient, more originary experience . . . of the secret" (Derrida 1995, 201). It is that which cannot and does not present itself; it is "not phenomenalizable" (Derrida 1992, 25). This secret is "an experience that does not make itself available to information" (Derrida 1995, 201). Given that it is not waiting in the wings to be revealed, it does not pertain to the category of knowledge; Derrida thus calls it "non-knowing" (1995, 201). In the context of literature, the unconditional secret ensures that a sentence can always mean something else; that meaning is undecidable; that reading is inexhaustible "endless interpretation" (1992, 34). The absolute secret or singularity of literature for Derrida secures the "right to say everything" (28) and anything, to fabricate without having to account for such fabrications. Indeed, an author cannot answer for her fiction. If she does, she is "treating [her] work as something other than literature" (Attridge 2011, 47). In any case, she can claim to tell the truth about her fiction—to say everything—and still not touch on this structuring secret (Derrida 1992, 29). So there is always something secret about this irreducible nonresponse. This principle holds true for democracy as much as literature for Derrida. As I explored in chapter 3, Derrida reads this excess as an absolute secret or singularity that must (and at the same time cannot) be tolerated by democracy (2001a, 59). Rather than material remnants left in the visible spectrum, like the secrets Paglen and Magid work with, this kind of secret leaves nothing but the aporia it puts in play: the (im)possibility of democracy; the (im)possibility of truth; the (im)possibility of pinning down, finally and forever, a text, another person, or even oneself. This secret resists being thought of as an aesthetic object or addressed through aesthetic judgment, attitude, encounter, or value, and thus it is therefore wholly different from the other categories of Figure 1.

It is important not to conflate the unconditional secret that Derrida writes about with a strategic position, but the former can certainly inspire the latter. In order to explore my earlier proposal of a radical response to the Snowden event, I will consider various experiments, both theoretical and material, with a secrecy of the left in chapter 6. This secrecy of the left will sometimes utilize the form of common, contextual secrets (masking or secret societies), but it also contends with the implications of the unconditional secret, particularly as these pertain to political collectivities. Here I simply want to recognize the way in which the art considered in this chapter constitutes an exploration of and provocation to the distribution of the sensible. As such, it can help us to hold on to the redistributive qualities and potential of the Snowden revelations, to configure secrets as a properly political subject. But I also want to acknowledge that this only gets us so far. Because I have viewed this art as belonging to one category in a schema mapping the relationship between secrecy and aesthetics (Figure 1), we are reminded of other forms of the secret. Artworks that address the play of contextual, open secrets sit close to the unconditional secret, the doubled unknown unknown, or irreducible singularity, which ensures my own interpretation of them cannot be final; they will always exceed the reading offered here. The secret in category D cannot be redistributed to become part of the sensible. It is as resistant to aesthetics as it is to knowledge; only a distribution in an internal sense, drawing on the etymology of *secretus* and its past participle, *secernere: se-* (apart) and *cernere* (separate). That is to say, the unconditional secret distributes only itself, destined to be other than or apart from itself, never self-present and locatable, always a moving target.

In the course of this chapter, I have explored a turn toward (and latterly away from) aesthetics, but not back toward knowledge. I have done so in order to reconceptualize a politics and aesthetics of the secret in the wake of the Snowden event. In the next chapter, I will contend that, contrary to popular thought, a move toward the secret does not have to be regressive, totalitarian, or statist. I will not be offering a classic defense of secrecy or the secret to the detriment of personal liberties. Rather, I want to think the secret and liberty otherwise as well as recalibrate the political and moral values attached to openness and secrecy, a historically contingent process I explored in chapter 1. An equitable distribution of the sensible, as Rancière (2004b) notes, may be necessary for politics to occur, but in order to prevent the hegemonic, data-driven settlement of shareveillance from resolidifying and containing redistributive attempts, we need to imagine and enact subjectivization and relationality through a play with secrecy.

# CHAPTER 6

# SECRETS OF THE LEFT
## A Right to Opacity

To return to a point I made in chapter 1: Although big tech, with its reliance on black box, discriminatory algorithms, and nontransparent business models, is also a contender today, it is the state that seems to have monopolized secrecy, so deep is its investment in covert surveillance and intelligence and secret military operations.[1] The so-called black budget in the United States alone for 2017, for example, included $73 billion for the National Intelligence Program and the Military Intelligence Program (ODNI 2017; Department of Defense 2017). In addition, the United States spends billions of dollars each year on a cumbersome, ever-expanding classification system; in 2017, for example, the government security classification costs amounted to over $18 billion (ISOO 2017). The expense and extent of this covert sector and its apparatus means that secrecy is marked by this perpetuation of power.

Because of this monopoly, progressive factions tend to steer clear of secrecy and instead praise transparency. Support for transparency in leftist politics might not be so surprising when we recall that the left has periodically conceived of resistance as organized, known, and internally transparent to itself, and revolution as dependent on exposing the secrets of class oppression and the workings of ideology. Lefebvre puts it like this: "It was on the basis of [an ideology of the transparency of space, which identifies knowledge, information, and communication] that people believed for quite a time that a revolutionary social transformation could be brought about by communication alone. 'Everything must be said! No time limit on speech! Everything must be written! Writing transforms language, therefore writing transforms society! Writing is a signifying practice!' Such agendas succeed only in conflating revolution and transparency" ([1974] 1991, 29). The "illusion of transparency turns out to be a transcendental illusion: a trap, operating on the basis of its own quasi-magical power" (29) in the revolutionary imaginary. Moreover, as we have seen, transparency has been articulated both to and by the neoliberal state in ways that hinder, not help, a progressive politics or equitable distribution. Should the left use or mimic (however playfully and idiosyncratically) forms of transparency that are deeply embedded within a shareveillant logic? What are the risks of taking such a position?

In using the term "the left" with regards to the contemporary American context, I am referring to a wide spectrum of groups, politicians, practices, and positions. These include institutionalist organizations like the Democratic Socialists of America; far-left Democratic Party or independent political figures such as Bernie Sanders and the members of the Squad (Alexandria Ocasio-Cortez, Ilhan Omar, Ayanna Pressley, and Rashida Tlaib); some manifestations of labor unionism; anticapitalist activist movements such as Occupy and its afterlives; rights-based movements that incorporate critiques of capital such as Black Lives Matter, queer activism, and socialist feminism; social justice activism like antifa groups; some forms of ecoactivism that consider capitalism as the engine of climate change; strands of more traditional communist organizing and thinking (Dean 2018); and finally discourses arising from new media forums such as "left Twitter" and podcasts like *Chapo Trap House* and *The Dig* from *Jacobin Magazine*. While broad, dispersed, constantly evolving, and heterogeneous, I will persist in using the term "the left" to indicate a politics that strives for more equitable alternatives to hegemonic distributions of social and economic power. If "the left" means anything, it is this desire for, openness to, and ability to conceive of change.

It is commonplace to find elements of the left defending liberal policies.[2] When faced with the actions of the Bush administration (including the NSA's warrantless eavesdropping program), for example, leftist factions understandably felt compelled to defend the basic principles of liberalism in terms of civil liberties. Therefore, as the secrecy of the Bush administration became an identifying feature, the left supported transparency as the only alternative to and resistance to government secrecy. Likewise, in the face of Trump's turn from administrative transparency (even while he continued to lay claim to other forms of transparency), the left had little option but to call for increased institutional transparency. Though pragmatic, the problem with such a position, as Wendy Brown puts it, is that "it does not facilitate a left challenge to neoliberalism if the Left still wishes to advocate in the long run for something other than liberal democracy in a capitalist socioeconomic order" (2005, 55). If the left supports the transparency policies implemented by neoliberal democracies under a logic of shareveillance, it risks valorizing the current manifestation of democracy as an inherently accountable system honorable enough to withstand any level of scrutiny. Representative (neo)liberal democracy is deemed fair simply by allowing scrutiny, rather than because of the economic or social policies being scrutinized. As it is strengthened, other visions of democracy—social, direct, or radical—become less visible and viable.

If the left champions transparency, then the opportunity to make a case for an alternative vision will have been missed. Transparency is a means to an end—good and fair government—not an end in itself. If the means supports ideologies the left cannot subscribe to or that render the ideal of democracy flawed, it may be necessary to find alternative routes to good, fair government as well as a different vision for what might constitute what is good and fair in this context.

Opening up a different route for leftist politics—one that will distinguish its ideals from mainstream forms of liberal democracy— does not mean that we have to dispense with transparency altogether. As I point out in the Introduction, transparency might constitute a floating signifier that is open to an ongoing contestation over meaning and can be articulated to radically different political projects (Laclau and Mouffe 1985). Transparency has no essential meaning outside of the discursive formations that invoke it or the historical context in which it is situated. This is why the left, although it needs to be wary of liberal and neoliberal championing of transparency, can still draw on it in the future when a new discursive formation will attribute new meanings to transparency. I am therefore not suggesting that all calls for transparency are misguided. There are salient and pressing reasons as to why the opaque nature of power causes concern, particularly for the disenfranchised who have been systematically rendered invisible.

However, if the intention is to mark out a particular space for leftist forms of democracy or politics, then the current articulations of both transparency and secrecy within shareveillance need to be questioned and both terms reappropriated and rehabilitated. In chapter 3, I discussed a radical transparency to come; in this chapter, I want to configure secrecy in a similar way. I ask what forms of politics, ethics, and being in common might it be possible to think if we pay attention to secrecy—radical secrecy—rather than transparency.[3]

Such work involves four stages. First, I offer some examples of resistant experiments with secret societies, masking, anonymity, and opacity more broadly. Second, I turn to digital experiments with secrecy that scramble the coordinates of shareveillance and offer what I have been calling the data multitude an alternative contract with data. Third, in order to reimagine subjectivity in the face of shareveillance, I invoke Édouard Glissant's (1997) right to opacity. Although he used this phrase to refer to the right not to comply with the demand to be knowable, understood, and transparent within a racialized, postcolonial epistemology, a right to opacity in the contexts this book is concerned with might mean, among other things, the demand not to be reduced to and interact with data in ways delimited by the state—that is, to resist the terms of engagement set by shareveillance. Fourth, I imagine the secret not as that which belongs to the state but as that which belongs to no one, and therefore everyone. With this in mind, I end by configuring secrecy as commons in order to invoke ways of being in common and of organizing that can respect singularity without collapsing into atomization. What might communities (or networks) of secrecy rather than communities of transparency suggest about the way we can think resistant or oppositional politics? For too long, secrecy and its productive possibilities have been obscured by the fear that it is always a gateway to microfascism and by a moral attachment to disclosure.[4] Recognizing this opens up a new way of understanding the political (and moral) alignments of concealment and disclosure.

## Secrecy and Opposition

Tactical secrecy is nothing new for nonhegemonic factions. In the historical account of secrecy in chapter 1, I considered the cover that secrecy provided for certain groups when they were discussing secular, democratic, and rationalist alternatives to the prevailing autocratic and religious order in eighteenth-century Europe. More visceral and perilous examples can be found in the methods of enslaved African Americans living under surveillance plantation conditions who risked "stealing away" to attend "an assortment of popular illegalities focused on contesting the authority of the slave-owning class and contravening the status of the enslaved as possession" (Hartman 1997, 66) and were by necessity acquainted with the need for hiding, disguise, and obfuscation when attempting to escape and avoid being returned by slave catchers. The covert system of aid, known as the underground railroad, offered to fugitive enslaved people by some abolitionists in the nineteenth century also provides an important historical precedent (Foner 2015). Simone Browne names the networks and practices of undersight involved with escape "dark sousveillance," which "charts possibilities and coordinates modes of responding to, challenging, and confronting a surveillance that was almost all-encompassing" (2015, 21).

Secrecy has also been periodically used by the nonstatist left. Believing that a successful revolution would need to exceed national boundaries, Mikhail Bakunin formed a secret international alliance in 1864, for example. As Robert Cutler points out, quoting Bakunin, "The reason the revolutionary organisation had to be secret was not only a tactical matter of survival" but "also for the strategic reason that if its existence was openly acknowledged, then it would become, like the State 'an artificial force outside the people'—and so lose the ability to fulfil its sole aim, which was 'to arouse, unite and organise spontaneous popular forces'" (2014, 21). Clandestine cells, we might also recall, have been a feature of resistance forces in occupied territory (such as the French Resistance in World War II) and terrorist organizations (such as Al-Qaeda).

Secrecy in the form of masking is a practical necessity for oppositional political factions needing to evade identification. The Zapatista Army of National Liberation in Mexico donned balaclavas to deindividualize their claim for autonomy for the Chiapas. In adopting this tactic, the Zapatistas, Bratich writes, "remind us that the State is always masked, and not just when its riot police wear armored disguises" (2007, 51). Obscuring identity and protecting against pepper spray with the strategic use of scarves, hoods, and glasses was the chosen mode of the "black bloc" in the 1990s (and since) when protesting against the worst excesses of globalization at the World Trade Organization and other emblems of globalized capital. Since the release of the film version of Alan Moore's graphic novel, *V for Vendetta* (dir. James McTeigue), in 2006, the stylized Guy Fawkes mask has been a popular shield for a broad range of activist groups, most prominently Anonymous and Occupy. Prodemocracy demonstrators in Hong Kong routinely wear physical face masks alongside using lasers to counter facial recognition technologies and taking measures to reduce their digital trace. During the coronavirus crisis, the mask has taken on new significance in public gatherings, including protests such as those associated with Black Lives Matter. The mask at these events is a signifier of community care, of self-protection; it is a way to evade the gaze of the police and counterprotesters. That white supremacists and gun-wielding antilockdown protesters have not masked up is not only because of their Covid-19 skepticism but also because they see their ideologies validated by Trump.[5]

It hardly needs pointing out here that negotiating and using secrecy has been a matter for survival for many groups subject to discrimination. As well as the extreme examples of hiding and disguise provided by enslaved African Americans in their quests for temporary and more permanent freedom, we could also look to the use of secret keeping, encoding, encryption, and even passing used by many different minorities. The politics of these practices, as well as their affective qualities for those who participate, obviously differ according to legal, religious, and cultural contexts. The closet, for example, holds different meanings in times and places where homosexuality is legal than when and where it is illegal. However, I do not wish to romanticize or overstate the use of secrecy thus far. Clearly, it has been used as much by regressive forces as progressive ones. The KKK's use of disguise, including (after the release in 1915 of D. W. Griffiths's *Birth of a Nation*) the iconic white hoods, while wielding racially motivated terror offers the obvious example, but we could also think about the way the so-called dark net provides a cloak for contraband.[6] Equally, as my reference to the closet indicates, secrecy is often culturally imposed rather than willingly used. Rather, the point is to acknowledge that the secrecy I am arguing for in this chapter enters into an existing lineage of praxis as well as aesthetic experimentation. There are also other, more theoretically oriented examples in which the secret, as idea, form, and practice, has provided cover and inspiration (and which have inspired my project in turn). Two experimental and radical collectives that span both ends of the twentieth century are of particular note for their singular commitment to the clandestine as an aesthetic and speculative force: Georges Bataille's secret society, Acéphale (1936–39), and the anonymous collective Tiqqun (1999–2001).[7]

Having been disappointed by the acrimonious breakdown of the short-lived anticommunist and antifascist group that included André Breton called Contre-Attaque (1935–36), Bataille and his associates came up with the idea of a clandestine sacrificial society as well as its public counterparts: the publication that shared Acéphale's name, and to a certain degree the Collège de Sociologie. Thanks to the archival work of Marina Galletti (2018)—I am tempted to write "detective work" in this context, given the complexities of recovering a history of a secret society whose adepts took seriously their oath to silence—a public, if fragmentary, account of Acéphale's rituals, oaths, and aims is now available (Bataille et al. 2018). The documents collected by Galletti offer tantalizing glimpses into the acephalic "religion" and its members, who included intellectuals of the day like Georges Ambrosino, Jacques Chavy, and Roger Caillois.[8]

Initiates were sent documents such as Acéphale's central philosophy and rules as well as a map of the forest of Marly, where nocturnal meetings would take place. Bataille assumed the pseudonym Dianus, taken from the mythological figure of an escaped enslaved man who committed regicide to assume the crown (Galletti 2018). The secret society was imbued with the sacred because for Bataille ([1967] 2013), it exemplified an economy of loss, which he placed in opposition to capitalist production and acquisition. Decapitation was the central motif (Acéphale translates as "headless") to represent a turn from Enlightenment reason, to indicate the idea of a leaderless hierarchy, and to reference Nietzsche's death of God (Galletti 2018, 20). The coming of war precipitated the disbanding of the society in general, but it was a specific incident—the refusal of the remaining adepts at the final meeting in the forest to sacrifice Bataille—that signaled the end for the radical philosopher (Patrick Waldberg qtd. in

Bataille et al. 2018, 456). Sacrifice was the ultimate ritual because the act would "bring together isolated individuals in a shared experience that exceeds their individual spheres of being" (Sweedler 2005, 347).

Disgusted with politics, even revolutionary politics, which he considered as not only too swayed by the promise and spoils of power but also unable to account for an essential violence and address "the fundamental aspirations of man" (Bataille 2018, 162), Bataille wanted a community that could regenerate or revolutionize society at large by instigating the kind of unorthodox values he championed throughout his oeuvre, including "expenditure, risk, loss, sex and death" (Stoekl 1985, xix). Long interested in marginal groups, some of which, such as Gnostics, practiced secret rites and dealt in esoteric knowledge, Bataille sought out the shadows not as an act of disengagement but to explore the limits of a metaphorical and literal decapitation in order to suppress reason and release the energy of living things.

While Bataille's project—to free radical primitive communal drives through Acéphale's sacrificial and secretive rituals—arises from a highly idiosyncratic mythology, it is clear that his interest in secrecy, his willingness to invest in it as much as more public projects, offers a useful model. He is notable for positioning secrecy as a regenerative and rejuvenating mode that can produce possibilities, affects, and effects. For Bataille, secrecy is a practice that makes something happen as much as, if not more than, open and more recognizably political interventions. Moreover, if Bataille wanted to "use secrecy as a weapon rather than a retreat" (Lütticken 2006, 32), such a weaponization might stand as a counteroffering to the routine weaponization of secrecy we find within contemporary securitization.

Tiqqun is a word derived from Hebrew (*tikkun olam*, "world repair") and was intended to refer to "small practices and rituals for mending creation and hastening the coming of the Messiah" (Caygill 2013, 195), but it has come to indicate social action more generally. Tiqqun is thus more than a name for the anonymous French, post-Situationist, poststructuralist, anarchist theory collective and its two journal issues. It is a philosophy in and of itself, and one that is expounded, albeit elliptically, in writings such as *Introduction to Civil War* ([2001] 2010) and *Theory of Bloom* ([2001] 2012). Drawing on the work of Deleuze and Guattari (e.g., 1987) Tiqqun describes itself as "the becoming-real, the becoming-practice of the world. Tiqqun is the process through which everything is revealed to be practice, that is, to take place within its own limits, within its own immanent signification. Tiqqun means that each act, conduct, and statement endowed with sense—act, conduct, and statement as event—spontaneously manifests its own metaphysics, its own community, its own party" ([2001] 2010, 39). Tiqqun indicates a performative act; it brings into being new ontologies. The writers' individual identities (and all that is carried within the logic of the proper name including reputation, value, career, property, and copyright) are sacrificed to the collective marker: Tiqqun.

After the dissolution of Tiqqun in 2001, some members went on to write and work under the equally anonymous collective Invisible Committee. (In fact, while the Invisible Committee chose to operate under the auspices of secrecy, the arrest of some of its members in 2008 charged with domestic terrorism quickly placed them under an unwelcome spotlight.) Despite the visibility demanded by such an encounter with authority and the law, Tiqqun's attempts at "desubjectivization," of becoming a "whatever singularity" ([2001] 2010, 46), chime with its larger project of "extending shadowy zones over the maps of Empire" (51), weakening bioinformatic strategies of control.[9] Highly influenced by the avant-garde Situationist International in general, and Guy Debord's critique of the society of the spectacle (1967) in particular, as well as Foucauldian biopower, Tiqqun developed a critique of the logic of consumerist, surveillance, and cybernetic capital, which demands and imposes certain forms of visibility and predictability. The shareveillant settlement explored in chapter 4 is a specific mode made possible by and within the general logic presciently identified by Tiqqun.

What is of most interest to me with respect to rehabilitating secrecy is the way in which Tiqqun calls for "interference," "haze," or "fog" as the "prime vector of revolt" in "The Cybernetic Hypothesis" ([2001] 2009, 49). Tiqqun writes,

> Fog is a vital response to the imperative of clarity, transparency, which is the first imprint of imperial power on bodies. To become foglike means that I finally take up the part of the shadows that command me and prevent me from believing all the fictions of direct democracy insofar as they intend to

ritualize the transparency of each person in their own interests, and of all persons in the interests of all. To become opaque like fog means recognizing that we don't represent anything, that we aren't identifiable; it means taking on the untotalizable character of the physical body as a political body; it means opening yourself up to still unknown possibilities. It means resisting with all your power any struggle for recognition. ([2001] 2009, 49)

Shadows, fog, and anonymity are instances of "internal defection" ([2001] 2011, 27) that Tiqqun suggests might interrupt how "the liberal State gives transparency to the fundamental opacity of the population" ([2001] 2010, 23). Secrecy (as anonymity, as obfuscation of the society of spectacle and retreat from information networks) again is positioned as that which makes something happen. "Fog makes revolt possible," for example, because it interferes with legibility and perception; and "haze" renders "indiscernible what is visible and what is invisible, what is information and what is an event" ([2001] 2009, 49). Resistance to "the tyranny of transparency which control imposes" (49) facilitates the emergence of alternative ways of thinking and living politically.

Tiqqun distances its project from Bataille's, which it sees as being too in thrall to the social formation of the secret society and its rituals: "It won't be a matter of reorganizing a few secret societies or conquering conspiracies like free-masonry, carbonarism, as the avant-gardes of the last century envisioned," writes Tiqqun ([2001] 2009, 50). Rather, *"establishing a zone of opacity* where people can circulate and experiment freely without bringing in the Empire's information flows, means producing 'anonymous singularities'" that will give rise to "a dense experience that can transform desires and the moments where they manifest themselves into something beyond desire, into a narrative, into a filled-out body" (50). Drawing on Hakim Bey's notion of a temporary autonomous zone (TAZ) (1985), Tiqqun calls for "zones of offensive opacity" (ZOO), which will initiate "an *irreversible disequilibrium*" ([2001] 2009, 50).[10] But just as Tiqqun distinguishes its project from Bataille's, it ends "The Cybernetic Hypothesis" by marking out the critical difference between TAZ and ZOO. The autonomy Bey imagines is, Tiqqun states, impoverished; it is a version

of "Californian ideology" that "poses autonomy as an attribute of individual or collective subjects," thus deliberately confusing "the 'self-
realization' of persons and the 'self-organization' of society" (51). Bey
designates them temporary because he has been unable to "[conceive]
of a struggle that merges with all of life" (51). Rather than a quality
of individuals, Tiqqun casts autonomy (within ZOO) as a condition
of possibility: that which "engenders multiplicities" enables mutating transformations of attack and withdrawal understood as "endless
experimentation" (51). Understanding autonomy in this way, Tiqqun
insists, can challenge the monopoly that Empire, "armed with cyber-
netics" (51), has on autonomy.

We may or may not align with the animating philosophies behind
the experimental secret society and anonymous collective described
here, and we have to take into account the very different historical and
technological conditions within which each arose. Nevertheless, it is
important to recognize the way in which secrecy and opacity are not
only animating revolutionary ideas but also providing cover in order
to share theories and revolutionary politics in ways that circumvent
certain traps of incorporation, traditional understandings of authorship (and ownership), and/or the surveillance capacities of the state.
While it is the animating, generative force of secrecy envisaged by
Bataille and Tiqqun that are of most relevance to this chapter, when I
come to consider in the Conclusion the ethical decision making about
what and when to share, and what and when to hold back, it will be
their (serious) play with opacity and openness that will resonate.

## Digital Secrecy

Creative "cuts" into what I am calling shareveillance, as part of what
Tiqqun imagines as spectacular, biopolitical, cybernetic capital, assume different forms. I am particularly interested in data obfuscation,
what Finn Brunton and Helen Nissenbaum term the "deliberate addition of ambiguous, confusing, or misleading information to interfere
with surveillance and data collection" (2015, 1). I am also interested
in digital opacity, a term that encompasses other methods that render users unreadable to data surveillance. Brunton and Nissenbaum
identify a number of different obfuscation strategies. They consider,
among other technologies, the Onion Router (TOR), which allows

for online anonymity through the combined tactics of encrypting communication and relaying it via several nodes on the internet to obscure the source and destination; TrackMeNot, a browser extension that floods search engines with random search terms to render algorithms ineffective; BitTorrent Hydra, which, when it was functioning, managed to confuse attempts by the content industry to identify illegal file sharers by adding random IP addresses; and the privacy plug-in FaceCloak, which encrypts genuine information offered to Facebook so that it can only be viewed by other friends who also use FaceCloak.

Online opacity can be achieved (albeit only partially or temporarily) by these obfuscation strategies. To these we can add other methods of deoptimizing or circumventing surveillance technologies such as tracking blockers like Ghostery, which intervene in consumer data surveillance by alerting users to, and in some cases disabling, cookies, tags, and beacons; and search engines like DuckDuckGo and Startpage, which allow for online searching without being tracked or profiled, as is the case with facilities like Google Search, the business model of which relies on the accumulation of consumer and user profiles and browsing habits. Equally, the now defunct Web 2.0 Suicide Machine, which scrambled a user's online identity by erasing individual data and friendship links on social media sites, would constitute a form of digital opacity.

While driven by privacy concerns and corporate confidentiality, the now discontinued Blackphone developed by Silent Circle offered mobile users a mode of communication built on a concept other than the form of sharing figured by shareveillance. Aptly, given what I write in chapter 4 about the way in which sharing operates at a protocological level with regards to the internet, one of the professed unique selling points of the phone is that it is "built on a fundamentally different protocol," as the website states.[11] The promotional video consists of a series of interviews with mobile users (or actors posing as mobile users) who are asked to read out the terms and conditions of use of the apps on their mobile phones. One woman stumbles on the fact that she has agreed to let an app change her call log. A man realizes he has given an app permission to record audio at any time without his confirmation. A woman is incredulous that an app can "modify calendar events and send e mails without [her] knowledge." Yet another mobile user looks concerned that an app can read his text messages and modify his contacts.

To back away from what Google's Eric Schmidt called "the creepy line" (qtd. in Saint 2010) and prevent leaky data, Blackphone uses its own operating system, offers compartmentalization facilities between work and social life in a way that goes against the grain of Facebook's integrated philosophy and real name policy, and aims to "put you in control of what you share." While it may reinforce the liberal notion of autonomy critiqued by Tiqqun, and its price prohibits general access to its privacy capital, Blackphone, like the other technologies described above, at the very least interrupts and asks us to question default modes of digital sharing and transparency norms through foregrounding forms of secrecy.

Owen Campbell-Moore offers a playful cut into shareveillance through digital opacity in the form of a Chrome browser extension he devised during his time at Oxford University. Using a technique known as JPEG steganography, Secretbook enables users to hide messages in photos on Facebook by making many visually imperceptible changes to encode the secret data.[12] Traditionally complex steganography tools are simplified and therefore somewhat democratized by Campbell-Moore. Here the act of sharing a photograph on and "with" Facebook belies another, more targeted, sharing: one that requires any receiver to have a decrypting password. Messages are thus hidden not only from other Facebook users but also from Facebook's scanning algorithms and profile-building analytics. Whereas cryptography can flag encoded communications to surveillants, steganography (within a platform like Facebook that has to deal with over 350 million photos being uploaded every day) has more chance of slipping secret messages through unnoticed.[13]

In terms laid out by Galloway and Thacker, such tactics and technologies afford nonexistence—a chance to be "unaccounted for" not necessarily because the subject is hiding but because the subject is invisible to a particular screen. They write, "One's data is there, but it keeps moving, of its own accord, in its own temporary autonomous ecology" (2007, 135). (Note here their careful use of "ecology" rather than "zone," indicating that they have taken heed of Tiqqun's warning that autonomy is heterogeneous and works on multiple planes and networks.) It could be argued that such interruptive cuts into shareveillance are isolated and that any disequilibrium they may introduce into the network is therefore limited in scope, that they do not offer pure examples of "zones of offensive opacity." Of data obfuscation in particular, Rob Horning (2015) warns that it is of very limited value: "The tactics of obfuscation don't scale," he argues. "The more people use them, the more incentive corporations and governments have to devote their superior resources to developing countertactics, thus quickly closing off whatever vulnerabilities were revealed."

Shoshana Zuboff also expresses doubts. She thinks such tactics are instances of "counter-declarations" that might be effective in discrete situations but that "leave the opposing facts [of surveillance capitalism] intact, acknowledging their persistence and thus paradoxically contributing to their legitimacy" (2019, 345). What is required, Zuboff argues, is a more forceful "synthetic declaration": a collective refusal that will "transform raw surveillance capitalism in favor of a digital future we can all call home" (345). In making this argument, she likens counterdeclarations to tunnels beneath the Berlin Wall. The tunnels offered respite and escape, but it was the collective demand for change that took the wall down. It is not by chance that she draws on a geopolitical situation that was a triumph for capitalism as well as democracy. For Zuboff, it is capitalism—what she calls reciprocal capitalism—as much as the sanctity of the individual that needs to be saved from the clutches of a surveillance imperative. However, capitalism has always surveilled because of its need to monitor spaces of labor, sociality, and domesticity, as well as to accumulate information about markets, debtors, and consumers.[14]

While I might not have the same idea as Zuboff as to what would constitute a structural change when it comes to surveillance capitalism, I share her emphasis on the necessity of structural change. I do, however, want to question the dispiriting account of counterdeclarative tunneling by positioning it as that which makes synthetic-declarative wall breaking possible. The tunnels from East to West Berlin, to pick up Zuboff's example, offered clandestine routes to new futures and collective critique. While individuals may have made that journey alone, they were counted among the growing number of defectors and dissidents—a collective body of refusal. While the flow of human traffic via these tunnels and other routes was one way, alternative political realities seeped back in via, for example, the mediated routes of pirate radio (such as Radio Glasnost, founded in the 1980s by Roland Jahn, a political exile from East Berlin), thereby bolstering local dissident groups.

Despite the limitations of data obfuscation and other forms of digital secrecy, "the very oppressive pervasiveness of capitalist realism means that even glimmers of alternative political and economic possibilities can have a disproportionately great effect" (Fisher 2009, 80–81). Moreover, if we understand that political-technological settlements like shareveillance are historically contingent and open to challenge and change, and that hegemony is a constant articulation and disarticulation between dominant ideologies and those elements that exceed or challenge it, then attempts to renegotiate the settlement or distribution are always significant.

As a particularly decisive cut or intervention, one that utilizes obfuscation to show the perils of sharing in the form of open data, a project published in 2015 by artist Paolo Cirio called *Obscurity* is noteworthy. In the United States, the publication of police photographs, or mug shots, of arrestees is legal under freedom of information and transparency laws in most states. Websites scrape mug shots that have been published elsewhere, mostly on sites belonging to law enforcement, and republish the photographs, requesting money from the arrestee to remove the picture and details. In *Obscurity*, Cirio and his collaborators developed a program to clone and scramble the data available on mug shot industry websites such as Mugshots.com, JustMugshots.com, and MugshotsOnline.com. Using almost identical domain names to these sites, Cirio's clone sites are uncanny. One might mistake them for the original at a quick glance. On closer inspection, they show hazy faces—misted mug shots—that are impossible to identify, and names have been changed. Cirio has singled out and enlarged some of the images from the clone sites in his shows. They serve as antiportraits, showing how each face has already been defaced (Figure 7).

While Cirio is most concerned with the right to be forgotten, as the issue has come to be referred to in the European Union after the landmark case in 2014 that ensured search engines are subject to the existing European Union data protection directive, we can also read this project as one that exposes the risks (of abuse and exploitation)

**FIGURE 7.** One of the obfuscated mug shots included in Paolo Cirio's project *Obscurity* (2015). Courtesy of the artist.

inherent to sharing and the limits and failures of some open data and transparency initiatives. In addition, the mug shot industry can be thought of as cynically aping the work undertaken by so-called data-preneurs to transform open data into profitable forms. After all, the websites Cirio is protesting against certainly have an entrepreneurial, creative approach to repurposing open data. In this way, they consti-tute a gruesome response to the call embedded in the Obama infor-mation imaginary described in chapter 2.

By cutting into shareveillance with opacity, Cirio demands that incarceration be seen not as a decontextualized, individualized problem but as a collective social issue for which we all have responsibility. Cirio (2015) writes, "Obscurity proposes a democratic judicial system that would help to understand crime as a community-related issue, bringing attention to the victims of mass incarceration in the U.S. and the unscrupulous criminal justice system and law enforcement agencies that created this situation." The project exposes the unethical cut of shareveillance with respect to a particular sociopolitical issue—in this case, how mug shot websites share data in such a way that presents incarceration as an asocial issue while in the process performing a second tier of punishment (shaming and extortion) on top of any lawfully imposed penalties. The project asks us to understand the political—and, crucially, racial—economy of criminalization and the carceral state in the United States. *Obscurity* cuts into this particular distribution with opacity in order to share anew. Creative interruptions of shareveillance can make ethical cuts and in the process show up the incisions that have constructed the neoliberal security settlement in which shareveillance plays a part.

## A Right to Opacity

These digital projects highlight concerns about information sharing and how surplus data and information are harnessed for profit in increasingly cynical ways. Obfuscation provides respite from processes that render human behavior and our data as capital. In this way it is political precisely because it questions the commercial appropriation of sharing and the capitalist realism underpinning acquiescence to data surveillance. It is also political because it deoptimizes the gaze of state security and its reliance on algorithmic governance. However, I also want to root these tactical interventions in a politics of and for the secret. Together, they constitute radical secrecy for the data multitude.

Derrida (2001a) professed a "taste for the secret." As discussed in chapters 3 and 5, rather than the common, contextual secret that hides somewhere waiting to be revealed (the secret that is, in principle at least, knowable), the secret of Derrida's formulation is unconditional. This irreducible excess, which never fully arrives and never fully presents itself, ensures an encounter with the other that should be understood in ethical terms. I have shown that for Derrida, this otherness must (but cannot) be respected by democracy. It has to allow for secrets as singularities (Derrida 1996); it has to play host to multiple singularities, including those who do not wish to respond, participate in, or belong to the public sphere. Democracy is nothing but the play between openness and secrecy, between belonging and nonbelonging, between sharing and not sharing. In taking account of singularities in this way, for Derrida, democracy is always "to come." It is an impossible (but necessary) project; true democracy would create belonging among people who will never belong.

In light of such a formulation, we should be concerned for those who do not want to adhere to the dominant elements of digital democracy, including transparency, veillance, and sharing. The subject of democracy is not simply one who is asked to be transparent to the state and to act on transparency. The subject is also, in the guise of Derrida's nonsovereign, non-self-coincident subject, constituted by a singularity, an unconditional secret, that prevents full capitulation to the demands or interpellation of transparency and sharing.

In a context different than the one I am engaged with, but mindful, I would wager, of Derrida's configuration of irreducible singularity, Glissant (1997) wrote about a right to opacity. Glissant conceptualized an ontological condition of minoritarian subjectivity and r(el)ationality that resists the demand to be knowable, understood, measured, categorized, and rendered transparent by the dominant Eurocentric order: readable within and reduced to its racialized and colonial terms. Opacity both problematizes and offers alternatives to systems of knowledge that produce the other as an object. This means not settling for an ethical relation to the other that is based in an idea of understanding and difference, but rather pursuing a "relation" based in a freedom made possible by the irreducible opacity of the other (Glissant 1997, 190)—with "relation" here being Glissant's term for a constantly changing and ungraspable system or totality that engenders encounters between diverse cultures that are based on equality and respect. Ultimately opacity interrupts assimilation and an exoticizing objectification; it resists a certain universalizing transparency. For Glissant (1989), opacity is freedom.

It is necessary before proceeding to pause on the term "right." The language and logic of rights, with its attendant humanism and universalism, seems at odds with much of the poststructuralist theory that I explicitly and implicitly rely on in this book in general and the posthuman digital assemblage I consider. But Glissant steers us away from humanism by advising us "to develop everywhere in defiance of a universalizing and reductive humanism, the theory of specifically opaque structures." Furthermore, he writes, "Humanity is perhaps not the 'image of man' but today the evergrowing network of recognized opaque structures" (1989, 133). We can therefore think of a right to opacity within the tradition of "rights revisionism" (Douzinas qtd. in Goulder 2015, 2), which positions rights not as the universal property of a cognizant and agential sovereign subject, as orthodox liberal discourse would have it, but rather a structuring human condition (whereby the category "human" is subject to endless revision—a point that has particular resonance in the context of race). Judith Butler writes, "The necessity of keeping our notion of the human open to a future articulation is essential to the project of international human rights discourse and politics" (2004, 36). Glissant's right to opacity is not an international human right in a legal sense, of course, but the point is salient. The minoritarian subject who has a right to opacity is always already rendered nonsovereign and nonuniversal by that very irreducible density of oneself, by opacity. The subject is as opaque to herself as she is to others.

With regards to collective digital politics, claiming a right to opacity seems more productive than a right to privacy. Whereas calls for privacy seem antithetical or irrelevant to collective politics, a right to opacity allows for a relationality not based on sanctioned identities and parameters of understanding. Glissant writes, "Opacities can coexist and converge" (1997, 190). In this relation, we would be able to conceive of the opacity of the other for us, without reproach for our opacity to the other. As Bratich puts it, "A right to secrecy would change the tenor of freedom from privacy's passive, individualized zone to an interactive exteriority of relations" (2007, 53). In the digital context, opacity might allow for identifications and subjectivities that circumvent or even refuse those prescribed by the governing laws and apparatus of shareveillance.

How to align the opaque subject with the idea of the data multitude put forth in the previous chapter? Rancière's equitable political name (the equivalent of "proletariat") has to take part in a way that will reshape the political-aesthetic configuration, whereas the opaque subject is resistant to strategies of visibility. Glissant's opacity is a relational ontological condition, whereas we can imagine the data multitude might use opacity tactically (in response to violating forms of power). Those who use tactical opacity can also be constituted by ontological opacity. Equally, the former can resonate with and shore up the latter. Moreover, in Rancière's (1992) recognition that processes of disidentification and declassification are essential to real politics, we can locate a place for opacity. What is important for my argument is the way in which the ethical is more aligned with secrecy than transparency in Glissant's writing. This configuration of the opaque subject offers us an alternative to the idea of the productive, vigilant, quantified, and transparent subject of shareveillant neoliberalism.

While respecting the origins of these concepts in philosophical work on democracy, responsibility, and literature with regards to Derrida, and the postcolonial with regards to Glissant, they can provide inspiration for thinking through the concerns of this book.[15] Derrida's unconditional secret highlights the violation (against singularity) at the heart of shareveillant practices, while a right to opacity would mean the demand not to be reduced to data and a resistance to consume and share data in ways defined by shareveillance. Placed side by side, these theories tell us that while some historically disenfranchised and discriminated against subjects continue to suffer more from the universalizing demands of transparency (whether administered through the datafied or Eurocentric gaze, if these can even be separated), all are constituted by an irreducible, unconditional secret and can therefore be violated by transparency demands (albeit to different degrees and with different consequences). When Glissant wrote "we clamor for the right to opacity for everyone" (1997, 194), he was writing within a postcolonial context in which only some (white Western subjects) had that right. Under datafied conditions, few are afforded this right, and those who do fall beyond the reach of datafication have already been rendered surplus by surveillance capitalism or shareveillance. It is less a right for those deemed unprofitable and more a marker of the many ways in which such lives are devalued.

In recognizing the ubiquity of nonopacity in digital contexts, I am not claiming that opacity is experienced as a universal constant, that all violations of opacity are identical, or that the burden of transparency falls evenly. This is clearly not the case. Rather, a right to opacity can be useful in different arenas of contestation without trying to claim an equivalence, not least because sometimes these arenas overlap. Some subjects are doubly afflicted by a lack of opacity—ontological and digital; and it is these subjects, rather than the newly violated (and otherwise privileged) subjects, who should be of primary concern. My invocation, far from erasing race from Glissant's concept, acknowledges the importance of thinking about race in the digital context. I recognize, however, that there are losses and gains, risks and rewards from this move.[16]

Rather than acts of publicity such as legal marches or online petitions, we need to meet the pervasive protocols of inequitable data surveillance used by the security state and the logic of shareveillance with forms of illegibility. We need, in short, a reimagined opacity. While Glissant saw opacity as the always already ontological condition or relation that power violates rather than that which subjects can actively acquire, opacity in the digital context can be invoked and enacted at a technological, aesthetic, and political level. There are some contradictions to grapple with. Zach Blas explains that for minoritarian subjects "who are most violently impacted by informatic identification standards," informatic opacity "is both liberating and oppressive"—oppressive because "becoming informatically opaque can have excruciating political consequences, such as the loss of basic human rights." Blas concludes, however, that "informatic opacity makes a more utopian gesture to exist without identification" (2018, 199). Such acts of tactical opacity are not the same as the unconditional secret or a right to opacity, but they maintain a link to the way in which those concepts interrupt the violence of transparency inherent in power. Such reformulations of the politics of the secret and opacity enable us to begin to rethink the role of sharing in a data ecology that demands visible, surveillable, quantifiable, and entrepreneurial subjects.

## Secrecy as Commons

A politics based not on privacy but opacity would not be a permanent and wholesale rejection of or retreat from the idea and practice of sharing (data, for our concerns). Opacity in this context would only ever be desirable if it allowed space to develop, paradoxically, a community-forming openness—relationality—that is based on the principle of the commons rather than its shareveillant manifestation.

The commons is a multifaceted term that "can be seen as an intellectual framework and political philosophy; . . . a set of social attitudes and commitments; . . . an experiential way of being and even a spiritual disposition; . . . an overarching worldview" (Bollier and Helfrich 2012). But in all of these framings of commons and commoning, questions of what is shared, and how, come to the fore (de Angelis 2007) in a way that calls into question the logic in which shareveillance is rooted. In other words, it is not only the enclosure, commodification, and privatization of previously communal natural resources, land, property, goods, services, or relations that the concept of commons challenges, but also the particular shape, place, and role sharing is given in any society.

Used more frequently in relation to environmental, institutional, labor, and species commons, the idea of "collective but decentralized control over resources" (de Peuter and Dyer-Witheford 2010, 30) is a productive one to think about secrecy. If the commons is to be a term that speaks of more than simply on-message, progressive themes (such as the endorsement of Creative Commons licenses for open access publishing, or the collective ownership of institutions like libraries, parks, or schools), it needs to be mobilized for those resources about which the left is more uncertain. Secrecy constitutes one of these problematic or unpalatable instances of a common resource that has been tainted by—and in recent years largely left to—the political right. But by thinking through "toxic" commons rather than only preapproved themes, the left avoids accusations of moralism (Brown 2001). If the left does not recognize secrecy as a common resource, not only will the right continue to "monopolize strategy" (Bratich 2007, 54), but also the link between transparency and moralism is in danger of being reinforced at the expense of an ethical decision (about the times and places in which transparency is or is not the best policy).

In this view, to pick up the example offered in chapter 3, what was potentially exciting or radical about a project like WikiLeaks, as well as its ability to remind us that there are other incarnations and modes of transparency out there, is not its identity as a group of cyberlibertarians intent on transparency in the service of accountability. In these aims, it was quite in keeping with a First Amendment liberal democratic tradition, as already pointed out. Rather, as a virtual, dispersed, nonstatist, largely anonymous cyborg assemblage (that claimed to be able to automate disclosure in the event of the detention of any one member), it treated secrecy as commons.[17] In other words, transparency, though certainly the most discussed aspect of the WikiLeaks project—the half of the story most applauded by the left—was arguably the least radical; the way in which the force of this transparency demanded a level of secrecy equivalent to that practiced by the state might be the most. We can think of this as the difference between the treatment of secrets per se as commons (which is tantamount to transparency) and of *secrecy* as commons.

As well as worrying about the risk to life haphazardly redacted disclosures might pose, the threats to national security, and the setbacks to open government initiatives, many critics of WikiLeaks point out that as an organization, it was itself far from transparent. Jim Barnett (2010), for example, writes, "If WikiLeaks really wants to promote transparency, it should start with its own operations." The short-lived OpenLeaks, created by disgruntled ex-WikiLeaker Daniel Domscheit-Berg, hoped to answer this call. On the now-defunct OpenLeaks website, the project claimed it would demand the same level of transparency from itself as other organizations: "We feel that a transparent approach is much better than cloak-and-dagger tactics, and believe that trust in us should be based on critical scrutiny—just as it should be for everyone else."[18] But WikiLeaks' opaque finances and mystery were not just an irony, an unfortunate hypocrisy, or an oversight that should be corrected in order to move WikiLeaks closer to the identity of a respectable NGO. WikiLeaks' clandestine modus operandi was not an aberrant feature of an otherwise admirably transparent project. Secrecy (as anonymity of sources, coded information, dispersed anonymous membership) was a condition of (im)possibility of the WikiLeaks (infra)structure.

In its cavalier approach to secrecy, WikiLeaks not only implicitly problematized the liberal democratic notion of transparency it at once explicitly sought to enact but also suggested a more nuanced notion of being in common than other calls to political action presume. In fact, we can detect in WikiLeaks a critique of community in line with the thought of Roberto Esposito (2009), and before him Jean-Luc Nancy (1991)—as well as Bataille (1970) and Maurice Blanchot (1988). There are well-rehearsed objections to such a reading.[19] The register in which these thinkers write tends to be epistemological, their concern being with transcendental and indeed quasi-transcendental modes of knowing, particularly in relation to the (non)knowability of the other, the other's secrecy, and the other's resistance to epistemological mastery. But to imagine that they simply ignore the political implications of this resistance would be to do a disservice to their work. The secret other, the other secret, the secret of the other, and the secret as the other—all were conterminously epistemological and political at their root.

Drawing on an exacting etymology of "communitas," Esposito writes, "The common is not characterized by what is proper but by what is improper or even more drastically, by the other; by a voiding, be it partial or whole, of property into its negative; by removing what is properly one's own that invests and decenters the proprietary subject, forcing him to take leave of himself, to alter himself" (2009, 7). The proprietary subject's singularity (understood as irrecuperable alterity) is extended, rather than relieved, by community. Moreover, the subject in community with other subjects suffers from its inability to own itself as proper. In the process, it forfeits not just epistemological and political grounding but also ontological and existential guarantees. "In the community," Esposito continues, "subjects do not find a principle of identification nor an aseptic enclosure within which they can establish transparent communication or even a content to be communicated. They don't find anything else except that void, that distance, that extraneousness that constitutes them as being missing from themselves" (7). In other words, what a community shares, what it has in common, is nonbelonging and otherness. It shares nonsharing. Even if we share secrets, there is a more constitutive secret conditioning the sharer in the first place. This is a secret the left has yet to come fully to terms with.

The commons in this view is radical not because of what it enables us to share, not because it offers a collective bond or power in numbers, but because it forces the subject to face otherness (within and between subjects)—or, as Glissant would have it, opacity. That is, although community might often be interpreted as an arena for sharing transparent statements, positive forms of knowledge, and revealed secrets, it is in fact a space in which subjects encounter secrets qua singularities (in terms of the absolute difference, the irreducible density, between subjects). The subject becomes more singular, not less, through a decentering, precisely because this removes it further from a generality under which it might be categorized. This being the fate of other subjects in the commons, however, the centrifugal movement applies to all. What results is a commons of shared atomism—an atomism that guarantees the secret and produces what could still be called a virtual community, with the caveat that that community remains secret to itself.

This is an important notion for the left, which has often wanted to gather all resources together in a united front. This secrecy of the commons does the reverse. It is disorganized resistance—not in the sense of incompetent organization, but in the sense of a pervasive organizing secret that makes the commons secret to itself and so all the more resistant. These subjects, or rather nonsubjects, are decentered and opaque and therefore cannot reflect themselves back to themselves. In a sense, the secret comes before subjectivity because it divides these nonsubjects from themselves as well as from the community, even if they all share in the same fate, which links them. It is a form of negative commons, rather than a positive commons of solidarity, identity, commitment, and knowledge.

In Nancy's work, the community is a multiplicity of singular existences that share nothing but mortality. Moreover, because of its incontrovertibility, this mortality, Nancy argues, cannot serve as the basis for any positive project or shared identity:

> The genuine community of mortal beings, or death as community, establishes their impossible communion. Community therefore occupies a singular place: it assumes the impossibility of its own immanence, the impossibility of a communitarian being in the form of a subject. In a certain sense community acknowledges and inscribes—this is its peculiar gesture—the impossibility of community. A community is not a project of fusion, or in some general way a productive or operative project—nor is it a project at all. . . . A community is the presentation to its members of their mortal truth. (1991, 15)

Nancy's Heideggerian allusions suggest that being-toward-death creates a fundamental isolation of all who share in it—that is, all mortal beings. We all share the secret of death, but it is different for each one of us; or rather, it is the same, but the mortality of mortal beings means that it affects my being only. Death is pure singularity, and there results a commons of mortality. Ian James explains, "Community reveals, or rather *is,* our exposure to the unmasterable limit of death, and thus our being together outside of all identity or work of subjectivity" (2006, 185). Because this community enables the subject's understanding of itself as radically isolated and individual, as outside itself, it is paradoxically the condition for the possibility of encountering the other (and of forming an ethical relation).

How does this relate to WikiLeaks? Derrida states that the concerns he has with the word "community"—for its associations with the common, the as-one (2001a, 25)—are eased somewhat when used in reference to "a community that is such only in an alliance that not only does not cancel out the singularity of the allies but, on the contrary, accentuates it" (24). Derrida, prompted by a question from Maurizio Ferraris, is talking about an interpretative "community" attending to a text that is "not closed in on itself" (24). However, I suggest that WikiLeaks, by respecting the singularity and otherness—that is, the secrecy—of the sources of knowledge it then makes transparent could be considered a community, but one without the idea of communion between self-present subjects.[20] But how was WikiLeaks different from any newspaper that maintains the anonymity of its sources? Though anonymous informants are still a characteristic of traditional journalism, confidential sources and journalists usually form a club of known people meeting in private. However, WikiLeaks was a technological–human assemblage that enabled automated data transfer between unidentified persons. It was a community that shared content but not necessarily identity (either nominal or social). Chelsea Manning, for example, did not have to share Julian Assange's more anarchic ambitions for radical transparency. The internet is instrumental to the appearance of WikiLeaks as an embodiment of a postcommunion community. It allows people to connect without compromising or downplaying their singularity. The internet, we could say, releases a community of singularity—the data multitude—from the burden of being an unproductive contradiction.

At the same time, the surveillance and open data capacities of the internet have also, as we have seen, made it deeply complicit with the violation of such singularity.

Some practical and theoretical experiments with secrecy show us that something valuable can take place, shift, or transform because of secrecy rather than (or as well as) transparency. If the radical left follows the moderate, liberal left by leaving secrecy to the enclosing, (in)securitizing forces of the right, it risks missing vital opportunities to explore forms of knowledge that do not conform to revelatory logic. It risks missing the chance to make something else happen. The secret is powerful, but not only for the opportunities of control and malfeasance the right, big tech, and the state have exploited. It can interrupt shareveillance and, as Bratich claims, "provide conditions for dissent and transformation" (2007, 506). But perhaps more important than acting as the inspiration for strategy, secrecy can open us to the affects, experiences, and transformations that nonpositive forms of knowledge (or nonknowledge) can set in motion. It can, when thought in relation to the work of Nancy, Esposito, Glissant, and Derrida, help us reevaluate the foundations of our being in common. The secret qua singularity, as opacity, can stage the ethical demand of radical otherness.

Such formulations lack political expediency. They cannot be the basis of a traditionally conceived movement or a positive community of action in the way that transparency can. However, to ignore this reconceived form of radical secrecy, to deny its status as a common resource or its demand on the way we conceive of our political identities, ethical responsibilities, and communities, means that it will remain a tool of ideology and power. It is my hope that the theories of and experiments with secrecy outlined in this chapter might enable us to begin to imagine a form of visibility that works for social justice rather than against it.

# CONCLUSION
## Toward Postsecrecy

Throughout this book, I have tried to challenge the meanings and values ascribed to secrecy and transparency in order to reappraise their political potential, to think through what part they might play in a more progressive political settlement than the one offered by many (neo)liberal democracies in general and the United States in particular today. As part of this process, I reversed the current consensus that positions secrecy on the one hand as suspect and transparency on the other as progressive. Drawing on Wendy Chun's (2006) coordinates, this aligns secrecy with control and transparency with freedom.[1] My challenge to these standard pairings is more than an intellectual exercise. I am interested in not only reconfiguring these points on the visibility spectrum but also in reconfiguring the very political-aesthetic conditions of that visibility spectrum.

Such a reversal of the binary logic at work here, as I pointed out in the Introduction, is only the first stage in a more thorough displacement. The latter is necessary if we are to avoid an uncritical romanticization (of secrecy's potential, for example) and not remain locked within dualistic thinking that lacks the agility needed to properly respond to the demands of the current conjuncture. (The reinterpretation of transparency and secrecy evident in the Trump information imaginary, explored in chapter 2, offers a pertinent case in point.) While tactical uses of secrecy and opacity might be necessary to interrupt and challenge shareveillance, the ultimate aim is not a political and cultural setting in which secrecy reigns and transparency is discredited. Rather, the goal is an equitable settlement in which a right to opacity is respected and in which radical forms of transparency, an openness to what openness means, supersede the neoliberal incarnation we are offered today. This is the work of the data multitude—that internally differentiated, distributed network aligned around situated and stratified experiences of data exploitation.

The goal is postsecrecy. I mean this not in the sense that the world, communication, data, and individuals would somehow be fully transparent after secrecy. Rather, I mean that we would be open to an understanding and experience of the political that is free from the false choice between secrecy and transparency as these terms are commonly understood and enacted today. The prefix "post-" points toward a particular way of thinking about the relation between secrecy and its others. In the same way that the "post-" of posthumanism can be read as "a paced and patient reckoning with what is at stake" (Badmington 2006, 266)—in the relationship between the human and nonhuman, for example—the "post-" in postsecrecy indicates a reckoning with and working through of our political investment in the secret from the angles of both concealment and revelation.

The antipolitical constraints of the settlement or distribution of shareveillance, outlined in chapter 4, illustrate how both secrecy and transparency can limit and even subvert freedom, equality, and agency. It is therefore important to approach secrecy and transparency free from old alliances and prejudices.

## Posting the Opposition

In chapter 3, I introduced a number of philosophical critiques of transparency, including the one we can extract from Derrida's writings. What becomes evident through a reading of this critique alongside his work on the unconditional secret is that it extends to a binary that would posit secrecy against transparency in any simple manner. This is the condition of instability that makes the retelling of any story of secrecy and transparency so problematic. Although it may be true that societies and states often favor one and turn against the other at particular cultural-historical moments (as can be seen in chapter 1), the relationship is far from resolved in those expressions of (perhaps moralistic or pragmatic or political) preference. Therefore, it is not only the case that continued investment in state secrecy, often itself covert, infects and destabilizes any public commitment to transparency, as became evident during the Obama administration, for example. It is also the case that secrecy and transparency are structuring conditions of (im)possibility of each other. They are inseparable in practice and in theory.

Despite political, academic, and cultural depictions of an either/or logic at work when it comes to secrecy and transparency, there are at least five compelling reasons why secrecy and transparency are not mutually exclusive, and therefore why the choice between them is false. I have already looked at some of these during the analytical work of this book, but for the sake of clarity, I summarize them here.

### 1. Transparency can be claimed by an opaque agent

For transparency to be known as transparency, there must be some agency (such as the media, the government, or an NGO) that legitimizes it as transparent; and because there is a legitimizing agent that does not itself have to be transparent, there is a limit to transparency. In this book, I have already looked at several examples of this: administrations that call for transparency but invoke executive privilege to operate beyond visibility; and the case of WikiLeaks, which labeled its content as transparent but did not apply transparency rules to its own organizational conduct. We might also add the various transparency reports that are becoming a tech industry standard. In these reports, companies like Google and Facebook reveal as much about government requests for information on its users as the classification system allows and outline content moderation and intellectual property policies. However, the reports are issued by companies whose business models rely on opaque algorithms to deliver content and advertisements and data extraction hidden within long and complex terms of use agreements. These examples illustrate more than hypocrisy. They show that nontransparency inhabits transparency when the latter is claimed, enacted, or imposed.

### 2. The secret is always already structuring transparency, and vice versa

One partial example in this book is Jodi Dean's configuration of the secret as generating publicity as the ideal of the public sphere, and a recognition that secret societies were important to the exploration of nascent democratic freedoms. But the purest expression of this relation as a two-way symbiosis is the discussion of democracy, first introduced in chapter 3. Democracy asks its subjects to be transparent, to participate in the public realm, and to be knowable members of the demos; but if it wants to resist sliding into totalitarianism, it must be able to tolerate secrets qua singularity—a desire not to belong to, or to be knowable members of, the demos. The singular secret licenses the movement toward the transparency of democracy, but it also prevents its full realization. In light of this, it makes no sense to talk of secrecy *or* transparency.

### 3. Subjects are constituted by both secrets and transparency

There is no choice to be made between secrets and transparency at the level of subjectivity. On the one hand, the secret has to declare itself as a secret to be secret. It must reveal if not its content, then its secret status, if only to the subject who bears the secret. If I am to possess and keep a secret, I must tell it to myself, and in that moment of keeping the secret (to myself), I have always already broken any promise to keep it. In the process, the secret's secret status is both undermined (through this partial revelation) and reinforced (by being identified as secret). Some minimal disclosure or transparency must therefore be present in this kind of commonplace secret.

However, on the other hand, if we consider twentieth-century reformulations of identity (not least the implications of the Freudian unconscious and Marxist false consciousness) and the critique of Rousseauist self-transparency referred to in chapters 1 and 3 (particularly Derrida's challenge to the concept of the sovereign subject), then this relation to the secret within the self can work the other way too. It can also mean that there is always something in us that is secret even to ourselves.

To be clear, the "impure" self-relation, the formulation of the non-self-coincident, nonsovereign subject, points toward a repeatability at the heart of consciousness, an absence in self-presence, a space between experience and experiencing, which means that in principle, we can never keep a secret; we are always already repeating, revealing, and being transparent even when we keep a secret. However, equally, the other in the self means that we are always secret to ourselves.

### 4. Because a secret is not a positive form of knowledge to begin with, any act of revelation in the service of transparency is compromised

Rather than a positive form, the secret is negative knowledge, or not known knowledge. Someone promises not to tell, to reveal, to speak of the secret. Because a secret does not declare itself in the fashion of more positive statements, it refutes this very negativity. "It is," as Derrida writes, "a negation that denies itself" (1987, 25). The secret therefore denies its own existence: "There is no secret *as such*" (26). But "this denial *[dénégation]* does not happen [to the secret] by accident; it is essential and originary" (25). It is an internal operation of the secret as secret. Moreover, because this essence is split through a self-denying negation, the secret creates its own other, "its own partition" (25). Crucially, transparency, or any other candidate nominated from the camp of openness, cannot be the absolute other of secrecy because the secret is already other to itself. A part of the secret is always already lost to itself, destabilizing any binary opposition between the two trajectories of secretion: toward the shadows and the light.

### 5. The unknowable is at work in the revealed

Even a revealed (commonplace) secret does not necessarily enter the realm of the transparent or the knowable. A told secret is perhaps simply unsecret in the same way that vampires are described as undead. The former is no more uncomplicatedly transparent than the latter is alive. Revelation, despite the way in which the problem is presented in liberal discourses around freedom of information, press freedom, open access, and so forth, is not the same as transparency.

We can take the photographs from Abu Ghraib prison in Iraq as an example, for what is revealed in those photos is far from transparent. The photographs can be, and have been, read through a number of different discourses (psychological, sexual) and through the vectors of race, class, and gender. However, the images themselves remain enigmatic, mysterious, dark, and troubling even as they seem to lay everything bare. They may be unsecret, but they remain opaque.

Of course (as fictional characters with superpowers like X-ray vision or telepathy soon realize), even that which is sold as transparent is not necessarily knowable either. Take, for example, the problem facing financial regulators in the United States before the financial crisis of 2007–8: "Between 1996 and 2005 alone, the federal government issued more than 30 major rules requiring new financial disclosure protocols, and the data has piled up. The [Security and Exchange Commission's] public document database, Edgar, now catalogs 200 gigabytes of filings each year—roughly 15 million pages of text—up from 35 gigabytes a decade ago. But the volume of data obscures more than it reveals; financial reporting has become so transparent as to be invisible" (Roth 2009). As my investigation into open government data in this book makes clear, data overload has led to a divorce between transparency and visibility. In this way, extreme transparency begins to have the same effect as secrecy.

Most information on the internet remains untouched, undigested, and outside the realm of knowledge because of the commercial imperative of search engines. Transparency will not ensure that all secrets become knowable; the algorithmic governance of for profit search will determine which secrets become knowable. The admission that transparency does not equal knowability is unpalatable because it goes against the grain of liberal orthodoxy; it goes against the call to democratize knowledge and free our data. The enduring belief in transparency persists in part because we like to think that revelation and transparency lead to more knowledge—to knowability. But the unknowable is always at play.

It is through the unknowable, the unconditional secret, that the opposition between secrecy and transparency unravels because it shows how the former is always already structuring the latter. Commonplace secrets—a conception most discussions of secrecy and transparency in public life rely on—privilege the unknown rather than the unknowable, something that became clear through an examination of different works of art that engage with an aesthetics of the secret in chapter 5. A shift occurs when we acknowledge that the unknowable is not such because it is enigmatic but rather because knowledge, an event, or a person or thing is not there, not fully present, in the way that we commonly understand them to be. Thus, in any communication, in any expression of knowledge, something is always held back. What is held back is in no way held in a reserve, ready to be discovered. Rather, there is a singular excess that cannot fully show itself. The implications of this are far reaching. Once a secret is revealed, in order to function in the public sphere, we have to be able to read, understand, share, and repeat it. In these new exchanges, there is a risk—a necessary risk—that our knowledge will be abused. This condition ensures that there is an unknowable at the heart of the knowable; we do not know in what ways our secret will be used. It can be known or revealed, again and again, in faithful or unfaithful forms. For Derrida, the absolute secret resides in the structural unknowability of the present (of events, meaning, texts). In this sense, there will always be something secret.

Being attentive to the unconditional secret has occasioned an awareness of and wariness about those times when secrets are discussed as conditional, contextual, and temporary, when too much faith is placed in the revelations that transparency mechanisms might enable. Understanding the opposition between secrecy and transparency to be politically expedient rather than philosophically sound is a crucial part of the postsecrecy process. The point of such a process is to create a space in which the politics and import of any act of secret keeping or transparency is not decided in advance—that is, to create a space in which sharing can be conceptualized and enacted beyond the shareveillant distribution of the sensible.

### Postsecret Decisions

While presenting themselves as acting on the side of the ethical, advocates of greater transparency are perhaps not being ethical at all, for they have already decided in advance what transparency is, as well as the identity of the secret and secrecy from which transparency is supposed to save us. Take this memorandum from Obama's time in office: "My Administration is committed to creating an unprecedented level of openness in Government. We will work together to ensure the public trust and establish a system of transparency, public participation, and collaboration. Openness will strengthen our democracy and promote efficiency and effectiveness in Government" (Executive

Office of the President 2009a). The language used in White House memoranda is obviously not going to demonstrate philosophical speculation, and I am not suggesting it should. However, it is clear that transparency is a fixed goal, not an object of debate or inquiry here. Would not any understanding of transparency worth its salt be subject to—and the result of—transparent processes such as public participation and collaboration? In this book, I have asked what a transparent transparency (an openness to openness that does not reinforce shareveillance) would look like. Such a transparency would certainly acknowledge and work with its real relation to the secret as outlined above.

The problem with much liberal discourse on transparency, exemplified by the Obama information imaginary and aspects of the transparency movement, is not only the accusation from the radical left that lip service to transparency is paid by the state to secure hegemony, but also that there is no responsible decision being made. All of the decisions about what constitutes transparency, secrecy, and democracy (and what is best for the public) have already been taken in a different political conjuncture to the one we are currently living through.

As it is put forward by Derrida, a responsible decision is that which is made without as many conditional secrets as possible; he writes that it is "necessary to know the most and best" (2001b, 54). But "between the widest, the most refined, the most necessary knowledge, and the responsible decision, an abyss remains" (54). At the same time we have to gather and use all that is knowable to us, if we are to make a decision that is truly ethical and responsible—that is, one that is not simply "the technical deployment of a cognitive apparatus" (Derrida 1992, 24) or the following of a clearly marked path—we also have to base this decision on an incalculable or unknowable calculation. It requires a leap into the unknowable—a leap into the arena of the unconditional secret. Being responsible might therefore require us not to view transparency and secrecy as discrete options that ask us to make a choice but rather to hold them in tension in order to make decisions about knowledge, secrets, accountability, and public access. There is always something left over when secrecy and transparency are presented as a way to differentiate presidential or governmental styles (as I discuss in chapter 2); when they dominate measurements of democracy; or when our only prescribed response to a whistle-blower like Snowden is to designate him a hero or a traitor (chapter 5). It is this excess that opens the way for the postsecret.

Postsecrecy would be free of the misconception that transparency and revelation offer the solution to democracy's problems. Other theorists have already expressed frustration with the store placed in transparency and revelation. Jodi Dean insists that transparency is beside the point: "All sorts of horrible political processes are perfectly transparent today. The problem is that people . . . are so enthralled to transparency that they have lost the will to fight." She calls for "decisive action" (2002, 174) as remedy. Alasdair Roberts makes a similar argument: "The significance of Abu Ghraib," he writes in this context, "may also lie in the extent to which we overestimated the catalytic effect of exposure" (2006, 238). For him, democracy has to involve the responsibility of the public to act on the information to which it has a right. Mark Fenster worries that "if there is no capable receiver at the end of the communicative act—then the transparency ideal is misplaced" (2017a, 139). Lawrence Lessig (2009) insists that technotransparency has to be accompanied by suggestions for reform to have any worth. Eve Kosofsky Sedgwick wonders, "What is the basis for assuming that [exposure] will surprise or disturb, never mind motivate, anyone to learn that a given social manifestation is artificial, self-contradictory, imitative, phantasmatic, or even violent?" (1993, 141). Jeremy Gilbert asserts that any tendency toward transparency "has to go beyond the mere telling of secrets and become real acts of what we might call . . . 'publication,' or 'publicity'" (2007, 38), which involves the politicization of an event or issue—that is, making them objects of debate, discussion, and intervention.

However, this radicalization of exposed secrets is only one element of the working through necessary in a postsecret politics: expose the ills of government, to be sure, and make those ills the subject of radical democratic debate. But total reliance on revelation (even when accompanied by action) risks a misunderstanding of the unconditional secret in which the unknowable rather than unknown is at work. If a new politics is based on a conventional notion of the secret, it will quickly begin to resemble the old. This can only lead to structural repetitions under the sign of difference.

By acknowledging the fragility of any community built on either

an embrace or denouncement of the (commonplace) secret; by understanding how both secrecy and transparency can be used to curtail
freedom; by imagining and enacting communities that can tolerate
and work with opacity; by accepting the role played by unknowability and the importance of secrets qua singularities in democracy—by
all these, we may be able to move away from the endless oscillation
between concealment and revelation. It is the work of postsecrecy to
find less artificial, ideological, and constricting points around which
democracy can pivot.

## Postsecret Academy

What might this all mean in practice? While the focus of this book has
been mainstream politics (looking at partisan politics, government
policies, public engagement with government data, and so forth), and
while I have offered ideas about how to interrupt configurations of
transparency and secrecy along the way, I am going to answer this
question more self-reflexively. In these closing paragraphs, I want to
consider what postsecrecy might mean for me as a cultural theorist
working in a British university. The nature of this work prompts daily
decisions about how and which knowledge will be revealed and ex-
changed, while the context of the contemporary university renders
me and my colleagues subject to various transparency measures
that are implemented for sometimes opaque reasons. I do so in the
hope that these observations reach beyond my own experiences and
prompt reflections on what postsecrecy might mean in other institutional contexts.

### Postsecret Reading

So-called symptomatic reading relies on a model of a disguised and
disguising textual surface and an unconscious, repressed depth that
skillful interpreters can unearth. In other words, the business of interpretation (of all kinds of texts) following the tenets of Marxist
and psychoanalytic literary and cultural theory seems to assume the
opacity of texts; they position readers as code breakers or detectives.
Turning against this mode of reading, some theorists have argued
for forms of postsymptomatic "surface reading," whether this be the

"reparative reading" that moves away from "paranoid reading" to pay attention to affect advocated by Sedgwick (1993), Franco Moretti's data-driven "distant reading" (2000), the cultural analytics developed by figures like Lev Manovich, or materialist approaches toward texts. Surface reading, Stephen Best and Sharon Marcus write, assumes the surface is "what is evident, perceptible, apprehensible in texts; what is neither hidden nor hiding; what, in the geometrical sense, has length and breadth but no thickness, and therefore covers no depth. A surface is what insists on being looked *at* rather than what we must train ourselves to see *through*" (2009, 9). They criticize symptomatic reading for operating under the desire to valorize the freedom (and heroism) of the critic and for repeatedly "finding" in a text the same repressed cause. Surface reading, by contrast, operates according to "a desire to be free from having a political agenda that determines in advance how we interpret texts" (16).

While trying to outline the pitfalls and obsolescence of symptomatic reading, Best and Marcus observe how Fredric Jameson's assumption "that domination can only do its work when veiled" now strikes them as "nostalgic" where it might once have seemed "paranoid" (2009, 2). They pinpoint blatantly, or transparently, racist twenty-first-century American events (such as the response to and coverage of Hurricane Katrina) to prove how a hermeneutics of suspicion is now superfluous. Their implication is that, since September 11, the obvious nature of the state's prejudices and abuses no longer requires readers to excavate such prejudices from ideological texts. We might think that Trump has trademarked such unashamedly open bigotry.[2]

Despite such a clear dismissal of the need for excavation, in a footnote after this observation, Best and Marcus write: "We note that there remain things that government powers go to extraordinary lengths to keep hidden, to keep as state secrets, 'extraordinary rendition' being one of them. A hermeneutics of suspicion in which understanding requires a subtle reading of the situation thus remains readily pertinent to the work of critique" (2009, 19). They refer the reader to Trevor Paglen's art practice, about which I write in chapter 5.

This footnote troubles the approach taken by Best and Marcus (2009). On the one hand, their argument rests on the belief that ideology is so open as to render hermeneutic interpretation redundant. On the other hand, the state—the primary generator of ideology—

clearly harbors secrets, a state of affairs that requires a "subtle reading of the situation." For Best and Marcus, it is not that the detection and exposure of secrets per se is poor practice, but rather that they want to stop a form of interpretation that presents open secrets as real secrets. Ideology might be fully transparent today, but there are still secrets of the state (and secrets of critical and literary theory) that need to be attended to.

Is surface reading a form of postsecrecy? In some cases, such as the hyperreading discussed by N. Katherine Hayles in *How We Think* (2012), surface reading seems to more fully acknowledge the coevolution of human and technological readers. That is, it might acknowledge the posthuman(ist) position that readers occupy today, which is essential if we are to understand and harness the networked, distributed nature of agency in postsecrecy. In addition, surface reading certainly seems to ask critics to approach texts in ethical ways, free from an already decided politics. This is all to the good. But in asking critics to approach texts without prejudice, Best and Marcus also demand that critics remain neutral once there. Some ethical decisions might take us toward, not away from, politics. Equally, what their footnote belies is that it may not be so easy to separate postideological open secrets from political secrets. And if we stop performing symptomatic readings of texts altogether, might we miss secrets in other realms?

Surface reading wants to be postsecret in a sense I am not using here: to be beyond a concern with secrets. But what Best and Marcus (2009) find, as their footnote suggests, is that there is no such beyond. Besides, there might be something paranoid about detecting, everywhere, paranoid reading. If postsecrecy is a working through of the hold that secrecy and transparency have over us, then postsecret reading would be one that negotiates the demands of depth and surface. It would need to avoid the worst excesses of symptomatic reading: the self-aggrandizement of the heroic detective-critic and approaching texts already knowing what one wants to find. Yet it would need to be attuned to the irreducible excess or remainder that nevertheless haunts a text because a surface is a limit point that reaches both upward and downward. The ethical decision of the reader is a decision that can take us above or below, or above and below, to follow what presents itself and that which cannot, and to consider the relationship between them.

*Postsecret Access*

While chapter 6 was interested in Acéphale and Tiqqun for the way they used secrecy, such groups, along with WikiLeaks, also offer examples of different kinds of publishing collectives. As such, they charged themselves with making decisions about what, when, and how to share knowledge and information, as well as what, when, and how to hold it back. Today, such decision making is becoming marginalized by norms of open access. Making one's work open access is heralded as the progressive way of sharing data, knowledge, and research. For example, U.K. Research and Innovation (formerly known as Research Council U.K.), a body that works with universities, research organizations, businesses, charities, and government, managing those bodies that award research grants, has embedded open access in its core values (RCUK 2018). Indeed, open access has become a condition of much research funding and is a stipulation of the United Kingdom's Research Excellence Framework exercise for any journal articles that hope to be included in a university's submission to it.

Gary Hall has tirelessly challenged standard ways of conceptualizing open access while applying the tenets of open access in more radical ways. For example, he remarks on the way in which open access is mostly envisaged and discussed in terms of how it augments scholarly publishing in traditional codex books, and consequently the way in which scholarly disciplines are imagined and organized. Open access, he notes, "is understood largely in terms of providing an increase in the amount of material that can be stored, the number of people who have access to it, the potential impact of that material, the range of distribution, the ease of information retrieval, reductions in staffing, production and reproduction costs and so forth. The argument then usually focuses on whether different aspects of this transformation can be considered to be a 'good' or a 'bad' thing" (2008, 10). To push forward the debate about digital open access, Hall calls for a rigorous consideration of how the unfixed and ephemeral nature of digital texts, "their undermining of the boundaries separating authors, editors, producers, users, consumers, humans and machines," and their ability to include and fuse sound, still and moving images "contain the potential, not merely to remediate older media forms, and thus deliver a preexisting and more-or-less unchanged content, albeit in a new way, but to transform fundamentally that content, and with it our relationship to knowledge" (10). Therefore, there might not be anything particularly or inherently radical about sharing knowledge through open access (even if this is more desirable than knowledge silos). What is radical about digital open access texts is that they have the potential to intervene in political-institutional pressures and legal frameworks placed on cultural production—and to alter ideological assumptions about what a text and an author can and should do and mean.

In order to experiment with such possibilities, a team led by Hall, of which I was a part, developed two series of online books. The first was named Liquid Books and the second Living Books About Life.[3] The books were made available on both a gratis (free) and libre (reuse) basis. While gratis is the more common incarnation of academic sharing, libre is the more contentious, "despite the fact that the ability to *re-use* material is actually an essential feature of what has become known as the Budapest–Bethesda–Berlin (BBB) definition of open access, which is one of the major agreements underlying the movements" (Adema and Hall 2013, 152). In addition to being available to read and reuse, Liquid Books and Living Books About Life are designed to give users the opportunity to reedit, rewrite, annotate, translate, and add to them in a shared, distributed, or networked model of authorship/curatorship. As the books link to and organize other open access materials across the internet, users can offer new links or reorganize the existing links into new themes. Such plasticity is enabled by the wiki platform. As an intervention into monetized forms of academic sharing qua publishing as well as an intervention into accepted forms of sharing in the guise of standard open access, these books were open on a read/write basis. Postsecrecy in this context would mean a reevaluation of sharing and openness (by pushing open access to its limits). It prompts self-examination on the part of scholars as to our role and investment in knowledge production, intellectual property, notions of authorship, and the political economy of circulation and distribution.

There will also be times when repositories and archives will need to resist such radical openness. Thinking about indigenous claims on and practices with knowledge, Kimberly Christen worries that "the celebration of openness, something that began as a reaction to corporate greed and the legal straightjacketing of creative works, has resulted in a *limited vocabulary* with which to discuss the ethical and cultural parameters of information circulation and access in the digital realm" (2012, 2874). Her experience of working on a free open source content management system to cater to the needs of indigenous peoples led her to conclude that such systems need to endorse ethical sharing. This meant developing information circulation that mirrors and respects the relational knowledge management of indigenous users. Against the edict that information should be free, a culturally dominant notion that Christen carefully critiques, access is not open by default but rather is restricted by local cultural protocols. The "Feminist Data Manifest-No" develops further a data science that respects indigeneity (Cifor et al. 2019). It is important to create databases and archives that enact secrecy and transparency—when we think of these as forms of information management—in ways that are attuned to cultural specificity, needs, and experience. I want to encapsulate such careful decision making (whether enacted by digital protocols and architecture, human cognition, or some combination of the two) in the face of culturally and politically contextual data, knowledge, and information by the term "secretarial ethics."

### Secretarial Ethics

The institutional experience of the modern British academic includes logging and tracking time through the Transparency Review Approach to Costing (TRAC) Time Allocation Survey (TAS); having annual performance reviews in which one's output is accounted for and goals set; having lectures recorded by Lecture Capture; having student feedback aggregated and collated; being assessed in the National Student Survey; having one's institution ranked in various league tables; and being subject to the auditing practices of the Research Excellence Framework and the Teaching Excellence Framework. The rise of audit culture in British universities is not a neutral process, but has accompanied "the transformation of the traditional liberal and Enlightenment idea of the university as a place of higher learning into the modern idea of the university as corporate enterprise whose primary concern is with market share, servicing the needs of commerce, maximizing economic return and investment, and gaining competitive advantage in the 'Global Knowledge Economy'" (Shore 2008, 282). In constantly reminding ourselves of this manifestation of neoliberalism, it becomes clear that our acquiescence to these processes of audit is a political matter. I am not suggesting that such auditing measures are greater than those implemented in other lines of work (I am sure it is less, and with fewer consequences). Nor am I claiming that they are more burdensome to academics than to those in other professions. Rather, I want to emphasize the way in which these often benign-looking transparency measures are ill-equipped to streamline or optimize an education and research environment supposed to produce intangible qualities such as critical thinking, as well as how their demands (and the market logic in which they are rooted) require academics who want to maintain integrity and intellectual autonomy to resort to forms of secrecy.

Sara Ahmed writes about her experience of this culture and the resulting necessity of knowing when to keep silent and when to keep certain things out of sight. In circumstances when speaking and revealing can be co-opted by empty rhetoric rather than ethics, silence and secrecy are strategies of resistance and displays of resilience. To illustrate, she recalls her involvement with producing a race equality action plan for her university at the behest of the Race Relations Amendment Act of 2001. Although she took great care to avoid writing a "happy diversity document" (2010, xviii), instead foregrounding whiteness as institutional, because the document was deemed "excellent," the vice chancellor interpreted this as meaning the university was succeeding in terms of racial equality. Ahmed reminds us that "documents that aim to reveal can be used to conceal what they reveal" (xviii). Consequently, she invokes the figure of the secretary to symbolize the need for discretion and secretion: "A secretary is one who is entrusted with secrets. Sometimes we need to keep the secrets and be worth this trust. Sometimes we need not to keep the secrets with which we are entrusted even if this means we become untrustworthy. What we do with what we are entrusted—whether we speak or keep silent—remains an important question" (xx). The secretary is therefore a model for those who see themselves as having to make a decision about when revealing, sharing, or acquiescing to transparency measures in institutional settings reinforces a politics that does not offer an equitable distribution of the sensible. Secretarial ethics are a form of postsecrecy.

Beyond the academy, one of my favorite examples of this kind of secretarial ethics (manifested as retreat) comes from the early twentieth century, when three to four thousand British suffragettes hid from enumerators during census night on April 2, 1911, which Jill Liddington (2014) terms "vanishing for the vote." Emily Davison, for example, hid in a cupboard inside the parliament building to avoid being part of a biopolitical exercise authorized by a government for which she could not vote. The militant Women's Social and Political Union (WSPU) hired the Aldwych roller-skating rink for an all-night session to avoid going home. The rink is no longer there, but its former location is across from my office. I always think of those suffragettes when walking down the grand curve of the Aldwych to class. The boycotters constituted only a fraction of the citizens included on the census, and the government declared the disruption negligible, but Liddington wagers that the protest, along with the lack of punitive action taken by the government, emboldened the movement in the months to come. Beyond statistics, she writes, there is a more important story. We should, she thinks, focus on the courage of those who did participate: "Prospective boycotters were right up against the Edwardian state, which had already rigorously pursued tax-resisters and forcibly fed suffragettes. We now know that not a single boycotter was dragged through the courts. On census night, they did not. So that perhaps three to four thousand women were prepared to take this risk remains indeed remarkable" (Liddington 2014, 232). These suffragettes entered the political realm of visibility when they had to, and they knew how to grab a headline, but they (visibly) retreated from being counted when doing so would optimize and bolster a system that offered them citizenship without adequate representation.

### Postsecret Sharing

Sharing suggests equitability and democratization, but, as I have shown in chapter 4, shares are not equally distributed, and access to data is compromised by certain conditions of access and the necessity for mediation and translation. At times we will need to demand meaningful, contextualized transparency about auditing measures carried out under the guise of progressive transparency. At other times, we may need to use collective withdrawal from the *dispositifs* that bind us. A right to opacity here means the right to refrain from sharing in, and being understood according to, a distribution that we may not support.

I want to end this book by summarizing what it is that academics can do to "cut well": deciding when, where, and how to share, and when to be guided by an ethic of openness and when to affirm a right to opacity even in the act of research and analysis. Again, I hope that some of this resonates with those in other contexts. As I point out above, we can adopt a radical approach to open access that goes beyond disseminating research to introduce forms of collaborative, radically open work. At the same time, we need to be mindful of the times when and places where a universal application of openness and open access to archives of, for example, indigenous information and knowledge violates the very people whom such archives are meant to serve. We can develop postsecret reading practices that avoid blindly repeating ideology critique while still being attuned to the opaque operations and erasures of discursive power. We can use a secretarial ethics in our institutional settings. In more general terms, we should not place too much faith in revelation or exposé alone, particularly given that this is the favored mode of both trustworthy and untrustworthy "news" sources, and sharing such revelations online accrues value for the platforms we use. We should contextualize and problematize invocations of openness and transparency. Finally, we should intervene in, rather than accept, dominant conditions of visibility.

In this reattunement of scholarship and practice, and in the echoes it can have beyond the university, sharing can be politicized through understanding it as a series of decisions and cuts. In a conjuncture that places a premium on the knowability and surveillability—that is, the transparency—of subjects, in which everyone must share her data and must come forth and be understood as data, imaginative cuts into shareveillance and experiments with and commitments to postsecrecy become ethical, political acts.

# ACKNOWLEDGMENTS

The acknowledgments in my first book were relatively short. A great deal more life has been lived during the germination and writing of this one. I've been thinking about this book during some of the most fulfilling and depleting experiences of my life. Many of the people I want to thank have been there through both.

First, I would like to extend my gratitude to those who have offered various forms of hands-on help as I undertook this project, whether in its current book form or in previous incarnations: Paul Myerscough, Matthew Potolsky, Amia Srinivasan, Emmanuel Alloa, Robert Smith, Neil Badmington, Ryan Bishop, Jem Gilbert, Joanna Zylinska, Gary Hall, and of course Doug Armato, Danielle Kasprzak, Zenyse Miller, and Mike Stoffel at the University of Minnesota Press.

I have been lucky enough to have made connections with excellent scholars in emerging intellectual subfields such as visibility studies, secrecy studies, conspiracy studies, and critical transparency studies. I thank all of them for taking me in different directions in this interdisciplinary project: Mark Fenster, Mikkel Flyverbom, Cynthia Stohl, Michael Stohl, Peter Knight, Tim Melley, Stefanos Geroulanos, Zach Blas, Jack Bratich, Susan Maret, Eva Horn, Michael Butter, Stef Aupers, Todor Histrov, Vian Bakir, and Greg Seigworth.

A number of people helped me to think about how I could put some of the more abstract ideas of this project into practice: Burak Arikan, Seb Franklin, Seda Gersus, James Smithies, Christopher Stewart, and Peter Woodbridge.

Thank you to my truly exceptional English department colleagues at King's College London, who are generously tolerant of my decidedly extraliterary interests. I extend special thanks to Janet Floyd, Richard Kirkland, and Anna Snaith, all of whom have headed the department during my time there, and to King's College London for a sabbatical that helped me write this book. I also want to thank Uta Balbier, who was the best colleague and confidant in the smallest research institute in the history of academia (RIP the Institute of North American Studies!).

I benefited enormously from the high-quality discussions in my MA course "Cultures of Secrecy" over the past few years. I have also been kept on my toes by the brilliant PhD candidates at King's (particularly Emily Brown, Rafael Lubner, Emily Montford, Christine Okoth, and Nadia Binti Rasidi). Beyond my own institution, I am grateful to everyone who has invited me to speak at academic, cultural, and policy-oriented institutions and those who came to listen and ask questions.

And because research does not happen in an ivory tower, I also want to thank people in my nonworking life.

Thank you to Stephen Armstrong for being my co-conspirator.

For open homes and hearts, I thank Polly Russell, Steve Rose, Dick and Mandy Russell, Julia Walsh, Jeremy Hayward, Louise Dodds, Caitlin Pitts, Sophie Smith, Amia Srinivasan, Paul Myerscough, Richard Vine, Robyn Pierce, Lucy Pope, Angela Martin, Nick McDowell, Hilary Cottam, Nigel Carter, Emma Kane, James Althaus, Anne Mensah, Kelly Sparks, Matt Herbert, Jay James, Victoria Hobbs, Clara Waissbein, Lola Oliyide, Esther Smith, and Zoë Compston.

For reminding me that "it is joy to be hidden, but disaster not to be found," as Donald Winnicott puts it, I want to thank Georgina.

Thank you to my parents, stepparents, siblings, and extended family for unconditional everything.

It would be remiss of me not to thank everyone who has picked up my kid, fed my kid, taught my kid, and loved my kid when I was too busy or tired to do it myself. It takes a village—or in my case, a city.

And last, I want to thank the kid herself—Eden—who is no longer such a kid, for trusting me with at least some of her secrets.

# NOTES

## Introduction

1. The workshop was called "Visible Mediations of Transparency: Changing Norms and Practices," held at King's College London, September 8, 2015. It was the fourth in a series of events, overseen by Vian Bakir, funded by the British Economic and Social Research Council; see http://data-psst.bangor.ac.uk/index.php.en.

2. In using this example, I want to leave aside the political hue of the claim for Catalan independence. Independence claims of this kind often operate beyond the left–right axis because on the one hand, any claim for autonomy can be read as a challenge to centralized power, but on the other, forms of essentialist identification or nationalist patriotism displace one another. Moreover, in Catalonia, the case for autonomy has often centered on the perceived unfairness of this relatively prosperous region paying more in taxes than it receives in funding, whereas poorer regions, such as Andalucía, receive more in funding than they contribute (Hinks 2017). The case for increased autonomy can be made by the left and right. Rather than supporting Catalan independence per se, then, we could see Xnet's intervention as protecting the right to have a say in the future of the region, whichever way the citizens of Catalonia voted, once the referendum had been called.

3. In not capitalizing "internet," I am heeding a point made by Mikkel Flyverbom: "Just like it would seem puzzling to talk about the Electricity or the Railway, it may be time to decapitalize the internet, and maybe even to leave the term behind. As technological innovations become integrated into our daily lives, we need to stop thinking of them as separate and grandiose" (2019, 27–28).

4. The European Commission's (2004) so-called Transparency Directive states: "Efficient, transparent and integrated securities markets

contribute to a genuine single market in the Community and foster growth and job creation by better allocation of capital by reducing costs."

5. For an etymology that emphasizes transparency's optical meanings and how these became associated with religious connotations, see Geroulanos (2017, 31–34).

6. Seb Franklin shifts the coordinates of this debate by offering an account of digitality as "a social logic that reaches beyond computational technologies" (2015, xxii). Thought as a process of discretization, digitality renders life "intelligible as value-creating labor" (19), which is an ever-expanding process under the logic of "control" (27).

7. I use the term "securitization" in this book after the meaning given by the Copenhagen school of security studies: the performative invocation of "security" in a way that socially constructs all kinds of issues as public threats (Wæver 1995).

8. I discuss this openness to openness in relation to radical transparency at the end of chapter 3.

## 1. The Changing Fortunes of Secrecy and Openness

1. Some countries implemented freedom of information laws earlier than the United States (Sweden in 1766 and Finland in 1951), but as Schudson (2015) points out, they did not have the same global influence.

2. In his *Annals* from 109 BCE, Tacitus describes Gaius Sallustius Crispus urging discretion and secrecy to Tiberias in the face of the murder Augustus's grandson. See Horn (2011).

3. By "statistics," Foucault is referring to "knowledge of the state, of the forces and resources that characterize a state at a given moment. For example: knowledge of the population, the measure of its quantity, mortality, natality; reckoning of the different categories of individuals in a state and of their wealth; assessment of the potential wealth available to the state, mines and forests, etcetera; assessment of the wealth in circulation, of the balance of trade, and measure of the effects of taxes and duties, all this data, and more besides" (2007, 354).

4. The production of secrecy discourse and its attendant ironies, not least in announcing and making visible that which is being labeled secret, is the dominant theme of a long entry on "secrecy" in the *Dictionary of Gnosis and Western Esotericism* (de Jong, Fanger, and Faivre 2006) split into three historical periods. Across the different sections, the contributors grapple with the tension between concealment and revelation played out in the desire to record and disseminate "secrets" in textual form.

5. When I look at the obfuscation used by privacy activists today in later

chapters, we will see this early tactical play with opacity repurposed for a digital era.

6. The esoteric secret knowledges Jütte is interested in are perhaps not easily compared to the military and security secrets of the state that preoccupy contemporary debates about secrecy. However, Jütte himself addresses this when he remarks, "Throughout the early modern period, secret knowledge often led Jews into the realm of the *arcana imperii*—especially when they were in contact with political authorities or with the courts of the nobility" (2015, 258).

7. In a history commissioned by the Central Intelligence Agency, P. K. Rose (2007) honors three patriots as the founding fathers of American intelligence: Franklin for covert action, Jay for counterintelligence, and Washington for acquisition of foreign intelligence.

8. Fenster puts it like this: "Transparency advocates had every reason to push for disclosure because the American constitutional system did not by itself solve the problem of bureaucratic information hoarding" (2017a, 64). However, here he is discussing transparency advocacy in the Nixon era.

9. At the same time he was extolling the virtues of openness, Wilson controlled information, creating pockets of opacity, through the Espionage Act (1917) and the Sedition Act (1918) during World War I (Schwarz 2015). Perhaps most controversially, he conducted the Paris Peace Conference behind closed doors even while advocating his fourteen points, which damned secrecy in diplomacy.

10. On the back of the FOIA, the Government in the Sunshine Act (1976) ensured that executive branch agencies hold open meetings. Other important legislation that placed value on openness include the Legislative Reorganization Act (1970), which approved continuous live television coverage of the chambers, and the Presidential Records Act (1978), which instituted public ownership of the official records of presidents and vice presidents.

11. An article in *Time* about the Roper Center's report notes, "There is no single question set that the center was able to use to trace feelings about transparency throughout the 50-year history of the FOIA: questions about the same topic (how much information should the government share with the people?) are phrased as matters of national security, size of government, press freedom or personal privacy, depending on the context" (Rothman 2016). We can tell much about the era and its concerns from the different ways in which questions about secrecy and openness are asked.

12. There are important precursors to *The Real World,* including *Candid Camera* (which began in 1948 and originally aired on ABC), cinema verité, activist films of the American counterculture, documentaries like *An American Family* (1973, PBS), and even Andy Warhol's Factory films (Quellette 2016).

13. This monopoly is perhaps only rivaled by the opaque practices and technologies of certain private sectors such as big tech, fossil fuels, pharmaceuticals, or medical insurance, each with its own way of praising transparency while operationalizing secrecy.

## 2. Information Imaginaries

1. OpenTheGovernment.org, 2009, "Secrecy Report Card 09," https://www.openthegovernment.org/sites/default/files/otg/SecrecyRC_2009.pdf.

2. "About," Data.gov, https://www.data.gov/about.

3. Beyond the United States, a report commissioned by the United Kingdom Cabinet Office explicitly states that one intention from the data released as part of its Transparency Agenda is to support the development of "social entrepreneurs" (O'Hara 2011, 5). In his foreword to "Open Data White Paper: Unleashing the Potential," presented to the British parliament in 2012, Francis Maude includes "demonstrating the value of open governance to economic growth" before "improved citizen engagement and empowerment" (5) when explaining the priorities of the British chairmanship of the Open Data Partnership, the motto of which is "transparency drives prosperity."

4. This is not the whole story. There are, for example, some potentially revealing apps made possible by freely available data that highlight possible connections between donations and votes (e.g., Greenhouse, http://allaregreen.us/). However, Lawrence Lessig (2009) argues that even the latter are greatly limited: "All the data in the world will not tell us whether a particular contribution bent a result by securing a vote or an act that otherwise would not have occurred."

5. Donald Trump signed presidential Executive Order 13823 on "Protecting America through Lawful Detention of Terrorists" (https://www.hsdl.org/?abstract&did=807881) on January 30, 2018, to keep the Guantánamo Bay facility open.

6. This noncompliance continued under the Trump administration (Aftergood 2018).

7. To this list of "transparency controversies," Mark Fenster adds "the Internal Revenue Service's secret targeting of Tea Party groups' tax exempt status; . . . and the response by the State Department and Central Intelligence Agency to the fatal attack of the U.S. Embassy in Benghazi, Libya" (2017a, 7).

8. I am thinking here of significant revelations such as the *Access Hollywood* recordings of Trump's derogatory remarks about women during the presidential race and witness testimonies during Trump's impeachment trial in 2020 from Gordon Sondland, who was at the time the U.S. ambassador

to the European Union, and career diplomat William B. Taylor Jr., among others, that Trump had directed a quid pro quo for military aid in Ukraine.

9. While we should allow for the possibility of differential nonresponse bias, a phenomenon that sees poll changes as caused by shifts in who responds to pollsters rather than a reflection of changes in public opinion, a Gallup poll conducted during the waning days of the impeachment process and released on February 4, 2020, saw Trump's job approval rating reach 49 percent. His rating among Republicans rose to 94 percent—up six percentage points from January 2020.

10. The transition period between administrations saw a flurry of interventions that involved transparency advocates, political historians, archivists, and environmental activists backing up federal data sets and Web pages for fear that a Trump administration would remove what was available (Gerstein 2016).

11. A White House report about a 2017 open data roundtable claims, "The Trump Administration expects that entire new ecosystems of businesses will prosper as agencies unlock data. Fueled by government data, entrepreneurs, and innovators will use open data for new ventures that create real-world value and American jobs" (White House 2017b).

12. The first initiative—to "publish a comprehensive federal data strategy"—was included in the President's Management Agenda in March 2018. The fifth—to "create agency-level chief data officers"—featured in the bipartisan OPEN Government Data Act of January 2019.

13. For example, on February 17, 2017, Trump tweeted, "The FAKE NEWS media . . . is not my enemy, it is the enemy of the American People!" And on July 19, 2018: "The Summit with Russia was a great success, except with the enemy of the people, the Fake News Media" (Twitter, @realDonaldTrump).

14. "Conspiracy theorist in chief" is the phrase that Tim Murphy (2016) uses.

15. For an insightful discussion of the play between the literal and the figural in conspiracy thinking, see Knight (2000).

## 3. Opaque Openness

1. See also Cukierman (2009), Lord (2006), and Tsoukas (1997).

2. The authors also recognize some programs that have been a success, such as restaurant hygiene initiatives in California.

3. Other commentators question the assumed link between transparency and trust with different emphases. Haridimos Tsoukas claims that "making more information on an expert system publicly available entails that

more opportunities for conflicting interpretations are created, and so it is less likely for trust to be achieved" (1997, 835). Similarly, Hood (2006b) points out that although it is impossible to prove that increased transparency results in less trust, we can say that the recorded decline of trust in government after 1970 indicates that, contrary to the claims of transparency advocates, there is no correspondence between increased transparency and trust. See also Hirschi (2018).

4. I will revisit and expand on this idea of the neoliberal *dispositif* in the following chapter in relation to Deleuze's thesis on the control society.

5. The case of France, which maintains a much closer relationship between intellectual and political life, is perhaps an exception to this, and Geroulanos (2017) accounts for why this might be the case. Even in contemporary French politics, however, Emmanuel Macron pays lip service to the Anglo-American rhetoric of transparency.

6. Geroulanos (2017) also considers Derrida within his cohort of postwar French thinkers who problematize transparency. He prioritizes Derrida's thoughts on *archē* writing and the idea that any form of inscription, including speech, is marked by violence, for it challenges the proposition that some forms of relation and communication can be transparent and authentic. See Derrida ([1967] 1997) and Geroulanos (2017).

7. I recognize that there are more positive accounts of globalization that focus on the ways in which local cultures resist, negotiate, and appropriate imported cultural texts and practices, giving more weight to reception and consumption than the power relations of production (e.g., Liebes and Katz 1990). Equally, the complexity of global flows that has been highlighted by Appadurai (1996) as well as by Deleuze and Guattari (1987) means that the homogenization feared by some proponents of the cultural imperialism thesis is impossible.

8. These contributions to CKAN are tracked on the Open Government Platform (OGPL) website (http://ogpl.github.io/tools/ckan-en.html).

9. Looking at the other term this book is concerned with—secrecy—we could offer a similar analysis of surveillance imperialism. Privacy International published a report in summer 2018 exposing the extent of the transfer of electronic surveillance capabilities around the globe: "Many of the recipient countries and agencies have a documented history of human rights abuses, meaning that in many cases, without appropriate safeguards and accountability, such assistance can facilitate gross abuses" (84).

10. Todd Sanders and Harry G. West usefully discuss transparency "as a key-word component to ideoscapes that travel the globe conveying notions fundamental to the operative logic of globalizing economic and political institutions" (2003, 10).

11. It is important to recall that WikiLeaks could receive and facilitate leaks from those who might benefit politically, but that does not necessarily mean that WikiLeaks shared the aims of those that did.

12. WikiLeaks, "What Is WikiLeaks," November 3, 2015, https://wikileaks.org/What-is-Wikileaks.html.

13. Citizen Ex, http://citizen-ex.com/.

14. Graph Commons, "About," https://graphcommons.com/about.

15. "My Facebook Invoice," https://docs.google.com/forms/d/e/1FAIpQLSfKtqRF8tTEJ3mzz7YhjvTmZQ72JyG9tbQ0mQIhTna73o0ciQ/viewform.

16. See Ahmed (2010) and my discussion of her framing in the Conclusion of this book.

## 4. Shareveillance

1. The "Feminist Data Manifest-No" (Cifor et al. 2019) is incisive on how and why experiences and markers of oppression need to be taken into account when assessing the ethicality of data collection, analysis, and scholarship.

2. The Open Data Institute in the United Kingdom, which works with public and private entities promoting innovation through open data, defines closed data as "data that can only be accessed by its subject, owner or holder" (Broad 2015).

3. This is not an unproblematic borrowing. The roots of Glissant's phrase in critical race theory are often erased and underplayed when invoked in other contexts. I would like to thank Zach Blas for introducing me to Glissant's thought some years ago and for questioning its use in different contexts.

4. It is not within the scope of this book to address the extra- or predigital history of sharing, but as Russell Belk writes, it is "likely the oldest type of consumption" (2010, 730).

5. Digital Keywords is a forum hosted by the University of Tulsa, which took inspiration from the fortieth anniversary of Raymond Williams's 1976 *Keywords* (http://culturedigitally.org/digital-keywords/). The entries were then published in a collection for Princeton University Press (Peters 2016).

6. Armitage made these comments during a response he gave at an event centered on James Bridle at the Whitechapel Gallery, "Systems Literacy," on January 29, 2016.

7. Instagram, "Data Policy," modified April 19, 2018, available via the Internet Archive (https://web.archive.org/web/20180423111924/https://help.instagram.com/519522125107875).

8. The covert collection of closed data transcends national boundaries. While we may make conscious or unconscious trade-offs with the nation-state in which we reside, we make no such deal with foreign surveillants. In terms of foreign state data surveillance, concern periodically arises around particular technologies—for example, Chinese-owned Huawei's 5G wireless and Byte-Dance's TikTok, or FaceApp from the Russian tech firm Wireless Lab. While surveillance capitalist practices mean that commercial data extraction can take place across national boundaries (although regulation like the European Union's GDPR certainly introduces friction), the panic around 5G, TikTok, and FaceApp are due to the perceived relationship such companies might have with the "hostile" states in which they operate rather than commercial uses of that data. I want to thank Richard Bingham for raising this issue.

9. There is also social value to be gained from the sharing of some big data, such as genomic and other health-related data. I discuss this in relation to the Covid-19 pandemic in the Preface.

10. Because "multitude" encompasses those traditionally excluded from notions of the proletariat (including unwaged laborers, the homeless, the unemployed, and members of the so-called underclass), Seb Franklin is concerned that Hardt and Negri's concept falls into the trap of valorizing the excluded and obscuring the difference between "those individuals and groups that are systematically excluded and those that are premised on the intentional evasion of capture" (Franklin 2015, 167). Franklin points out the problem of assigning revolutionary status to a surplus that by definition has already been captured by capital before being deemed superfluous. The logic and violence of control to judge the value of life pervades. Franklin looks to Deleuze's "vacuoles of non-communication" as "circuit breakers" that can "elude control" (Deleuze 1995, 175) and to Tiqqun's ([2001] 2009) fog as more promising ideas. He does so because of the ways they foreground "a limit to control that is based on the impossibility of capturing certain phenomena in the first place" (Franklin 2015, 167). I will explore fog and opacity in terms of excess in later chapters, but I will do so alongside a reframing of the multitude as connected through experiences of datafication. The data multitude differs from Hardt and Negri's formulation in that it necessarily acknowledges the reach of control to determine the value of each constituent. All data surplus has been rendered profitable; indeed, data surplus is at the core of data capitalism because it is sold rather than used to optimize the system. To be sure, some data subjects are more valuable than others, but all are valuable in the way they contribute to aggregate data sets.

11. I invoke the figure of the hacker with caution here, not least because the free labor model underlying the hacker ethic has been exploited by big tech. See Wark (2013).

## 5. Aesthetics of the Secret

1. Several relatively recent exhibitions have approached secrecy in direct and indirect ways. For example, Tate Modern's *Exposed: Voyeurism, Surveillance and the Camera* (2010) considered surveillance; the International Centre of Photography's exhibition, *Public, Private, Secret* (2016), considered the relationship between secrecy and social media; *A Secret Service: Art, Compulsion, Concealment* (2007) looked at questions of visibility; *Staging Disorder,* curated by Christopher Stewart and Esther Teichmann (2015), took as its subject secretive military training sites; *For Opacity* (2018) at the Drawing Centre in New York focused on opacity and identity; and the New York Metropolitan Museum of Art's *Everything Is Connected* (2018) focused on conspiracy. Artists who might on occasion be described as working with an aesthetics of the secret, although with different concerns and in a variety of ways, include Rosella Biscotti, Zach Blas, Sophie Calle, James Coupe, Hasan Elahi, Goldin+Senneby, Mishka Henner, Jenny Holzer, Simon Menner, Simon Norfolk, Seth Price, Taryn Simon, and Gillian Wearing.

2. See the Rasmussen Report poll from June 19, 2013 (https://www .rasmussenreports.com/public_content/politics/general_politics/june_ 2013/12_see_nsa_leaker_snowden_as_hero_21_as_traitor).

3. Much of the legislation that followed the Snowden revelations, both in the United States and elsewhere, has not necessarily reduced the state's surveillance capacities but rather has merely legalized what were previously covert, arguably illegal or extralegal, practices. In the United Kingdom, the Data Retention and Investigatory Powers Act of 2014, and its successor, the Investigatory Powers Bill of 2016, known as the Snooper's Charter, authorized far-reaching surveillance. In the United States, the FISA Amendments Reauthorization Act of 2017, Section 702, signed into law by President Trump on January 19, 2018, allows the NSA to continue methods of surveillance that incidentally sweeps data from U.S. citizens who are, by law, protected from warrantless surveillance.

4. The cognitive terms in the table refer to remarks made by Donald Rumsfeld in a Defense Department briefing on February 12, 2002. Although there are potential problems with relying on language from the context of a securitization project (and I do not wish to valorize Rumsfeld's thinking), I invoke it for the way it brings into focus the politics of visibility. Distributions of the sensible are often matters of life and death. Aesthetics is a part of, rather than apart from, that process. I want to thank Renée Ridgway for her thoughts on this.

5. In an added layer to this artwork and its story, the San Francisco Museum of Modern Art initiated a project to recompose the erased picture through infrared scanning technology.

6. This is often cited as the reason why the revelations failed to exercise more citizens. At some level, this argument goes, citizens already understood themselves as surveilled subjects, not least because of the revelations during the Bush administration in 2005 about warrantless wiretapping (Risen and Lichtblau 2005).

## 6. Secrets of the Left

1. Shoshana Zuboff's account of what Eric Schmidt has called Google's hiding strategy confirms that big tech is wedded to secrecy: "Once Google's leadership understood the commercial power of behavioral surplus . . . Google employees were not to speak about what the patent had referred to as its 'novel methods, apparatus, message formats and/or data structures' or confirm any rumors about flowing cash. Hiding was not a post hoc strategy; it was baked into the cake that would become surveillance capitalism" (2019, 88–89).

2. I should reiterate here that transparency is not only championed by liberals. A representative of the libertarian Cato Institute explains the widespread appeal in the United States: "Transparency is a pan-ideological good. Libertarians and conservatives want more transparency to reduce demand for government. Liberals see opportunity to validate government and root-out corruption" (qtd. in Triplett 2010). However, transparency has become predominantly associated with progressive liberalism in the United States and is a prime feature of the current manifestation of liberal democracy.

3. Jack Bratich has an excellent article on these very questions. He too asks, "In an age where secrecy is virtually everywhere as a strategy of domination, can we begin to experiment with an insurgent secrecy, a minor secrecy, or a popular secrecy?" (2007, 47). I am indebted to his thinking on this matter.

4. Leif Wenar writes, "Some may . . . think that a more transparent system is morally better in itself, or that transparency is constitutive of a system that has some other virtue like justice" (2006, 8).

5. Various artists have explored masking to highlight the hegemonic and securitizing function of surveillance. As political gesture, artist Zach Blas developed a series called "Facial Weaponization Suite." This series comprises unreadable masks for communities discriminated against or marked by biometric surveillance. Adam Harvey, another contemporary artist, has created antidrone wear, constructed of fabric that evades the visualizing and identifying capacities of thermal imaging drones (Rhee 2016). Such overtly political art repurposes a long-standing aesthetic interest in masks and their place in ritual, play, or dissembling for the twenty-first century.

6. The KKK is a complex example because, as Alison Kinney (2016) explains, "Anonymity wasn't quite the point: While the hoods could assure their wearers' personal anonymity, their force came from declaring membership in a safe, privileged identity that was anything but secret. The hoods . . . helped rebrand the Klan as a popular, patriotic, money-making, white clubhouse movement."

7. This turn to Tiqqun is perhaps surprising in a (lightly) deconstructive project such as *Radical Secrecy,* given the hostile remarks about deconstruction to be found in *Introduction to Civil War* ([2001] 2010). However, as Tobias C. Van Veen (2010) points out, just after these remarks in sections 57 and 58, Tiqqun adapts the Derridean thesis of supplementarity.

8. This was a very male cohort, although Milo Sweedler (2005) writes engagingly about the simultaneously marginal and central role that Laure (Colette Peignot) played in the secret society.

9. Tiqqun's reference to Empire draws on Hardt and Negri. Tiqqun writes, "Empire is when the means of production have become the means of control and the means of control the means of production" ([2001] 2010, 56).

10. Bey, a pseudonym for Peter Lamborn Wilson, writes, "The TAZ exists not only beyond Control but also beyond definition, beyond gazing and naming as acts of enslaving, beyond the understanding of the State, beyond the State's ability to *see*" (1985, 162).

11. Silent Circle, "Enterprise Mobile Privacy Platform," n.d., https://www.silentcircle.com/products-and-solutions/technology/.

12. Secretbook is no longer available as an extension via app stores or at Campbell-Moore's personal Web pages, but the CNET download site describes it (https://download.cnet.com/Secretbook/3000-33362_4-75902 432.html).

13. Campbell-Moore (2013) does admit that "the goal of this project was to demonstrate a proof of concept of performing steganography on a social network with JPEG recompression, not to provide total security. Hence this application is only suitable for casual users and is totally useless for serious applications such as terrorism since detection would not be difficult for organisations such as the NSA."

14. Felix Stalder makes a similar point about the long relationship between capital and surveillance in a Nettime mailing list post from February 11, 2019.

15. There are other thinkers that I could draw on here, including Maurice Blanchot (1990) and his right to disappear; Foucault and his acknowledgement that although silence and secrecy "are a shelter for power . . . they also loosen its holds and provide for relatively obscure areas of tolerance" (1978, 100–101); and Roland Barthes's "right to be silent—a possibility of keeping

silent" (2005, 23). Nicholas de Villiers (2012) invokes the two latter examples to illustrate how opacity is used as a queering tactic.

16. I thank Rafael Lubner for pressing me on what is at stake in turning to Glissant to understand the digital context, given the latter's technophobic stance (Blas 2018). I also thank Katherine McKittrick for highlighting, in her eloquent readings of Glissant in her Twitter feed (@demonicground) and elsewhere, the risks of such an enterprise.

17. In a statement to the press on the day of Julian Assange's arrest in London, December 7, 2010, his lawyer, Mark Stephens, commented that WikiLeaks is a "virtual journalistic community around the world," indicating that its work could not be halted by the arrest of one person (qtd. in Weaver and Adams 2010). Assange himself had earlier remarked, "The Cablegate archive has been spread . . . to over 100,000 people in encrypted form." He added, "If something happens to us, the key parts will be released automatically." Although Assange's assumption of the role of spokesperson rendered him as an individual far from secret, the structure of secrecy remained an instrumental element of WikiLeaks.

18. OpenLeaks FAQ, archived at https://web.archive.org/web/2012 0607052431/http://www.openleaks.org/content/faq.shtml.

19. Christopher Fynsk, for example, warns, "One cannot work to institute or realize this thought of community" (1991, xi). The idea of an operative inoperative community or of applying Nancy's thought to politics might lead to frustration. But Fynsk also states, "The impossibility of immediately translating this thought into a political program does not dictate political paralysis." Rather, we must "rethink the very concept of political practice" (xi).

20. It should be noted with respect to this issue that Chelsea Manning was only arrested because of a failure in her own ability to keep a secret, not a failure of the WikiLeaks technology to do so. She revealed her intention to leak the classified information to hacker Adrian Lamo, who later informed the FBI.

### Conclusion

1. Chun's 2006 landmark study challenges these coordinates by arguing that for control technology to be sold as freedom, as was the case with the internet, it had to become fictionalized, and freedom had to be reduced to control. As a way out, she draws on the work of Jean-Luc Nancy to argue that freedom always exceeds control.

2. There are many examples to draw on, but perhaps the most telling is Trump's July 14, 2019, tweet that suggested progressive congresswomen

of color should "go back and help fix the totally broken and crime infested places from which they came" (Twitter, @realDonaldTrump).

3. Liquid Books can be found at http://liquidbooks.pbworks.com/w/page/11135951/FrontPage and Living Books About Life at http://www.livingbooksaboutlife.org/. The other series editor for the Living Books About Life project is Joanna Zylinska; members of the project team include Sigi Jöttkandt, David Ottina, and Pete Woodbridge.

# BIBLIOGRAPHY

Adams, John. 1854. *The Works of John Adams, Second President of the United States.* Volume 9. London: Little, Brown.

Adams, Rachel. 2017. "The Creation of 'A World after Its Own Image': A Genealogy of Transparency." PhD diss., University of Cape Town.

Adema, Janneka, and Gary Hall. 2013. "The Political Nature of the Book: Artists' Books and Radical Open Access." *New Formations* 78:138–56.

Adorno, Theodor. (1951) 1974. *Minima Moralia: Reflections from Damaged Life.* Translated by Edmund F. N. Jephcott. London: Verso.

Adorno, Theodor, and Max Horkheimer. (1944) 2002. *Dialectic of Enlightenment.* Translated by Edmund F. N. Jephcott. Stanford, Calif.: Stanford University Press.

Aftergood, Steven. 2009. "Reducing Government Secrecy: Finding What Works." *Yale Law and Policy Review* 27 (2): 399–416.

Aftergood, Steven. 2018. "Secrecy about Secrecy: The State Secrets Privilege." *Secrecy News,* June 20, 2018. https://fas.org/blogs/secrecy/2018/06/state-secrets-reporting/.

Aftergood, Steven. 2019. "White House Rebuffs Declassification, Disclosure Requirements." Federation of American Scientists, December 23, 2019. https://fas.org/blogs/secrecy/2019/12/white-house-rebuffs/.

Agrippa, Cornelius. (1510) 1992. *De Occulta Philosophia Libri Tres.* Edited by V. Perronne Compagni. Leiden: Brill.

Ahmed, Sara. 2010. Foreword to *Secrecy and Silence in the Research Process: Feminist Reflections,* edited by Róisín Ryan-Flood and Rosalind Gill, xvi–xxi. London: Routledge.

Alloa, Emmanuel. 2018. "Transparency: A Magic Concept of Modernity." In Alloa and Thomä 2018b, 21–56.

Alloa, Emmanuel, and Dieter Thomä. 2018a. "Transparency: Thinking Through an Opaque Concept." In Alloa and Thomä 2018b, 1–14.

Alloa, Emmanuel, and Dieter Thomä, eds. 2018b. *Transparency, Society, and Subjectivity: Critical Perspectives.* London: Palgrave.

Althusser, Louis. 1971. "Ideology and Ideological State Apparatuses." In *Lenin and Philosophy, and Other Essays.* Translated by B. Brewster, 127–88. London: New Left.

Anburajan, Aswini. 2007. "Obama Open to Limited Legalization." MSNBC, November 25, 2007. Available via the Internet Archive, https://web .archive.org/web/20071126054403/http://firstread.msnbc.msn.com/ archive/2007/11/25/479649.aspx.

Andrejevic, Mark, and Kelly Gates. 2014. "Big Data Surveillance: Introduction." *Surveillance and Society* 12 (2): 185–96. https://doi.org/10.24908/ ss.v12i2.5242.

Appadurai, Arjun. 1996. *Modernity at Large: Cultural Dimensions of Globalization.* Minneapolis: University of Minnesota Press.

Arendt, Hannah. (1967) 2000. "Truth and Politics." In *The Portable Hannah Arendt,* edited by Peter Baehr, 545–75. New York: Penguin.

Armstrong, Stephen. 2017. "Catalonia Plots Digital Government in Exile in Bid for Independence." *Wired,* October 9, 2017. https://www.wired .co.uk/article/catalan-government-independence-internet-spain.

Assange, Julian. 2006. "State and Terrorist Conspiracies." http://cryptome .org/0002/ja-conspiracies.pdf.

Assange, Julian. 2010. "Don't Shoot the Messenger for Revealing Uncomfortable Truths." *Australian,* December 8, 2010. https://www.theaus tralian.com.au/.

Associated Press. 2009. "White House Will Publicly Release Visitor Blogs." *Guardian,* September 4, 2009. https://www.theguardian.com/.

Attridge, Derek. 2011. *Reading and Responsibility: Deconstruction's Traces.* Edinburgh: Edinburgh University Press.

Bacon, Francis. 1826. *The Works of Francis Bacon, Baron of Verulam, Viscount St. Alban, and Lord High Chancellor of England.* Volume 1. London: F. C. and J. Rivington.

Badmington, Neil. 2006. "Cultural Studies and the Post-human(ities)." In *New Cultural Studies: Adventures in Theory,* edited by Clare Birchall and Gary Hall, 260–72. Edinburgh: Edinburgh University Press.

Bailey, Dennis. 2004. *The Open Society Paradox: Why the Twenty-First Century Calls for More Openness, Not Less.* Washington, D.C.: Brassey's.

Bailyn, Bernard. 1967. *The Ideological Origins of the American Revolution.* Cambridge, Mass.: Belknap.

Barder, Owen. 2010. "Transparency Will Make Aid Work Better." *Guardian,* December 21, 2010. https://www.theguardian.com/.

Barnett, Jim. 2010. "WikiLeaks and a Failure of Transparency." Nieman Jour-

nalism Lab, Harvard University, July 29, 2010. https://www.niemanlab
.org/2010/07/wikileaks-and-a-failure-of-transparency/.

Barone, Siegfried D. 2006. *Secrecy in the Bush Administration.* New York:
Nova.

Barthes, Roland. 2005. *The Neutral: Lecture Course at the Collège de France,
1977–1978.* Translated by Rosalind E. Krauss and Denis Hollier. New
York: Columbia University Press.

Bataille, Georges. (1967) 2013. *The Accursed Share: Volume 1.* Translated by
Robert Hurley. New York: Zone Books.

Bataille, Georges. 1970. *Oeuvres Complètes, Volume 1.* Paris: Gallimard.

Bataille, Georges, Roger Caillois, Michel Leiris, Pierre Klossowski, and
André Masson. 2018. *The Sacred Conspiracy: The Internal Papers of the
Secret Society of Acéphale and Lectures to the College of Sociology.* Edited
by Marina Galletti and Alasdair Brotchie. Translated by Natasha Lehrer,
John Harman, and Meyer Barash. London: Atlas.

Baudrillard, Jean. 1983. *Simulations.* Los Angeles: Semiotext(e).

Baudrillard, Jean. 1990. *Fatal Strategies.* Los Angeles: Semiotext(e).

Baume, Sandrine. 2011. "Transparency in the Handling of Public Affairs:
Origins and Meaning of a Requirement." Paper presented at the First
Global Conference on Transparency Research, Rutgers University,
Newark, N.J., May 19–20, 2011.

Baume, Sandrine. 2018. "Publicity and Transparency: The Itinerary of a
Subtle Distinction." In Alloa and Thomä 2018b, 203–24.

Beck, John. 2014. "The Purloined Landscape: Photography and Power in
the American West." *Tate Papers,* no. 21, April 3, 2014. https://www.tate
.org.uk/research/publications/tate-papers/21/the-purloined-landscape
-photography-and-power-in-the-american-west#footnoteref15_x49lu42.

Belk, Russell. 2010. "Sharing." *Journal of Consumer Research* 36 (5): 715–34.

Benkler, Yochai. 2006. *The Wealth of Networks: How Social Production Transforms Markets and Freedom.* New Haven, Conn.: Yale University Press.

Bennington, Geoffrey. 2011. "Kant's Open Secret." *Theory, Culture, and Society* 28 (7–8): 26–40.

Bentham, Jeremy. (1790) 1843. "Bentham's Draught for the Organization of
Judicial Establishments." In *The Works of Jeremy Bentham,* edited by John
Bowering, 4:305–406. Edinburgh: William Tait.

Bentham, Jeremy. (1791) 1843. "Panopticon; or The Inspection-House." In
*The Works of Jeremy Bentham,* edited by John Bowering, 4:37–172. Edinburgh: William Tait.

Bentham, Jeremy. (1791) 1999. *The Collected Works of Jeremy Bentham: Political Tactics.* Edited by Michael James, Cyprian Blamires, and Cathering
Pease-Watson. Oxford: Oxford University Press.

Best, Stephen, and Sharon Marcus. 2009. "Surface Reading: An Introduction." *Representations* 108 (1): 1–21.

Bey, Hakim. 1985. *TAZ: The Temporary Autonomous Zone, Ontological Anarchy, Poetic Terrorism.* New York: Autonomedia.

Birchall, Clare. 2006. *Knowledge Goes Pop: From Conspiracy Theory to Gossip.* Oxford: Berg.

Birkinshaw, Patrick. 2006. "Transparency as a Human Right." In *Transparency: The Key to Better Governance,* edited by Christopher Hood and David Heald, 47–59. Oxford: Oxford University Press.

Blanchot, Maurice. 1988. *The Unavowable Community.* Translated by Pierre Joris. New York: Station Hill Press.

Blanchot, Maurice. 1990. *Foucault/Blanchot.* Translated by Brian Massumi and Jeffrey Mehlman. New York: Zone Books.

Blas, Zach. 2018. "Informatic Opacity." In *Posthuman Glossary,* edited by Rosi Braidotti and Maria Hlavajova, 198–99. London: Bloomsbury Academic.

Blumenthal, Paul. 2010. "The History of Transparency—Part 1: Opening the Channels of Information to the People in the 18th Century." Sunlight Foundation, March 23, 2010. https://sunlightfoundation .com/2010/03/23/the-history-of-transparency-part-1-opening-the -channels-of-information-to-the-people-in-the-18th-century/.

Bok, Sissela. 1982. *Secrets: On the Ethics of Concealment and Revelation.* Oxford: Oxford University Press.

Bollier, David, and Silke Helfrich. 2012. "Introduction: The Commons as a Transformative Vision." *The Wealth of the Commons: A World Beyond Market and State.* http://wealthofthecommons.org/essay/intro duction-commons-transformative-vision.

Brandeis, Louis. 1913. "Other People's Money." *Harper's Weekly,* November 29, 1913.

Bratich, Jack. 2007. "Popular Secrecy and Occultural Studies." *Cultural Studies* 21 (1): 42–58.

Bratich, Jack. 2008. *Conspiracy Panics: Political Rationality and Popular Culture.* New York: SUNY Press.

Broad, Ellen. 2015. "Closed, Shared, Open Data: What's in a Name?" Open Data Institute, September 9, 2015. http://oldsite.theodi.org/blog/ closed-shared-open-data-whats-in-a-name.

Brooke, Heather. 2010. *The Silent State.* London: Heinemann.

Brown, Wendy. 2001. *Politics Out of History.* Princeton, N.J.: Princeton University Press.

Brown, Wendy. 2005. *Edgework: Critical Essays on Knowledge and Politics.* Princeton, N.J.: Princeton University Press.

Browne, Simone. 2015. *Dark Matters: On the Surveillance of Blackness.* Durham, N.C.: Duke University Press.

Brunton, Finn, and Helen Nissenbaum. 2015. *Obfuscation: A User's Guide for Privacy and Protest.* Cambridge, Mass.: MIT Press.

Bulajewski, Mike. 2014. "The Cult of Sharing." Metareader, August 5, 2014. http://www.metareader.org/post/the-cult-of-sharing.html.

Butler, Judith. 2004. *Undoing Gender.* New York: Routledge.

Butter, Michael. 2014. *Plots, Designs, and Schemes: American Conspiracy Theories from the Puritans to the Present.* Berlin: De Gruyter.

Campbell-Moore, Owen. 2013. "Hide Secret Messages in Facebook Photos Using This New Chrome Extension." Owen Campbell-Moore (blog), April 6, 2013. Available via the Internet Archive, https://web.archive.org/web/20130410072023/http://www.owencampbellmoore.com/blog/2013/04/hide-secret-messages-in-facebook-photos-using-this-new-chrome-extension/.

Caygill, Howard. 2013. *On Resistance: A Philosophy of Defiance.* London: Bloomsbury.

Chakrabarty, Dipesh. 2009. "The Climate of History: Four Theses." *Critical Inquiry* 35 (2): 197–222.

Chapman, Danny, Ryan Panchadsaram, and John Paul Farmer. 2013. "Introducing Alpha.Data.gov." White House, Office of Science and Technology Policy, January 28, 2013. https://obamawhitehouse.archives.gov/blog/2013/01/28/introducing-alphadatagov.

Christen, Kimberly. 2012. "Does Information Really Want to Be Free? Indigenous Knowledge Systems and the Question of Openness." *International Journal of Communication* 6:2870–93.

Chun, Wendy Hui Kyong. 2006. *Control and Freedom: Power and Paranoia in the Age of Fiber Optics.* Cambridge, Mass.: MIT Press.

Cifor, Marika, Patricia Garcia, T. L. Cowan, Jasmine Rault, Tonia Sutherland, Anita Say Chan, Jennifer Rode, Anna Lauren Hoffman, Niloufar Salehi, and Lisa Nakamura. 2019. "Feminist Data Manifest-No." https://www.manifestno.com/.

Cirio, Paolo. 2015. "About the Obscurity Project." https://obscurity.online/?/l/About/#Participatory.

Clapmarius, Arnold. 1605. *De Arcanis Rerumpublicarum.* Bremen, Germany.

Clough, Patricia, Karen Gregory, Benjamin Haber, and R. Joshua Scannel. 2014. "The Datalogical Turn." In *Non-representational Methodologies: Re-envisaging Research,* edited by Phillip Vannini, 146–64. London: Routledge.

Clymer, Adam. 2003. "Government Openness at Issue as Bush Holds On to Records." *New York Times,* January 3, 2003. https://www.nytimes.com/.

Cohen, Kris. 2017. "Fake News Isn't a Truth Problem, It's a Personhood Problem." Chapati Mystery, January 22, 2017. https://www.chapati mystery.com/archives/fake_news_isnt_a_truth_problem_its_a_per sonhood_problem.html.

Cohen, Marshall, and Holmes Lybrand. 2019. "Fact-Checking Trump Claims He's 'The Most Transparent' President in U.S. History." CNN, May 25, 2019. https://edition.cnn.com/2019/05/24/politics/trump -claims-most-transparent-president-fact-check/index.html.

Comaroff, Jean, and John Comaroff. 2003. "Transparent Fictions; or The Conspiracies of a Liberal Imagination: An Afterward." In *Transparency and Conspiracy: Ethnographies of Suspicion in the New World Order,* edited by Harry G. West and Todd Sanders, 287–99. Durham, N.C.: Duke University Press.

Connelly, Matthew. 2014. "The Radical Transparency of the American Republic." London School of Economics public lecture, October 21, 2014. Audio, 1:26:00. https://www.lse.ac.uk/lse-player?id=2648.

Cross, Harold. 1953. *The People's Right to Know.* New York: Columbia University Press.

Cukierman, Alex. 2009. "The Limits of Transparency." *Economic Notes* 38 (1–2): 1–37.

Cutler, Robert. 2014. "Bakunin's Anti-Jacobinism: 'Secret Societies' for Self-Emancipating Collectivist Social Revolution." *Anarchist Studies* 22 (2): 17–27.

Davis, David Brion. 1971. *The Fear of Conspiracy: Images of Un-American Subversion from Revolution to the Present.* Ithaca, N.Y.: Cornell University Press.

de Angelis, Massimo. 2007. *The Beginning of History: Value Struggles and Global Capital.* London: Pluto.

de Jong, Albert, Claire Fanger, and Antione Faivre. 2006. "Secrecy." In *Dictionary of Gnosis and Western Esotericism,* edited by J. Hanegraaff Wouter, Antoine Faivre, Roelof van den Broek, and Jean-Pierre Brach, 2:1050–61. Leiden: Brill.

de Nesnera, André. 2013. "Is NSA Leaker Edward Snowden a Traitor?" Voice of America, August 8, 2013. https://www.voanews.com/usa/ nsa-leaker-edward-snowden-traitor.

de Peuter, Greig, and Nick Dyer-Witheford. 2010. "Commons and Cooperatives." *Affinities* 4 (1): 30–56.

de Villiers, Nicholas. 2012. *Opacity and the Closet: Queer Tactics in Foucault, Barthes, and Warhol.* Minneapolis: University of Minnesota Press.

Dean, Jodi. 1998. *Aliens in America.* Ithaca, N.Y.: Cornell University Press.

Dean, Jodi. 2002. *Publicity's Secret: How Technoculture Capitalizes on Democracy.* Ithaca, N.Y.: Cornell University Press.

Dean, Jodi. 2005. "Communicative Capitalism: Circulation and the Foreclosure of Politics." *Cultural Politics* 1 (1): 51–74.

Dean, Jodi. 2009. *Democracy and Other Neoliberal Fantasies: Communicative Capitalism and Left Politics.* Durham, N.C.: Duke University Press.

Dean, Jodi. 2017. "Not Him, Us (And We Aren't Populists)." *Theory and Event* 20 (1): 38–44.

Dean, Jodi. 2018. *The Communist Horizon.* London: Verso.

Dean, John W. 2004. *Worse than Watergate: The Secret Presidency of George W. Bush.* New York: Little, Brown.

Debord, Guy. 1967. *La Société du Spectacle.* Paris: Buchet-Chastel.

Deleuze, Gilles. 1992. "Postscript on the Societies of Control." *October* 59:3–7.

Deleuze, Gilles. 1995. "Control and Becoming: Gilles Deleuze in Conversation with Antonio Negri." In *Negotiations.* Translated by Martin Joughin, 169–76. New York: Columbia University Press.

Deleuze, Gilles, and Félix Guattari. 1987. *A Thousand Plateaus.* Translated by Brian Massumi. Minneapolis: University of Minnesota Press.

Department of Defense. 2017. "Department of Defense Releases Budget Figure for 2017 Military Intelligence Program (MIP)." November 1, 2017. https://www.defense.gov/Newsroom/Releases/Release/Article/1360019/department-of-defense-releases-budget-figure-for-2017-military-intelligence-pro/source/GovDelivery/.

Department of Justice. 1993. "FOIA Update." October 4, 1993. https://www.justice.gov/oip/blog/foia-update-attorney-general-renos-foia-memorandum.

Department of Justice. 2001. "Memorandum for the Heads of All Federal Departments and Agencies." October 12, 2001. https://www.justice.gov/archive/oip/011012.htm.

Department of Justice. 2009. "Policies and Procedures Governing Invocation of the State Secrets Privilege." September 23, 2009. https://www.justice.gov/sites/default/files/opa/legacy/2009/09/23/state-secret-privileges.pdf.

Derrida, Jacques. (1967) 1997. *Of Grammatology.* Translated by Gayatri Chakravorty Spivak. Baltimore, Md.: Johns Hopkins University Press.

Derrida, Jacques. 1987. "How to Avoid Speaking: Denials." Translated by Ken Friden. In *Languages of the Unsayable: The Play of Negativity in Literature and Literary Theory,* edited by Sandford Budick and Wolfgang Iser, 3–70. Stanford, Calif.: Stanford University Press.

Derrida, Jacques. 1988. *Limited Inc.* Translated by Samuel Weber. Evanston, Ill.: Northwesten University Press.

Derrida, Jacques. 1992. "Passions: An Oblique Offering." In *Derrida: A Critical Reader,* edited by David Wood, 5–36. Translated by David Wood. Oxford: Blackwell.

Derrida, Jacques. 1995. *Points . . . : Interviews, 1974–1994.* Stanford, Calif.: Stanford University Press.

Derrida, Jacques. 1996. "Remarks on Deconstruction and Pragmatism." In *Deconstruction and Pragmatism,* edited by Chantalle Mouffe, 79–90. London: Routledge.

Derrida, Jacques. 2001a. *A Taste for the Secret.* Cambridge: Polity.

Derrida, Jacques. 2001b. *On Forgiveness.* Translated by Mark Dooley and Michael Hughes. London: Routledge.

Diamond, Jeremy. 2017. "Spicer: Trump Didn't Mean Wiretapping When He Tweeted about Wiretapping." CNN, March 14, 2017. https://www.cnn.com/2017/03/13/politics/sean-spicer-donald-trump-wiretapping/index.html.

Duffy, Nick. 2016. "19 PinkNews Stories People Want the Internet to Forget." *PinkNews,* February 2, 2016. https://www.pinknews.co.uk/2016/02/02/bbc-stars-to-crystal-meth-in-anus-19-pinknews-stories-people-want-the-internet-to-forget/.

Elmer, Greg. 2003. *Profiling Machines: Mapping the Personal Information Economy.* Cambridge, Mass.: MIT Press.

Environmental Data and Governance Initiative. 2018. "Changing the Digital Climate." https://envirodatagov.org/wp-content/uploads/2018/01/Part-3-Changing-the-Digital-Climate.pdf.

Esposito, Roberto. 2009. *Communitas: The Origin and Destiny of Community.* Translated by Timothy Campbell. Stanford, Calif.: Stanford University Press.

European Commission. 2004. "E.C. Directive 2004/109/EC of the European Parliament and the Council of 15th December 2004 on the Harmonization of Transparency Requirements in Relation to Information about Issuers Whose Securities Are Admitted to Trading on a Regulated Market and Amending Directive 2001/34/EC, OJ 2004 L 390/38." *Official Journal of the European Union,* December 31, 2004. http://eurlex.europa.eu/LexUriServ/LexUriServ.do?uri=OJ:L:2004:390:0038:0057:EN:PDF.

Everett, Anna. 2009. "The Afrogeek-in-Chief: Obama and Our New Media Ecology." *Journal of Visual Culture* 8 (2): 193–96.

Executive Office of the President. 2009a. "Memorandum for the Heads of Executive Departments and Agencies: Transparency and Open

Government." January 21, 2009. https://www.archives.gov/files/cui/documents/2009-WH-memo-on-transparency-and-open-government.pdf.

Executive Office of the President. 2009b. "Memorandum for the Heads of Executive Departments and Agencies: Freedom of Information Act." January 21, 2009. https://obamawhitehouse.archives.gov/the-press-office/freedom-information-act.

Executive Office of the President. 2009c. "Memorandum for the Heads of Executive Departments and Agencies: Open Government Directive." December 8, 2009. https://obamawhitehouse.archives.gov/open/documents/open-government-directive.

Executive Office of the President. 2009d. "Executive Order 13491: Ensuring Lawful Interrogations." *Federal Register*, January 22, 2009. https://www.federalregister.gov/documents/2009/01/27/E9-1885/ensuring-lawful-interrogations.

Feinberg, Lotte E. 2001. "Mr. Justice Brandeis and the Creation of the *Federal Register*." *Public Administration Review* 61:359–70.

Fenster, Mark. 2010. "Seeing the State: Transparency as Metaphor." *Administrative Law Review* 62 (3): 617–72. http://scholarship.law.ufl.edu/cgi/viewcontent.cgi?article=1571&context=facultypub.

Fenster, Mark. 2017a. *The Transparency Fix: Secrets, Leaks and Uncontrollable Information*. Stanford, Calif.: Stanford University Press.

Fenster, Mark. 2017b. "Transparency in Trump's America." *Governance*, January 2017, 173–75.

Fenton, Natalie. 2016. *Digital, Political, Radical*. Cambridge: Polity.

Fisher, Mark. 2009. *Capitalist Realism: Is There No Alternative?* London: Zero Books.

Fiske, John. 1993. *Power Plays, Power Works*. London: Verso.

Fluck, Matthew. 2016. "Theory, 'Truthers,' and Transparency: Reflecting on Knowledge in the Twenty-First Century." *Review of International Studies* 42 (1): 48–73.

Flyverbom, Mikkel. 2019. *The Digital Prism: Transparency and Managed Visibilities in a Datafied World*. Cambridge: Cambridge University Press.

Flyverbom, Mikkel, Paul Leonardi, Cynthia Stohl, and Michael Stohl. 2016. "The Management of Visibilities in the Digital Age—Introduction." *International Journal of Communication* 10:98–109.

Foner, Eric. 2015. *Gateway to Freedom: The Hidden History of America's Fugitive Slaves*. Oxford: Oxford University Press.

Foucault, Michel. 1978. *The History of Sexuality: Volume 1*. Translated by Robert Hurley. New York: Pantheon.

Foucault, Michel. 1980. "The Eye of Power." In *Power/Knowledge: Selected*

*Interviews and Other Writings, 1972–1977,* edited by Colin Gordon, 146–65. Translated by Colin Gordon. New York: Pantheon.

Foucault, Michel. 2007. *Security, Territory, Population: Lectures at the Collège de France, 1977–78.* Edited by Michael Senellart. Translated by Graham Burchell. New York: Palgrave Macmillan.

Franklin, Seb. 2015. *Control: Digitality as Cultural Logic.* Cambridge, Mass.: MIT Press.

Froomkin, Dan. 2009. "A Pretty Good Place to Start." *Washington Post,* January 22, 2009. https://www.washingtonpost.com/.

Fung, Archon, Mary Graham, and David Weil. 2007. *Full Disclosure: The Perils and Promise of Transparency.* Cambridge: Cambridge University Press.

Fynsk, Christopher. 1991. "Experiences of Finitude." Foreword to Jean-Luc Nancy, *The Inoperative Community,* edited by Peter Connor, vii–xxxv. Translated by Peter Connor, Lisa Garbus, Michael Holland, and Simona Sawhney. Minneapolis: University of Minnesota Press.

Galletti, Marina. 2018. "The Secret Society of Acéphale: 'A Community of the Heart.'" In *The Sacred Conspiracy: The Internal Papers of the Secret Society of Acéphale and Lectures to the College of Sociology,* by Georges Bataille, Roger Caillois, Michel Leiris, Pierre Klossowski, and André Masson, edited by Marina Galletti and Alasdair Brotchie, 19–49. London: Atlas Press.

Galloway, Alexander. 2004. *Protocol: How Control Exists after Decentralization.* Cambridge, Mass.: MIT Press.

Galloway, Alexander, and Eugene Thacker. 2007. *The Exploit: A Theory of Networks.* Minneapolis: University of Minnesota Press.

Garsten, Christina, and Monica Lindh de Montoya. 2008. "Examining the Politics of Transparency." Introduction to *Transparency in a New Global Order: Unveiling Organizational Visions,* edited by Christina Garsten and Monica Lindh de Montoya, 1–24. Cheltenham: Edward Elgar.

Gearen, Sarah. 2013. "Innovators Using Federal Data to Help Consumers Make Informed Decisions." U.S. Department of the Treasury, April 16, 2013. https://www.treasury.gov/connect/blog/Pages/Innovators -Using-Federal-Data-to-Help-Consumers-Make-Informed-Decisions .aspx.

Geroulanos, Stefanos. 2017. *Transparency in Post-war France: A Critical History of the Present.* Stanford, Calif.: Stanford University Press.

Gerstein, Josh. 2016. "Fears Rise of Trump-Era 'Memory Hole' in Federal Data." *Politico,* December 13, 2016. https://www.politico.com/ story/2016/12/trump-federal-data-fears-232591.

Gilbert, Jeremy. 2007. "Public Secrets: 'Being-with' in an Era of Perpetual Disclosure." *Cultural Studies* 21 (1): 22–41.

Gilbert, Jeremy. 2008. *Anticapitalism and Culture: Radical Theory and Popular Politics.* Oxford: Berg.

Giri, Saroj. 2010. "WikiLeaks beyond WikiLeaks?" Meta Mute, December 16, 2010. https://www.metamute.org/en/articles/WikiLeaks_beyond_WikiLeaks.

Gitelman, Lisa, and Virginia Jackson. 2013. Introduction to *Raw Data Is an Oxymoron,* edited by Lisa Gitelman, 1–14. Cambridge, Mass.: MIT Press.

Glissant, Édouard. 1989. *Caribbean Discourse: Selected Essays.* Translated by J. Michael Dash. Charlottesville: University Press of Virginia.

Glissant, Édouard. 1997. *Poetics of Relation.* Translated by Betsy Wing. Ann Arbor: Michigan University Press.

Goldstein, Brett, and Lauren Dyson, eds. 2013. *Beyond Transparency: Open Data and the Future of Civic Innovation.* San Francisco, Calif.: Code for America Press.

Gosseries, Axel, and Tom Parr. 2018. "Publicity." In *Stanford Encyclopedia of Philosophy,* edited by Edward N. Zalta. https://plato.stanford.edu/archives/win2018/entries/publicity/.

Goulder, Ben. 2015. *Foucault and the Politics of Rights.* Stanford, Calif.: Stanford University Press.

Grotta, Gerald L. 1971. "Philip Freneau's Crusade for Open Sessions of the U.S. Senate." *Journalism Quarterly* 48:667–71.

Guardian. 2009. "Secret Prisons: Obama's Order to Close 'Black Sites.'" *Guardian,* January 23, 2009. https://www.theguardian.com/.

Gustafsson, Henrik. 2013. "Foresight, Hindsight and State Secrecy in the American West: The Geopolitical Aesthetics of Trevor Paglen." *Journal of Visual Culture* 12 (1): 148–64.

Habermas, Jürgen. (1964) 1991. *The Structural Transformation of the Public Sphere.* Translated by Thomas Berger. Cambridge, Mass.: MIT Press.

Hall, Gary. 2008. *Digitize This Book! The Politics of New Media, or Why We Need Open Access Now.* Minneapolis: University of Minnesota Press.

Hall, Gary. 2016. *The Uberfication of the University.* Minneapolis: University of Minnesota Press.

Hamilton, Alexander. 1788. "The Executive Department Further Considered." Federalist No. 70. *New York Packet,* March 15, 1788.

Han, Byung-Chul. 2015. *The Transparency Society.* Stanford, Calif.: Stanford University Press.

Hansen, Hans Krause, Lars Thøger Christensen, and Mikkel Flyverbom. 2015. "Introduction: Logics of Transparency in Late Modernity: Paradoxes, Mediation and Governance." *European Journal of Social Theory* 18 (2): 117–31.

Hardt, Michael. 2003. "Harman–Hardt Debate: The Working Class or the Multitude." Marxists Internet Archive, January 2003. https://www.marxists.org/archive/harman/2003/01/debate-hardt.html.

Hardt, Michael. 2004. *Multitude: War and Democracy in the Age of Empire.* New York: Penguin.

Hardt, Michael, and Antonio Negri. 2000. *Empire.* Cambridge, Mass.: Harvard University Press.

Hardtwig, Wolfgang. 1989. "Eliteanspruch und Geheimnis in den Geheimgesellschaften des 18. Jahrhunderts." In *Aufklärung und Aeheimgesellschaftern: Zur politischen Funktion und Sozialstruktur der Fremaurerlogen im 18. Jahrhundert,* edited by Helmut Reinalter, 63–86. Munich: Oldenbourg.

Harrison, Ross. 1983. *Bentham.* London: Routledge.

Hartman, Saidiya. 1997. *Scenes of Subjection: Terror, Slavery, and Self-Making in Nineteenth Century America.* Oxford: Oxford University Press.

Hayles, Katherine N. 2012. *How We Think: Digital Media and Contemporary Technogenesis.* Chicago: University of Chicago Press.

Hegel, G. W. F. (1807) 1977. *Phenomenology of Spirit.* Translated by A. V. Miller. Oxford: Oxford University Press.

Herb, Jeremy, and Justin Sink. 2013. "Sen. Feinstein Calls Snowden's NSA Leaks an 'Act of Treason.'" *The Hill,* October 6, 2013. https://thehill.com/policy/defense/304573-sen-feinstein-snowdens-leaks-are-treason.

High Level Expert Group on Fake News (HLEG). 2018. "Final Report of the High Level Expert Group on Fake News and Online Disinformation." European Commission, March 12, 2018. https://ec.europa.eu/digital-single-market/en/news/final-report-high-level-expert-group-fake-news-and-online-disinformation.

Hill Collins, Patricia. 1990. *Black Feminist Thought: Knowledge, Consciousness and the Politics of Empowerment.* New York: Routledge.

Hinks, Joseph. 2017. "Catalonia Just Voted for Independence from Spain. Here's Why That Is Unlikely to Happen." *Time,* October 2, 2017. https://time.com/4964559/catalan-independence-referendum-spain/.

Hirschi, Caspar. 2018. "Regulation and Transparency as Rituals of Distrust." In Alloa and Thomä 2018b, 225–42.

Hirschman, Albert O. 1991. *The Rhetoric of Reaction.* Cambridge, Mass.: Belknap.

Hofstadter, Richard. 1964. "The Paranoid Style in American Politics." *Harper's Magazine,* November 1964, 77–86.

Hood, Christopher. 2006a. "Beyond Exchanging First Principles? Some Closing Comments." In *Transparency: The Key to Better Governance?,* edited by Christopher Hood and David Heald, 211–25. Oxford: Oxford University Press.

Hood, Christopher. 2006b. "Transparency in Historical Perspective." In *Transparency: The Key to Better Governance?*, edited by Christopher Hood and David Heald, 3–23. Oxford: Oxford University Press.

Horkheimer, Max. (1941) 1989. "Notes on Institute Activities." In *Critical Theory and Society: A Reader*, edited by Stephen E. Bronner and Douglas Kellner, 264–66. New York: Routledge.

Horn, Eva. 2011. "Logics of Political Secrecy." *Theory, Culture, and Society* 28 (7–8): 103–22.

Horning, Rob. 2015. "Hide and Seek: The Problem with Obfuscation." Review of *Obfuscation: A User's Guide for Privacy and Protest*, by Helen Nissenbaum and Finn Brunton. *L.A. Review of Books*, November 10, 2015. https://lareviewofbooks.org/article/hide-and-seek-the-problem -with-obfuscation/.

Howarth, David. 2004. "Hegemony, Political Subjectivity and Radical De- ¹nocracy." In *Laclau: A Critical Reader*, edited by Simon Critchley and Oliver Marchart, 256–76. London: Routledge.

Igo, Sarah E. 2018. *The Known Citizen: A History of Privacy in Modern America*. Cambridge, Mass.: Harvard University Press.

Information Security Oversight Office (ISOO). 2017. "2017 Report to the President." https://www.archives.gov/files/isoo/reports/2017-annual -report.pdf.

Ingram, George. 2018. "How Better Aid Transparency Will Help Tackle Global Development Challenges." Brookings Institution, June 21, 2018. https://www.brookings.edu/blog/up-front/2018/06/21/how-better -aid-transparency-will-help-tackle-global-development-challenges/.

Ingram, Matthew. 2013. "Even the CIA Is Struggling to Deal with the Volume of Real-Time Social Data." Gigaom, March 20, 2013. https:// gigaom.com/2013/03/20/even-the-cia-is-struggling-to-deal-with-the -volume-of-real-time-social-data/.

Isin, Engin, and Evelyn Ruppert. 2015. *Being Digital Citizens*. London: Rowman & Littlefield.

James, Ian. 2006. *The Fragmentary Demand: An Introduction to the Philosophy of Jean-Luc Nancy*. Stanford, Calif.: Stanford University Press.

Jameson, Fredric. 1988. "Cognitive Mapping." In *Marxism and the Interpretation of Culture*, edited by Cary Nelson and Lawrence Grossberg, 347–60. London: Macmillan.

Jarosinski, Eric. 2009. "Of Stones and Glass Houses: Minima Moralia as Critique of Transparency." In *Language without Soil: Adorno and Late*

*Philosophical Modernity,* edited by Gerhard Richter, 157–71. New York: Fordham University Press.

Jay, John. 1788. "The Powers of the Senate." Federalist No. 64. *Independent Journal,* March 5, 1788.

John, Nicholas A. 2013. "Sharing and Web 2.0: The Emergence of a Keyword." *New Media and Society* 15 (2): 167–82.

John, Nicholas A. 2014. "Sharing [Draft] [#DigitalKeywords]." Culture Digitally, May 27, 2014. http://culturedigitally.org/2014/05/sharing-draft-digitalkeywords/.

Johnson, Jenna. 2016. "'A Lot of People Are Saying . . .': How Trump Spreads Conspiracies and Innuendoes." *Washington Post,* June 13, 2016. https://www.washingtonpost.com/.

Johnson, M. Eric, Dan McGuire, and Nicholas D. Willey. 2008. "The Evolution of the Peer-to-Peer File Sharing Industry and the Security Risks for Users." Paper presented at the 41st Hawaii International Conference on System Sciences (HICSS), Waikoloa, Hawaii, January 8–10, 2008. https://www.computer.org/csdl/proceedings/2008/hicss/12O mNy3iFtz.

Johnston, David. 2009. "U.S. Says Rendition to Continue, but with More Oversight." *New York Times,* August 24, 2009. https://www.nytimes.com/.

Jütte, Daniel. 2015. *The Age of Secrecy: Jews, Christians, and the Economy of Secrets, 1400–1800.* Translated by Jeremiah Riemer. New Haven, Conn.: Yale University Press.

Kant, Immanuel. (1781) 1998. *Critique of Pure Reason.* Edited and translated by Paul Guyer and Allen Wood. Cambridge: Cambridge University Press.

Kant, Immanuel. (1784) 2001. "Answer to the Question: What Is Enlightenment?" In *Basic Writings of Kant,* edited by Allen W. Wood, 133–42. Translated by Thomas K. Abbott. New York: Modern Library.

Kant, Immanuel. (1795) 1996. "Toward Perpetual Peace." In *Practical Philosophy,* edited by Mary Gregor, 8:343–86. Translated by Mary Gregor. Cambridge: Cambridge University Press.

Keeley, Brian, and Patrick Love. 2010. "From Crisis to Recovery: The Causes, Course and Consequences of the Great Recession." *OECD Insights.* https://www.oecd.org/insights/46156144.pdf.

Kember, Sarah, and Joanna Zylinska. 2012. *Life after New Media: Mediation as Vital Process.* Cambridge, Mass.: MIT Press.

Kennedy, John F. 1961. "The President and the Press: Address before the American Newspaper Publishers Association, April 27, 1961." Waldorf-Astoria Hotel, New York City. John F. Kennedy Presidential Library and Museum. https://www.jfklibrary.org/archives/other-resources/john-f-kennedy-speeches/american-newspaper-publishers-association-19610427.

Kinney, Alison. 2016. "How the Klan Got Its Hood." *New Republic,* January 8, 2016. https://newrepublic.com/article/127242/klan-got-hood.

Kitchin, Rob. 2014. *The Data Revolution: Big Data, Open Data, Data Infrastructures, and Their Consequences.* London: Sage.

Knight, Peter. 2000. *Conspiracy Culture: From Kennedy to "The X-Files."* London: Routledge.

Knott, Stephen F. 1996. *Secret and Sanctioned: Covert Operations and the American Presidency.* Oxford: Oxford University Press.

Koselleck, Reinhart. 1988. *Critique and Crisis: Enlightenment and the Pathogenesis of Modern Society.* Cambridge, Mass.: MIT Press.

Laclau, Ernesto. 2007. *Emancipation(s).* London: Verso.

Laclau, Ernesto, and Chantalle Mouffe. 1985. *Hegemony and Socialist Strategy.* New York: Knopf Doubleday.

Lazzarato, Maurizio. 2009. "Neoliberalism in Action: Inequality, Insecurity and the Reconstitution of the Social." *Theory, Culture, and Society* 26 (6): 109–33.

Lee, Pamela M. 2011. "Open Secret: On the Work of Art between Disclosure and Redaction." *Artforum,* May 2011. https://www.artforum.com/print/201105/open-secret-the-work-of-art-between-disclosure-and-redaction-28060.

Lefebvre, Henri. (1962) 1995. *Introduction to Modernity.* Translated by John Moore. London: Verso.

Lefebvre, Henri. (1974) 1991. *The Production of Space.* Translated by Donald Nicholson-Smith. Oxford: Blackwell.

Leonard, J. William. 2004. *Remarks to the National Classification Management Society's Annual Training Seminar.* Washington, D.C.: Information Security Oversight Office.

Lessig, Lawrence. 2009. "Against Transparency." *New Republic,* October 9, 2009. https://newrepublic.com/article/70097/against-transparency.

Lichtblau, Eric. 2004. "Material Given to Congress in 2002 Is Now Classified." *New York Times,* May 20, 2004. https://www.nytimes.com/.

Lichtblau, Eric. 2006. "Bush Defends Spy Program and Denies Misleading Public." *New York Times,* January 2, 2006. https://www.nytimes.com/.

Liddington, Jill. 2014. *Vanishing for the Vote: Suffrage, Citizenship, and the Battle for the Census.* Manchester: Manchester University Press.

Liebes, Tamar, and Elihu Katz. 1990. *The Export of Meaning: Cross-Cultural Readings of "Dallas."* Oxford: Oxford University Press.

Lippard, Lucy. 1973. *The Dematerialization of the Art Object.* Oakland: University of California Press.

Lockridge, Kenneth. 1974. *Literacy in Colonial New England: An Enquiry into the Social Context of Literacy in the Early Modern West.* London: Norton.

Long, Pamela O. 2001. *Openness, Secrecy, Authorship: Technical Arts and the Culture of Knowledge from Antiquity to the Renaissance.* Baltimore, Md.: Johns Hopkins University Press.

Lord, Kristen M. 2006. *The Perils and Promise of Global Transparency.* Albany: SUNY Press.

Lovink, Geert. 2017. *Social Media Abyss: Critical Internet Cultures and the Forces of Negation.* New York: Wiley.

Lütticken, Sven. 2006. *Secret Publicity: Essays on Contemporary Art.* Rotterdam: NAi.

Lyotard, Jean-François. 1984. *The Postmodern Condition: A Report on Knowledge.* Translated by Geoffrey Bennington and Brian Massumi. Minneapolis: University of Minnesota Press.

Lyotard, Jean-François. 1991. *The Inhuman: Reflections on Time.* Translated by Geoffrey Bennington and Rachel Bowlby. London: Polity.

MacCabe, Colin. 1995. Preface to *The Geopolitical Aesthetic: Cinema and Space in the World System,* by Fredric Jameson, ix–xvi. Bloomington: Indiana University Press.

Mace, Matt. 2016. "Tesco Boss Calls for Greater Transparency to Tackle Food Waste." Edie.net, December 6, 2016. https://www.edie.net/news/5/Tesco-chief-calls-for-greater-reporting-transparency-to-tackle-food-waste/.

MacKinnon, Catharine. 1989. *Toward a Feminist Theory of the State.* Cambridge, Mass.: Harvard University Press.

Madison, James. (1787) 2003. *Journal of the Federal Convention.* Edited by Erastus Howard Scott. Clark, N.J.: Lawbook Exchange.

Magid, Jill. 2009a. *Becoming Tarden.* London: Tate Modern.

Magid, Jill. 2009b. Letter to the deputy director general of AIVD, August 26, 2009. Available via the Internet Archive, https://web.archive.org/web/20091008101905/http://www.becomingtarden.net/index.php?page=letter.

Magid, Jill. 2012. "Artist Talk." The Modern (podcast), Modern Art Museum of Fort Worth, March 4, 2012. Audio, 1:12:09. https://www.themodern.org/podcast/jill-magid.

Malloy, Daniel. 2005. "Dialectic and Enlightenment: The Concept of Enlightenment in Hegel and Horkheimer–Adorno." *Auslegung* 27 (2): 43–60.

Mann, Steve. 2013. "Veillance and Reciprocal Transparency: Surveillance versus Sousveillance, AR Glass, Lifeglogging, and Wearable Computing." http://wearcam.org/veillance/veillance.pdf.

Manyika, James, Michael Chui, Diana Farrell, Steve Van Kuiken, Peter Groves, and Elizabeth Almasi Doshi. 2013. "Open Data: Unlocking Innovation and Performance with Liquid Information." McKinsey Digital, McKinsey Global Institute, October 1, 2013. https://www.mckinsey .com/business-functions/mckinsey-digital/our-insights/open-data -unlocking-innovation-and-performance-with-liquid-information.

Marin, Louis. 1998. *Cross-Readings.* Translated by Jane Marie Todd. Atlantic Highlands, N.J.: Humanities.

Marquardt, James J. 2011. *Transparency and American Primacy in World Politics.* Farnham, U.K.: Ashgate.

Marx, Karl. (1887) 1976. *Capital, Volume 1.* London: Penguin.

Masco, Joseph. 2014. *The Theatre of Operations: National Security Affect from the Cold War to the War on Terror.* Durham, N.C.: Duke University Press.

Maude, Francis. 2012. "Open Data White Paper: Unleashing the Potential." July 12, 2012. https://assets.publishing.service.gov.uk/government/ uploads/system/uploads/attachment_data/file/78946/CM8353_acc .pdf.

McDermott, John. 2015. "WTF Is Data Leakage?" Digiday, January 27, 2015. https://digiday.com/media/what-is-data-leakage/.

McStay, Andrew. 2014. *Privacy and Philosophy: New Media and Affective Protocol.* Bern: Peter Lang.

Melley, Tim. 2012. *The Covert Sphere: Secrecy, Fiction, and the National Security State.* Ithaca, N.Y.: Cornell.

Mellinger, Gwyneth. 2015. "Washington Confidential: A Double Standard Gives Way to the People's Right to Know." *Journalism and Mass Communication Quarterly* 92 (4): 857–76.

Merlan, Anna. 2019. *Republic of Lies: American Conspiracy Theorists and Their Surprising Rise to Power.* London: Random House.

Miller, Ellen, and Michael Klein. 2009. "Too Much Transparency? (Part 2)." *New Republic,* October 11, 2009. https://newrepublic.com/article /70160/tnr-debate-too-much-transparency-part-ii.

Mirzoeff, Nicholas. 2011. *The Right to Look: A Counterhistory of Visuality.* Durham, N.C.: Duke University Press.

Moretti, Franco. 2000. "Conjectures on World Literature." *New Left Review* 1:54–68.

Morozov, Evgeny. 2013. *To Save Everything, Click Here: Technology, Solutionism, and the Urge to Fix Problems that Don't Exist.* London: Allen Lane.

Moynihan, Patrick. 1998. *Secrecy: The American Experience.* New Haven, Conn.: Yale University Press.

Muirhead, Russell, and Nancy L. Rosenblum. 2019. *A Lot of People Are Saying*. Princeton, N.J.: Princeton University Press.

Murphy, Katharine. 2014. "Edward Snowden a Traitor but U.S. Spy Review Is Welcome, Says Julie Bishop." *Guardian*, January 23, 2014. https://www.theguardian.com/.

Murphy, Tim. 2016. "How Donald Trump Became Conspiracy Theorist in Chief." *Mother Jones*, November/December 2016. https://www.motherjones.com/politics/2016/10/trump-infowars-alex-jones-clinton-conspiracy-theories/.

Nancy, Jean-Luc. 1991. *The Inoperative Community*. Translated by Peter Connor, Lisa Garbus, Michael Holland, and Simona Sawhney. Minneapolis: University of Minnesota Press.

NBC. 2014. "Edward Snowden: #Traitor or #Patriot." NBC News. http://interactive.nbcnews.com/nightly-news/williams-snowden/.

Noble, Safiya Umoja. 2018. *Algorithms of Oppression: How Search Engines Reinforce Racism*. New York: New York University Press.

Nowotny, Stefan. 2011. "Publicity and Secrecy: Variations on Intertwining Use." *Open! Platform for Art, Culture and the Public Domain* 22: 26–35.

Obama, Barack. 1995. *Dreams from My Father*. New York: Times.

Obama, Barack. 2009. "Speech on National Security." *New York Times*, January 21, 2009. https://www.nytimes.com/.

Obama, Barack. 2013. "Transcript: Obama's Remarks on NSA Controversy." *Wall Street Journal*, June 7, 2013. https://www.wsj.com/.

Obrist, Barbara. 1982. *Les débuts de l'imaginerie alchemique (XIVe–XVe siècles)*. Paris: Le Sycomore.

Office of the Director of National Intelligence (ODNI). 2017. "DNI Releases Appropriated Budget Figure for 2017 National Intelligence Program." October 3, 2017. https://www.dni.gov/index.php/newsroom/press-releases/item/1810-dni-releases-appropriated-budget-figure-for-2017-national-intelligence-program.

O'Hara, Kieron. 2011. *Transparent Government, Not Transparent Citizens: A Report on Privacy and Transparency for the Cabinet Office*. Cabinet Office, Gov.uk. http://www.cabinetoffice.gov.uk/sites/default/files/resources/transparency-and-privacy-review-annex-a.pdf.

Oliver, Eric, and Thomas Wood. 2016. "A New Poll Shows 52% of Republicans Actually Think Trump Won the Popular Vote." *Washington Post*, December 18, 2016. https://www.washingtonpost.com.

Oliver, Julian. 2012. "The Transparency Grenade." https://transparencygrenade.com/.

O'Neill, Onora. 2002. "Trust and Transparency." *Reith Lectures*, BBC

Radio 4, April 26, 2002. Audio, 43:00. https://www.bbc.co.uk/pro
grammes/p00gpzcz.

Open Data Institute HQ (ODIHQ). 2015. "The Economic Impact of
Open Data: What Do We Already Know?" Open Data Institute (ODI),
Medium, November 2, 2015. https://medium.com/@ODIHQ/the
-economic-impact-of-open-data-what-do-we-already-know-1a119c1958
a0#.t3b53aa8j.

Organisation for Economic Co-operation and Development (OECD). 2017.
"New Approach Needed to Tackle Rising Drug Prices." January 16, 2017.
http://www.oecd.org/health/new-approach-needed-to-tackle-rising
-drug-prices.htm.

Paglen, Trevor. 2008. *I Could Tell You but Then You Would Have to Be Destroyed by Me: Emblems from the Pentagon's Black World.* Brooklyn: Mel-
ville House.

Paglen, Trevor. 2009. "Blank Spots on the Map." Talks at Google, You-
Tube, February 17, 2009. Video, 59:37. https://www.youtube.com/
watch?v=mApBa2qKVDM.

Paglen, Trevor. 2014. "Art as Evidence." Transmediale 2014 keynote address, Haus der Kulturen der Welt, Berlin, January 30, 2014. Transmediale, YouTube, January 31, 2014. Video, 23:03. https://www.youtube
.com/watch?v=SDxue3jGAug.

Palazzo, Giovanni Antonio. 1604. *Discorso del governo e della ragion vera di
Stato.* Naples: G. B. Sottile.

Pasquale, Frank. 2015. *The Black Box Society: The Secret Algorithms that
Control Money and Information.* Cambridge, Mass.: Harvard University
Press.

Patel-Carstairs, Sunita. 2017. "Fox Pulls Andrew Napolitano Off Air after
GCHQ Trump Wiretap Claim." Sky News, March 21, 2017. https://
news.sky.com/story/fox-pulls-andrew-napolitano-off-air-after-gchq
-trump-wiretap-claim-10809396.

Peters, Benjamin, ed. 2016. *Digital Keywords: A Vocabulary of Information
Society and Culture.* Princeton, N.J.: Princeton University Press.

Phillip, Abby D. 2013. "House Speaker John Boehner: NSA Leaker a
'Traitor.'" *ABC News,* June 11, 2013. https://abcnews.go.com/blogs/
politics/2013/06/house-speaker-john-boehner-nsa-leaker-a-traitor/.

Pomerantsev, Peter. 2017. "The Rise of the Postmodern President." *News-
night,* March 16, 2017. https://www.bbc.co.uk/programmes/p04x293b.

Postema, Gerald. 2014. "The Soul of Justice: Bentham on Publicity, Law, and
the Rule of Law." In *Bentham's Theory of Law and Public Opinion,* edited
by Xiaobo Zhai and Michael Quinn, 40–62. Cambridge: Cambridge
University Press.

Potolsky, Matthew. 2019. *The National Security Sublime: On the Aesthetics of Government Secrecy*. London: Routledge.

Powers, Richard Gid. 1998. Introduction to *Secrecy: The American Experience*, by Patrick Moynihan, 1–58. New Haven, Conn.: Yale University Press.

Privacy International. 2018. "Teach 'Em to Phish: State Sponsors of Surveillance." July 2018. https://privacyinternational.org/report/2159/teach-em-phish-state-sponsors-surveillance.

Quellette, Laurie. 2016. *A Companion to Reality Television*. Hoboken, N.J.: Wiley.

Rancière, Jacques. 1992. "Politics, Identification, and Subjectivization." *October* 61:58–64.

Rancière, Jacques. 1999. *Disagreement: Politics and Philosophy*. Translated by Julie Rose. Minneapolis: University of Minnesota Press.

Rancière, Jacques. 2004a. *The Philosopher and His Poor*. Edited by Andrew Parker. Translated by John Drury, Corinne Oster, and Andrew Parker. Durham, N.C.: Duke University Press.

Rancière, Jacques. 2004b. *The Politics of Aesthetics: Distribution of the Sensible*. Translated by Gabriel Rockhill. London: Continuum.

Rancière, Jacques. 2010. *Dissensus: On Politics and Aesthetics*. Edited and translated by Steven Corcoran. London: Continuum.

Rauschenberg, Robert. 2007. "Erased de Kooning." Svsugvcarter, YouTube, May 15, 2007. Video, 4:26. https://www.youtube.com/watch?v=tpCWh3IFtDQ.

Reichardt, Rolf. 1998. "Light against Darkness: The Visual Representations of a Central Enlightenment Concept." *Representations* 61:95–148.

Remnick, David. 2010. "The Invention of Barack Obama." *Guardian,* April 24, 2010. https://www.theguardian.com/.

Research Council U.K. (RCUK). 2018. "Policy on Open Access." https://www.ukri.org/files/legacy/oadocs/ukri-open-access-principles-and-high-level-policy-pdf.

Reuters. 2013. "Protesters March in Washington against NSA Spying." October 26, 2013. https://www.reuters.com/article/us-usa-security-protest-idUSBRE99P0B420131027.

Reuters/Ipsos. 2020. "Press Release: Reuters/Ipsos Poll: Trump Taxes and Financial Records." https://fingfx.thomsonreuters.com/gfx/mkt/qzjvqndaxpx/Topline%20Reuters%20Trump%20Taxes%2009%2029%202020.pdf.

Rhee, Jennifer. 2016. "Adam Harvey's 'Anti-drone' Wear in Three Sites of Opacity." *Camera Obscura* 31 (2): 175–85.

Risen, James. 2016. "If Donald Trump Targets Journalists, Thank Obama." *New York Times*, December 30, 2016. https://www.nytimes.com/.

Risen, James. 2018. "The Biggest Secret: My Life as a *New York Times* Reporter in the Shadow of the War on Terror." Intercept, January 3, 2018. https://theintercept.com/2018/01/03/my-life-as-a-new-york-times-reporter-in-the-shadow-of-the-war-on-terror/.

Risen, James, and Eric Lichtblau. 2005. "Bush Lets U.S. Spy on Callers without Courts." *New York Times*, December 16, 2005. https://www.nytimes.com/.

Roberts, Alistair. 2006. *Blacked Out: Government Secrecy in the Information Age*. Cambridge: Cambridge University Press.

Rockhill, Gabriel. 2004. "Glossary of Technical Terms." In *The Politics of Aesthetics: The Distribution of the Sensible*, by Jacques Rancière, 80–93. London: Continuum.

Roper Center for Public Opinion Research. 2016. "The Public and Its Right to Know." June 27, 2016. https://ropercenter.cornell.edu/blog/public-and-its-right-know.

Rose, P. K. 2007. "The Founding Fathers of American Intelligence." Central Intelligence Agency, March 16, 2007; last update July 7, 2008. https://www.cia.gov/library/center-for-the-study-of-intelligence/csi-publications/books-and-monographs/the-founding-fathers-of-american-intelligence/art-1.html.

Roth, Daniel. 2009. "Road Map for Financial Recovery: Radical Transparency Now!" *Wired* 17 (3), February 23, 2009. https://www.wired.com/2009/02/wp-reboot/.

Rothman, Lily. 2016. "FOIA at 50: How American Views of Transparency Have Changed." *Time*, July 21, 2016. https://time.com/4408574/foia-50-american-transparency-polls/.

Rousseau, Jean-Jacques. (1762) 2002. *"The Social Contract" and "The First and Second Discourses."* Edited by Susan Dunn. New Haven, Conn.: Yale University Press.

Rousseau, Jean-Jacques. (1764) 1953. *The Confessions of Jean Jacques Rousseau*. Translated by J. M. Cohen. Harmondsworth: Penguin.

Ruppert, Evelyn. 2015. "Doing the Transparent State: Open Government Data as Performance Indicators." In *The World of Indicators: The Making of Governmental Knowledge through Quantification*, edited by Richard Rottenburg, Sally E. Merry, Johanna Mugler, and Soon-Joon Park, 127–50. Cambridge: Cambridge University Press.

Sagar, Rahul. 2013. *Secrets and Leaks: The Dilemma of State Secrecy*. Princeton, N.J.: Princeton University Press.

Saint, Nick. 2010. "Eric Schmidt: Google's Policy Is to 'Get Right up to the Creepy Line and Not Cross It.'" *Business Insider,* October 1, 2010. https://www.businessinsider.com/eric-schmidt-googles-policy-is-to-get-right-up-to-the-creepy-line-and-not-cross-it-2010-10?op=1&r=US&IR=T.

Sanders, Todd, and Harry G. West. 2003. "Power Revealed and Concealed in the New World Order." In *Transparency and Conspiracy: Ethnographies of Suspicion in the New World Order,* edited by Todd Sanders and Harry G. West, 1–37. Durham, N.C.: Duke University Press.

Sassen, Saskia. 2006. *Territory, Authority, Rights: From Medieval to Global Assemblages.* Princeton, N.J.: Princeton University Press.

Scherer, Michael. 2017. "Can President Trump Handle the Truth?" *Time,* March 23, 2017. https://time.com/4710614/donald-trump-fbi-surveil lance-house-intelligence-committee/.

Schmitt, Mark. 2010. "Transparency for What?" *American Prospect,* February 15, 2010. https://prospect.org/special-report/transparency-what/.

Schudson, Michael. 2015. *The Rise of the Right to Know: Politics and the Culture of Transparency, 1945–1975.* Cambridge, Mass.: Harvard University Press.

Schulman, Loren DeJong, and Alice Friend. 2018. "The Pentagon's Transparency Problem." *Foreign Affairs,* May 2, 2018. https://www.foreignaffairs.com/articles/united-states/2018-05-02/pentagons-trans parency-problem.

Schwarz, Frederick A. O. 2015. *Democracy in the Dark: The Seduction of Government Secrecy.* New York: New Press.

Sedgwick, Eve Kosofsky. 1993. "Paranoid Reading and Reparative Reading, or You're So Paranoid, You Probably Think This Essay Is About You." In *Touching Feeling: Affect, Pedagogy, Performativity.* Durham, N.C.: Duke University Press.

Shane, Scott. 2009. "ACLU Lawyers Mine Documents for Truth." *New York Times,* August 29, 2009. https://www.nytimes.com/.

Shirky, Clay. 2008. *Here Comes Everybody: The Power of Organizing without Organizations.* London: Penguin.

Shore, Cris. 2008. "Audit Culture and Illiberal Governance: Universities and the Politics of Accountability." *Anthropological Theory* 8 (3): 278–98.

Sidgwick, Henry. (1874) 1907. *The Methods of Ethics.* 7th ed. London: Macmillan.

Siegel, Barry. 2008. *Claim of Privilege.* New York: Harper Collins.

Simmel, Georg. 1906. "The Sociology of Secrecy and of Secret Societies." *American Journal of Sociology* 11 (4): 441–98.

Spivack, Nova. 2013. "The Post-privacy World." *Wired,* July 2013. https://www.wired.com/insights/2013/07/the-post-privacy-world/.

Spivak, Gayatri Chakravorty. 2009. "The Modern Prince . . . 'To Come'?" *Journal of Visual Culture* 8:191–93.

Stalder, Felix. 2011. "The Fight over Transparency." *Open* 22:8–22.

Starobinski, Jean. 1988. *Jean-Jacques Rousseau: Transparency and Obstruction.* Translated by Arthur Goldhammer. Chicago: University of Chicago Press.

Steel, Emily, Callum Locke, Emily Cadman, and Ben Freese. 2013. "How Much Is Your Personal Data Worth?" *Financial Times,* June 12, 2013. https://ig.ft.com/how-much-is-your-personal-data-worth/.

Stern, Alena. 2018. "Open Data Policy and Freedom of Information Law: Understanding the Relationship between the Twin Pillars of Access to Information." Sunlight Foundation. https://sunlightfoundation.com/wp-content/uploads/2018/10/alena-white-paper-PDF.pdf.

Stoekl, Allan. 1985. Introduction to *Visions of Excess: Selected Writings, 1927–1939,* by Georges Bataille, edited by Allan Stoekl, ix–xxv. Minneapolis: University of Minnesota Press.

Stolberg, Sheryl Gay. 2009a. "Obama Finds that Washington's Habits of Secrecy Die Hard." *New York Times,* April 5, 2009. https://www.nytimes.com/.

Stolberg, Sheryl Gay. 2009b. "On First Day, Obama Quickly Sets a New Tone." *New York Times,* January 21, 2009. https://www.nytimes.com/.

Strathern, Marilyn. 2000. *Audit Cultures: Anthropological Studies in Accountability, Ethics, and the Academy.* London: Routledge.

Strauss, Leo. 1988. *Persecution and the Art of Writing.* Chicago: University of Chicago Press.

Strohm, Chris, and Del Quentin Wilber. 2014. "Pentagon Says Snowden Took Most U.S. Secrets Ever: Rogers." Bloomberg, January 10, 2014. https://www.bloomberg.com/news/articles/2014-01-09/pentagon-finds-snowden-took-1-7-million-files-rogers-says.

Suskind, Ron. 2004. "Faith, Certainty and the Presidency of George W. Bush." *New York Times,* October 17, 2004. https://www.nytimes.com/.

Sweedler, Milo. 2005. "From the Sacred Conspiracy to the Unavowable Community: Bataille, Blanchot and Laure's Le Sacre." *French Studies* 19 (3): 338–50.

Tanke, Joseph. 2011. *Jacques Rancière: An Introduction.* London: Continuum.

Taussig, Michael. 1999. *Defacement: Public Secrecy and the Labor of the Negative.* Stanford, Calif.: Stanford University Press.

Timm, Trevor. 2014. "Beware the Surveillance Reform Trojan Horse: What's Not in the New NSA Laws?" *Guardian,* May 29, 2014. https://www.theguardian.com/.

Tiqqun. (2001) 2009. "Cybernetic Hypothesis." The Anarchist Library.

https://theanarchistlibrary.org/library/tiqqun-the-cybernetic-hypoth esis.pdf.

Tiqqun. (2001) 2010. *Introduction to Civil War*. Translated by Alexander Galloway and Jason Smith. Los Angeles: Semiotext(e).

Tiqqun. (2001) 2011. *This Is Not a Program*. Translated by Joshua David Jordan. Los Angeles: Semiotoext(e).

Tiqqun. (2001) 2012. *Theory of Bloom*. Translated by Robert Hurley. Berkeley, Calif.: LBC.

Transparency International. n.d. "Tools to Support Transparency in Local Governance." https://www.transparency.org/en/publications/tools-to -support-transparency-in-local-governance.

Triplett, Michael. 2010. "Transparency Group Taking Government Openness to the People." Mediaite, March 18, 2010. https://www.mediaite .com/online/transparency-group-taking-government-openness-to -the-people/.

Trump, Donald J. 2016. "Donald Trump's Speech Responding to Assault Accusations." West Palm Beach, Fla. *PBS News Hour,* NPR, October 13, 2016. Video, 48:19, and transcript. https://www.npr .org/2016/10/13/497857068/transcript-donald-trumps-speech-re sponding-to-assault-accusations.

Tsoukas, Haridimos. 1997. "The Tyranny of Light: The Temptations and Paradoxes of the Information Society." *Futures* 29 (9): 827–43.

Van Dijck, José. 2013. *The Culture of Connectivity: A Critical History of Social Media*. Oxford: Oxford University Press.

Van Veen, Tobias C. 2010. "Contesting Civil War: Tiqqun and Agamben." Fugitive Philosophy (blog), June 30, 2010. http://fugitive.quad rantcrossing.org/2010/06/contesting-civil-war/.

Visser, Nick. 2017. "Trump Administration Increasingly at Odds with U.S. Intelligence Community." Huffington Post, February 16, 2017. https:// www.huffpost.com.

Voigts, Manfred. 1995. *Das Geheimnisvolle Verschwinden des Geheimnisses: Ein Versuch*. Vienna: Passagen.

Wæver, Ole. 1995. "Securitization and Desecuritization." In *On Security,* edited by Ronnie Lipschutz, 46–86. New York: Columbia University Press.

Walker, Hunter, and Jana Winter. 2020. "White Supremacists Discussed Using Coronavirus as a Bio Weapon." *Huffington Post,* March 21, 2020. https://www.huffpost.com.

Wallace, Rob, Alex Liebman, Luis Fernando Chavez, and Rodrick Wallace. 2020. "Covid-19 and Circuits of Capital." *Monthly Review,* March 28, 2020. https://monthlyreview.org/2020/05/01/covid-19-and-circuits-of -capital/.

Wark, McKenzie. 2013. "Courting Vectoralists: An Interview with McKenzie Wark on the 10 Year Anniversary of *A Hacker Manifesto.*" Conducted by Melissa Gregg. *L.A. Review of Books,* December 17, 2013. https://lareviewofbooks.org/article/courting-vectoralists-interview-mckenzie-wark-10-year-anniversary-hacker-manifesto/.

Washington, George. (1777) 1983. Letter from private collection of Walter Pforzheimer. Reprinted in *Yale Alumni Magazine and Journal,* December 1983.

Washington Post. 1966. "Freedom of Information." Editorial. *Washington Post,* July 6, 1966.

Weaver, Matthew, and Richard Adams. 2010. "WikiLeaks U.S. Embassy Cables: Live Updates." *Guardian,* December 7, 2010. https://www.theguardian.com/.

Wenar, Leif. 2006. "Accountability in International Development Aid." *Ethics and International Affairs* 20 (1): 1–23.

White House. 2017a. "Executive Order: Enhancing Public Safety in the Interior of the United States." January 25, 2017. https://www.whitehouse.gov/presidential-actions/executive-order-enhancing-public-safety-interior-united-states/.

White House. 2017b. "Fueling American Innovation and Economic Growth with Open Data." August 11, 2017. https://www.whitehouse.gov/articles/fueling-american-innovation-economic-growth-open-data/.

White House Office of the Press Secretary. 2014. "Fact Sheet: The Administration's Proposal for Ending the Section 215 Bulk Telephony Metadata Program." March 27, 2014. https://obamawhitehouse.archives.gov/the-press-office/2014/03/27/fact-sheet-administration-s-proposal-ending-section-215-bulk-telephony-m.

Williams, Raymond. 1976. *Keywords: A Vocabulary of Culture and Society.* London: Fontana.

Wilson, Woodrow. (1913) 2018. *The New Freedom: A Call for the Emancipation of the Generous Energies of a People.* n.p.: Books on Demand.

Wise Bauer, Susan. 2008. "Why Public Confession Speaks to a Secular America." History News Network, Columbian College of Arts and Sciences, George Washington University, November 9, 2008. http://hnn.us/articles/56587.html.

Wittel, Andreas. 2011. "Qualities of Sharing and Their Transformations in the Digital Age." *International Review of Information Ethics* 15:3–8.

Wittes, Benjamin. 2009. *Legislating the War on Terror.* Washington, D.C.: Brookings Institution.

Wolf, Michael. 2018. *Fire and Fury: Inside the Trump White House.* New York: Little, Brown.

Wood, Gordon. 1982. "Conspiracy and the Paranoid Style: Causality and Deceit in the Eighteenth Century." *William and Mary Quarterly* 39 (3): 401–41.

World Bank. 2014. "Open Data for Economic Growth." http://www .worldbank.org/content/dam/Worldbank/document/Open-Data-for -Economic-Growth.pdf.

World Social Forum. 2002. "Charter of Principles." Approved in 2001. World Social Forum of Transformative Economies. https://transformadora .org/en/about/principles.

Yvon Lambert. 2009. Press release for *The Thicker the Glass*, by Jill Magid. http://www.jillmagid.com/exhibitions/the-thicker-the-glass-yvon -lambert-paris-2009-2.

Zito, Salena. 2016. "Taking Trump Seriously, Not Literally." *Atlantic*, September 23, 2016. https://www.theatlantic.com/politics/archive/2016/09/ trump-makes-his-case-in-pittsburgh/501335/.

Žižek, Slavoj. 1995. *Mapping Ideology*. London: Verso.

Zuboff, Shoshana. 2015. "Big Other: Surveillance Capitalism and the Prospects of an Information Civilization." *Journal of Information Technology* 30:75–89.

Zuboff, Shoshana. 2019. *The Age of Surveillance Capitalism: The Fight for a Human Future at the New Frontier of Power*. London: Profile.

# INDEX

(continued from p. ii)

**CLARE BIRCHALL** is reader in contemporary culture in the English department at King's College London. She is author of *Knowledge Goes Pop: From Conspiracy Theory to Gossip* and *Shareveillance: The Dangers of Openly Sharing and Covertly Collecting Data* (Minnesota, 2018), as well as coeditor of *New Cultural Studies: Adventures in Theory*.